"*The Summer of Beer and Whiskey* is full of great stories and interesting tidbits of history." —*The Ft. Wayne News-Sentinel*

"[A] fine history . . . Like a pitcher seamlessly targeting his pitches around the plate, Achorn weaves a story rife with facts and anecdotes." —*Plain Dealer*

"Funny, quirky and way out of baseball's vast left field." —*American History*

"I really can't praise *The Summer of Beer and Whiskey* enough, as it is truly one of my favorite books that I have ever read. Don't let the topic of baseball pigeonhole this title, there is something that anyone and everyone can enjoy in Achorn's masterful retelling of one of the more colorful episodes in sports history." —*NeuFeuter Blog*

"Achorn . . . does a terrific job of sketching this world and just how much fun everyone was having. . . . That summer of 1883 was the breakthrough, the time when a new league could come out of nowhere and not just challenge the status quo but break it. Looked at this history from the right angle, you can almost argue that the book is *Moneyball* from 130 years ago." —*Wall Street Journal*

"*The Summer of Beer and Whiskey* provides an interesting snapshot of the game during the decades it fought to define itself and professionalize into something resembling the modern day. . . . Perhaps the greatest strength of Achorn's work is that he presents the games and its characters in a way to make them instantly recognizable as sports personalities well represented in today's game. The narratives of the strident press, the arrogant star, the buffoonish ownership and the 'feel good' player who makes it are no different . . . than in 1883, even 130 years later. The game was different, but the people aren't, and in that context, it makes it much easier to relate to their efforts, failures, and successes." —Bluebird Banter.com (Toronto)

Praise for *The Summer of Beer and Whiskey*

"The time machine travels back to the 1880s as brewer Chris von der Ahe purchases the forerunner of the St. Louis Cardinals, with the singular purpose of selling more beer." —*The Daily Beast*

"*The Summer of Beer and Whiskey* hinges on the hard-fought 1883 pennant race between Von der Ahe's ascendant Browns and the Philadelphia Athletics. The book is rich in newspaper accounts of the race, along with accompanying caricatures of the players. But Achorn also includes insightful digressions on topics ranging from the sport's persistent problems with racism and alcoholism to the peculiarities of 19th-century baseball, which featured barehanded fielders, one umpire per contest, and pitchers who could take a slight running start before each throw."
—*St. Louis Post Dispatch*

"For fans, each season's crop of baseball books is like a literary Christmas. [*The Summer of Beer and Whiskey* is one] of this year's treasures."
—*Chicago Tribune*

"When it comes to baseball history, Edward Achorn has carved out his own territory, re-animating the 19th century game." —*Los Angeles Times*

"[Baseball's] colorful early days and characters, especially Chris von der Ahe, could hardly have hoped for a better retelling than Ed Achorn's."
—*The Weekly Standard*

"Achorn . . . turns his attention to old-time professional baseball, visiting the nascent days of the American Association, more notably, the American Association that turned baseball into a nationally beloved sport. . . .[An] entertaining history of baseball's overlooked early years."
—*Publishers Weekly*

"A realistic and colorful look at early professional baseball."
—*Providence Journal*

"*The Summer of Beer and Whiskey* strengthens the baseball fan's understanding of that raw, unvarnished era of baseball 130 years ago that eventually evolved into the smooth product we see today. Achorn writes passionately and presents an excellent history lesson." —*Tampa Tribune*

"A thoroughly researched and charmingly written account of a sensational pennant race populated by outsized characters" —*Oregonian*

"Achorn's gift for storytelling shines in the climactic games of the season. Vivid scenes put the reader in the stands as pitchers pelt batters, fielders crash through fences and the forces of nature whip up a blinding ninth-inning dust 'hurricane.'" —*Minneapolis Star-Tribune*

"A thoroughly enjoyable re-creation of the gusto, guts, glory and grime of the game's early days. —***Kirkus Reviews***

"Recording history is one thing. Giving it life beyond the ink on a page is another. Edward Achorn is on the list of authors who understands the difference. He doesn't merely mine and present dusty facts—and there are plenty of those to go around—he crafts thousands of stray historical threads into a rich tapestry that offers more than just a glimpse into his subject, in this case post–Civil War America and the origins of professional baseball. . . . *The Summer of Beer and Whiskey* is very much a story that goes beyond baseball. It reveals more about the evolution of popular culture—from entertainment and sports to media and celebrity. In many ways, it serves as a primer for how America got where it is today."
—**The Times News** (Madison, Wisconsin)

"A wonderful, unsentimental history of the men who bequeathed the game to us." —**Murray Polnar, History News Network**

"The author makes a convincing case that it was an exceptionally entertaining time to be a baseball fan in St. Louis."
—**Bill Littlefield, NPR's "Only a Game"**

"Combining the narrative skills of a sportswriter with a historian's depth of knowledge and stockpile of detail, Achorn has produced a book that is both entertaining and informative." —*The New Yorker*

THE SUMMER
OF BEER
AND WHISKEY

How Brewers, Barkeeps, Rowdies,
Immigrants, and a Wild Pennant Fight
Made Baseball America's Game

EDWARD ACHORN

PUBLICAFFAIRS
NEW YORK

PublicAffairs books are available at special discounts for bulk purchases in the U.S.
by corporations, institutions, and other organizations. For more information, please
contact the Special Markets Department at the Perseus Books Group, 2300 Chestnut
Street, Suite 200, Philadelphia, PA 19103, call (800) 810-4145, ext. 5000, or e-mail
special.markets@perseusbooks.com.

Book design by Linda Mark

Library of Congress Cataloging-in-Publication Data
    Achorn, Edward.
    The summer of beer and whiskey : how brewers, barkeeps, rowdies, immigrants,
    and a wild pennant fight made baseball America's game / Edward Achorn.
        pages cm
    Includes bibliographical references and index.
        ISBN 978-1-61039-260-0 (hardcover : alk. paper)—ISBN 978-1-61039-261-7 (e-book)
    1. American Association (Baseball league : 1882–1891)—History. 2. Baseball—United
    States—History. I. Title.
    GV875.A57.A35 2013
    796.3570973—dc23
                                                                    2013000200
    ISBN 978-1-61039-377-5 (paperback)

10 9 8 7 6 5 4 3 2 1

To my children, Jean, Matt, and Josh

CONTENTS

[Chris Von der Ahe] did as much for baseball in St. Louis and the country at large as any man ever associated with the game.

—AL SPINK,
THE NATIONAL GAME, 1910

In the next century, when baseball will be in the hands of posterity, and the present votaries and exponents gone to their long sleep, the Bancroft of the national game will place Chris Von der Ahe where he rightfully belongs.

—TED SULLIVAN,
HUMOROUS STORIES OF THE BALL FIELD, 1903

PREFACE:
THE LOVE AFFAIR

A T 10:22 P.M. ON THE NIGHT OF OCTOBER 28, 2011, A MUSCULAR, six-foot-four left-handed batter and devout Christian, David Murphy of the Texas Rangers, took a swift hack at a 97-mile-per-hour fast-ball and launched a long fly ball to left field. Red-jacketed fans in the St. Louis crowd of 47,399 were already on their feet yelling, waving white "Rally Squirrel" towels in honor of the American gray squirrel whose re-peated dashes across the field had prophesied the Cardinals' improbable upset of the Philadelphia Phillies in the Division Series playoffs three weeks earlier. As the ball soared into the night, Cardinals left fielder Allen Craig sprinted hard, turned around, and, backpedaling, thrust up his left arm, framed by the wall's giant picture of the Cards' legendary pitcher and showman Dizzy Dean, star of the Depression-era champions known as the Gashouse Gang. Fans fixed their eyes on the dying arc, bracing to bellow ear-splitting screams. When Craig's glove swallowed the ball, they jumped up and down, slapped backs, shook hands, hugged, laughed, wept. Ecstatic young athletes in white and red uniforms swarmed over the field, forming a mound atop closer Jason Motte. Fireworks boomed over the stadium, splashing piercing colors into the sky that were reflected beyond center field on the Gateway Arch, symbol of the city's critical role in America's bold westward expansion. Another splendid page in St. Louis history had been written.

It was one of those unthinkable finishes that make baseball so magical. On August 27, the St. Louis Cardinals had languished in third place in the wildcard race, ten and a half games behind, written off by everyone but themselves. They fought back frantically and, with a win on the last day of the regular season, actually snuck into the playoffs. They then pushed aside the highly touted Phillies and the hard-hitting Milwaukee Brewers to make it all the way to the World Series, where they would be up against the heavily favored Texas Rangers. Twice in Game Six, they had been on the brink of elimination, down to their last strike, but the stars spectacularly aligned in their favor, and they survived, somehow, to triumph in the eleventh inning. And now they were World Champions, sending millions of Cardinals fans across America into paroxysms of joy. Gushing with pride, General Manager John Mozeliak declared: "We have the greatest fans in the world."

The people of St. Louis seemed determined to prove it. Two days later they filled Busch Stadium and lined downtown streets for a parade celebrating their baseball miracle. A team of eight massive Clydesdale steeds pulled a scarlet red Budweiser beer wagon, symbol of Anheuser-Busch's longtime association with the team and St. Louis's love for the amber beverage that had been made internationally famous by the city's German immigrant brewers. Manager Tony La Russa smiled and waved from the seat of honor atop the wagon, alongside green-clad liverymen.

But few, if any, of the hundreds of thousands celebrating that afternoon paused to reflect on the founder of their beloved team, the shrewd and amusing man to whom they owed a good deal of their joy this day. Most in the crowd had never even heard the name of Chris Von der Ahe, let alone his story. This immigrant grocer and saloonkeeper dived into baseball even before he thoroughly mastered the English language. With cheap tickets, Sunday ball, and beer, he grabbed control of the dying game in St. Louis and, in a turnaround at least as improbable and dramatic as the one engineered by the 2011 Cardinals, infused it with new life and popularity—while perhaps saving all of professional baseball in the bargain. Von der Ahe also played a role in founding a flamboyant new major league, whose influence echoes loudly through Major League Baseball to this day.

Von der Ahe did not act alone, of course. He was one of a gang of owners and players who revived the game by creating a dazzlingly colorful professional sports league known as the American Association. This book tells their tale—the tale of how baseball, under their guidance, extended its reach to fans of all classes and became more truly America's game. It tells of the extraordinary passion for baseball they helped to ignite in cities such as St. Louis, Philadelphia, New York, Pittsburgh, Cincinnati, Baltimore, Louisville, and Columbus. Our vehicle to reconnect with this fascinating world will be the cycle that is the essence of baseball—a single season, from April's soaring expectations to September's aching sorrows.

To be sure, the American Association's summer of 1883 has been utterly foreign to all but the most intrepid baseball historians. But in many ways it transformed and even saved the game, dramatically increasing its popularity and demonstrating that, however unpredictable professional baseball might be, it could be played honestly. It was the year America went baseball mad—a season of struggle and passions featuring a wild pennant race. It was filled with memorable characters—and often hilarious twists and turns, so wonderful that only baseball could have invented them. It is a season that marvelously opens a window, as baseball always does, into the culture of America of its time—the harsh struggle, the cruel and mocking racism, the heavy drinking, and the triumphant, glorious spirit of individual achievement of the day.

To get oriented, it might be helpful to know something about the American Association, the major league that functioned alongside the National League from 1882 through 1891. It was not the progenitor of today's American League, which became a major league in 1901, though it did demonstrate that there was good money to be made in a competing league. Formally in existence for just nine years, the American Association might seem short-lived—long gone and long forgotten. But in a very real sense, it is still thriving today. In 1892, the Association merged with the National League, which had been founded in 1876, much as the upstart American Football League merged with the more venerable National Football League in 1970. Four former American Association teams became keystone National League franchises: Pittsburgh (today's Pirates), St. Louis (today's Cardinals), Cincinnati (today's Reds), and Brooklyn (today's Los Angeles Dodgers). The newly merged league was called the National League and American Association of Professional Base Ball Clubs—a real mouthful, understandably shortened in common usage to National League, though perhaps unfortunately so, since the Association and its great contribution to baseball were thereby largely forgotten.

The franchise that became known as the Cardinals—and plays one of the starring roles in this book—was originally called the St. Louis Browns. This club is not to be confused with the St. Louis Browns of the American League, 1901–1953, who moved to Baltimore and became today's Orioles. Those Browns simply borrowed the name, by then no longer in use, of the storied franchise founded by Von der Ahe.

Big-league baseball imported much more than ball clubs from the American Association. The Association powerfully transformed baseball, making it more open and accessible. Decades before Jackie Robinson, it featured two black ballplayers, breaking the color line for a time in Jim Crow America. The big leagues also eventually adopted the Association's Sunday ball, ballpark beer, and spirit of reckless fun that was at the heart of the organization from the beginning—qualities that, to one degree or another, live on to this day, just like the St. Louis Cardinals.

And it began, as so much of baseball does, with a most improbable character. . . .

1

In the Big Inning

EVERYBODY WHO KNEW CHRIS VON DER AHE, IT SEEMS, HAD A story about him—about his colossal pomposity; his wonderful generosity; his red-faced rages that inevitably recoiled catastrophically on himself; his thick German accent and wobbly use of the English language; and his insatiable appetite for beer, beautiful young women, song, and life. As a baseball owner, he was George Steinbrenner, Charlie Finley, and Bill Veeck rolled into one—haughty, temperamental, driven to win, wildly experimental, and madly in love with a dazzling show. He had a splash of Yogi Berra in him, too, which surfaced in his expression of Zen-like axioms.

He struck some observers as the quintessential cartoon of a German immigrant: moon-faced and strawberry-nosed, with twinkling eyes, a bushy mustache, and an emerging pot belly that pushed on the vest of his loud checkered three-piece suit. One contemporary reporter observed: "His taste was given to trombone tailory. He liked hilarious habiliments. Large checks in light hues were his favorite colors. He adored tan shoes and pearl-gray hats." Describing Von der Ahe's appearance at one owners' meeting, an admiring reporter noted that the German "wore a flashy suit of clothes and a smile that would stretch across the Ohio River." Sportswriter and former ballplayer Tim Murnane compared him to Cyrano de Bergerac, the joyful, flamboyant lover of women and life cursed with a comical appearance. Chris was fond of "large things. He wears a No. 8 hat, No. 10 shoes and sports a 48-carat diamond on his shirt front."

Many stories suggest that Von der Ahe's knowledge of the game was less than encyclopedic. We hear in one 1885 article that he bragged to his off-and-on press secretary, David L. Reid, when the two were meeting at his ballpark:

"Dave, dis vas de piggest diamond in de country."

"No, Chris," replied Dave, "all diamonds are the same size."

"Vell," replied Chris, "it vas de piggest infield, anyhow."

Since Von der Ahe traveled with his team frequently and made complicated deals to obtain very good ballplayers, such colossal ignorance seems beyond belief. Yet many contemporary accounts, including from people who admired him, attest that he never quite seemed to grasp the intricacies of baseball. "Often after his team lost a game," his longtime manager, Charlie Comiskey, recalled, "Chris would dash into the club's dressing room, single out a certain player and shout, 'Vy did you drop dat ball, eh?' He took every muff as a personal affront and seemed to think the poor players could explain in well chosen words why they happened to muff." On other occasions, he tried to inspire players with clubhouse addresses characterized by his memorable flair for language. One reporter claimed he once delivered this warning about "lushing," or excessive drinking: "See here now; I don't vant some foolishness from you fellows. I vant you to stop dis slushing and play ball.

Chris Von der Ahe
(Library of Congress)

Of you vin de scampinship I gif you all a suit of clothes and a benefit-game extra and of you don't you vill haf to eat snowballs all vinter."

His use of English made even his friends laugh. Longtime Baltimore Orioles manager Billy Barnie recalled introducing a couple of traveling reporters to the St. Louis owner one day, back when it was rare for sportswriters to accompany teams on road trips. "Poys, I am awful glad to see you and velcome you to St. Lewis," Von der Ahe declared. "Ofer there is my pox. It is at your exposal." Admonished once for letting some good players go, Von der Ahe wrung his hands and moaned, "Vy, oh vy, didn't I take mine own advice?"

A man of immense pride in his achievements, he once gathered his friends to show off his flashy new horse and light buggy, parked outside of his Grand Avenue beer garden. Chris dramatically climbed in, drove nearly all the way to Natural Bridge Road, turned around, and began a wild half-mile gallop down the wide avenue toward his associates. To his friends' horror, the horse sped past the café in a frenzy, collided with a telephone pole, catapulted Von der Ahe into the mire, "and galloped wildly up the hill, dragging the remnants of the rig behind it." Von der Ahe was lugged back inside, had the mud and grime washed off of him, and downed a couple of stiff drinks to revive his spirits. He then barked to an assistant, "Take dot blanked blanked horse back to der barn unt starve him to deat. Don't give him noddings to eat but hay und oats."

He was an insatiable womanizer, a failing that made him a figure of ridicule in the papers and virtually ruined his life. On a roasting hot Sunday night in St. Louis in August 1885, while his wife, Emma, was sitting on the steps in front of their home at 3613 St. Louis Avenue, he came careening around the corner, crashing his carriage. Out spilled a pretty young blonde named Miss Kittey Dewey, who escaped serious injury but not a tongue-lashing from Mrs. Von der Ahe. When Miss Dewey had the nerve to show up at Von der Ahe's Sportsman's Park a month later, Emma crept up on her, pulled a soda bottle from the folds of her dress, and brought it crashing down on the young woman's head. On another occasion, a man showed up at Emma's front door to complain that Von der Ahe was sleeping with his wife. Emma eventually divorced Von der Ahe, charging that he stayed "out late at night in the company of women of ill-repute" and "violated his marital vows not only in St. Louis, but traveled with women of bad character from place to place." But Von der Ahe didn't learn. At the age of forty-six, he took up with a gold-digging twenty-one-year-old named Della Wells. After he married Della in 1896, one Miss Annie Kaiser came forward, a "handsome young woman" who had worked for Von der Ahe and his first wife as a servant before the couple got divorced. Miss Kaiser claimed he had promised to marry *her*, and that they had been planning to set a date. Von der Ahe and Della soon divorced, and Chris, having resolved the breach-of-promise lawsuit, married the servant girl who brought it against him. All this proved enormously costly.

A portable theater of the absurd seemed to follow Von der Ahe around all his days. But how many of these tales were true? Nineteenth-century newspaper reporters, handed the priceless gift of this oversized personality, transformed him into something approaching a pure ethnic stereotype: the German immigrant as a bombastic rube, known as a "Dutchman," who must be constantly corrected by his smarter, American-born associates. Yet the historical record reveals a much more complex character than the one constantly lampooned in the papers. His contemporaries knew him as a brilliant showman and risk-taker, a man who, though he often wore his heart on his sleeve, worked harder and had a keener vision of baseball's potential than almost all of his contemporaries. "He is shrewd, cunning and pugnacious," observed one reporter who knew him well. "His methods are drive, drive, drive and keep on driving." Another reporter, studying an "irregular" face that smiled more than it frowned, formed a strong impression of his willpower: "Base ball vicissitudes have not turned his hair gray. He looks like a man who could strike out vigorously when the sea becomes troublesome and who could keep his head well above the waves when other powerful swimmers begin to think of sinking."

<hr />

VON DER AHE'S RISE TO BASEBALL GLORY STARTED WITH THE immigrant's dream of getting rich in America. By the late 1870s, as the proprietor of a thriving grocery store, saloon, and boardinghouse in St. Louis's West End, half a block from Grand Avenue Park, he was well on his way to his goal. He operated a beer garden on the property, and, after games, baseball fanatics flocked into his place for a tall mug of lager and a bite to eat. They might enjoy sprightly polkas and popular tunes, played by a small band, before heading home after dusk on the horse-drawn streetcars. On the city's sweltering summer afternoons, the lush green leaves overhead formed a cooling canopy that rustled in the breeze, helping to capture some of St. Louis's intense dust and heat. It was "one of the peculiarities of German customs" that parents readily brought their young ones to such drinking places, noted the 1878 book *A Tour of St. Louis*. "It is often the case that a family consisting of husband and wife and half a dozen children may be observed seated at a table, sipping fresh, foaming beer, and eating pretzels."

Germans had poured into the Midwest from the 1830s through the 1880s as part of a mass exodus from their homeland. They were fleeing hard times, bad harvests, bullying bureaucrats, and the brutality of war for a better, freer life. The crackdown that followed the revolutions of 1848, in particular, drove many German liberals to America, where some became distinguished leaders in the antislavery and workers' rights movements. By 1880, some 54,901 of the 350,518 people in St. Louis—more than 15 percent—were German-born. They had nourished their dreams on books of advice like *The Germans in America* (1851), by a Boston pastor named F. W. Bogen. "A great blessing meets the German emigrant the moment he steps upon these shores," Bogen promised. "He comes into a free country; free from the oppression of despotism, free from privileged orders and monopolies, free from the pressure of intolerable taxes and imposts, free from constraint in matters of belief and conscience." Many Germans were drawn to the idea of a young, dynamic country where their talent and strenuous work mattered more than the whims of government bureaucrats or the accident of birth.

The Germans brought with them something called *gemutlichkeit*—a compound of "conviviality, camaraderie and good fellowship, love of celebrations, card-playing, praise of [the] German way of life, and all these washed over by flowing kegs of good lager beer." *Lippincott's Magazine* explained to its readers in April 1883: "Beer and wine the German looks upon as gifts of God, to be enjoyed in moderation for lightening the cares of life and adding to its pleasures; and Sunday afternoon is devoted, by all who do not belong to the stricter Protestant sects, to recreation."

Many native-born Americans frowned on such ideas. The *New York Times*, the voice of the eastern Protestant establishment, with its affection for blue laws and prohibition, hoped these aliens would soon outgrow their Old World habits: "In the old countries, where freedom is smothered, drinking may be necessary to drown the depressing influences of despotism; but here, where freedom woos the mind to culture, no such beastly compensation is called for, and we believe we have said sufficient to prove that our German fellow-citizens are born for higher and nobler uses than for schnapps and lager-bier." The *Cincinnati Enquirer*, in contrast, insisted that German beer actually helped to civilize America. "Formerly Americans drank scarcely anything else than whisky, frequently very bad whisky, and the consequence was quarreling, strife and fights. Now Americans drink almost as much beer as the Germans do, and whereas Americans used to pour everything down their throats standing, they now sit down good naturedly and chat over a good glass of beer, without flying into one another's hair."

It wasn't long before the number of beer gardens operating on Sundays in St. Louis became something of a national scandal, as easterners complained of a steady assault on the sanctity of the Lord's Day. Though St. Louis was predominantly Christian, "it cannot be claimed that its inhabitants are pious, in the sense of the word as understood in Boston," admitted the authors of *A Tour of St. Louis*. St. Louis residents—some descended from French Catholics, who shared the German attitude toward Sundays—burst from their homes on the Lord's Day, filling the streets with laughter and chatter as they made their way to such "umbrageous enclosures" as beer gardens. "Music, dancing, ball games, and other amusements are indulged in with a zest which shows the intensity of pleasure realized from them by the participants." For them, such pleasures were "soul-feasts."

In St. Louis, immigrants encountered a thriving but rough city at the cultural crossroads of America—one part southern in its charm, gentility, and large black population; one part northern in its relentless jockeying for money; and one part cowboy outpost, the traditional departure point for those intrepid souls making the journey for the Wild West on Conestoga wagons. By the 1880s, few of the city's 300 miles of roadway had been paved, leaving St. Louis to be plagued by wind-whipped dust in dry weather and slimy mud during the wet season. The sewer system was poor, and polluted wells were a source of deadly diarrhea and fever.

Strangers had great difficulty finding their way around, since the city did not bestir itself to install street signs until it hosted the 1896 Republican National Convention. People made their way about the city on bob-tail cars—small, 15-foot-long streetcars drawn along rails, pulled by one horse or two donkeys, and typically overflowing with passengers, some precariously clinging to the outside.

Before the Civil War, St. Louis had been a major steamboat hub, and those magnificent, brightly colored "floating palaces" formed "a forest of smokestacks along the banks," one German immigrant recalled. But, in ever-changing America, that gaudy world vanished almost overnight. By the 1880s, railroads, which could move people and goods much faster and cheaper than steamboats, had stolen much of the boats' business.

Von der Ahe's St. Louis was a booming place, the sixth largest city in America as of 1880. Thick coal smoke hung over the city, making the morning light seem feeble and gray long after dawn. "These Western cities exhale a tainted breath, stifle themselves in the fumes of their own prosperity," wrote a visiting writer for *Harper's Magazine*. On brutally hot summer days, St. Louis residents strolled across the great Eads Bridge, or found relief in sidewalk cafés that made the *Harper's* reporter think of Paris boulevards: "Little tables are put out in the front of the principal restaurants," he wrote, "and the guests chatter and sip refreshments at them, under the glowing gas-lights, till a late hour."

———◦———

VON DER AHE HAD FOUND HIS WAY HERE FROM 4,000 MILES AWAY. He was born on October 2, 1848, in Hille, a fastidious farming village in the green region of Westphalia in Prussia. Christened Christian Frederick Wilhelm Von der Ahe, he took his name from his father, who had been named, like *his* father, after Frederick the Great. Chris was the oldest of nine children, several of whom died in childhood. He was baptized in the Evangelist Church, signifying he was Protestant, probably Lutheran. The elder Von der Ahe was an ambitious and successful grain dealer and merchant, but death struck him down early, in 1864, when he was only forty. Chris was sixteen. Three years later, he faced compulsory service in the Prussian military, with its harsh discipline and officers in spiked helmets. Fearing dismemberment or death in the wars of German unification, the young man dodged it all by emigrating in 1867. To get out of Germany, he may have lied to officials, telling them he was born in 1851, and thus too young to serve, a fictional birthdate he maintained throughout his life, presumably to avoid arrest should he ever return to his native land. The fib is preserved on his gravestone and in various official documents. In any case, he found his way to a ship, most likely in Hamburg or Bremen, that was bound for New York City.

The voyage across took about seventeen days by steamer, the form of transportation used by most immigrants by the late 1860s. Stacked atop each other in berths, sometimes four rows high, the immigrants were crammed into a dark hold that reeked of vomit, rancid food, and unbathed humanity—a Petrie dish for lice, infectious disease, and death. Saltwater seeped into the steerage through ventilation holes, adding dampness and cold to the misery. Their troubles did not end in New York. The moment the travelers stepped off the boat and tried to regain their land legs, swarms of money-grubbing Americans were poised to fleece them. Immigrants knew that they could seek help at the German Immigration Society, a charitable institution established to assist those coming to America. But con artists went to the trouble of setting up fake German societies; some newcomers went to them, to be parted from whatever little money they had brought.

Soon after landing in New York, Von der Ahe set out for the Midwest. He arrived as the city's economy was staggering into a postwar slump. Day and night, hungry, haggard men thronged the St. Louis headquarters of the German Immigration Society, in the basement of Tivoli Hall on Elm Street, desperate for work. But Von der Ahe, bright and ambitious, landed a job as a grocery clerk in the city's West End. Within a few years of his arrival, he was co-owner of a combination grocery store and saloon on the corner of Sullivan and Spring. In those times, "any grocery store worth its salt was attached directly through a swinging door to a saloon," one St. Louis resident recalled.

On March 3, 1870, when he was twenty-one, Von der Ahe married twenty-year-old Emma Hoffmann, a Missouri-born daughter of German immigrants. Nine months later, their only son, Edward, was born. In 1872, Chris boldly bought out his business partner, staking his life's savings of $1,125, and when one of his debtors died, Von der Ahe moved his business into a two-and-a-half-story boardinghouse a block south, at the corner of Grand and St. Louis. He delved into ward politics, working on behalf of the pro-immigrant, antiprohibition Democratic Party, and befriended a rising state representative named John Joseph O'Neill, soon to be elected to Congress. In short, Von der Ahe had acquired a family, a growing business, a place in the community, and political connections. In time, he had a feed and flour store and butcher shop, three horses, three delivery wagons, a stable, nine rooms over the store, and an office on the first floor. He could boast of $75,000 in annual sales. The business he had built was a testament to the American dream. But Von der Ahe craved more money, fame, and respect.

He intended to win them through, of all things, an odd American obsession that was then called base ball—two words. One of his neighbors, a Swiss immigrant named Augustus Solari, ran an enclosed baseball grounds right down the street named Grand Avenue Park. Solari had overseen its erection on what was then a cornfield on the outskirts of town. He then rented it out to a series of teams, most notably the superb St. Louis Brown Stockings, a major-league club from 1875 through 1877. Intrigued, Von der Ahe began contemplating how his saloon business could exploit its proximity to the ballpark, "as he might have become interested in pretzels, peanuts or any other incitant to thirst and beer drinking," according to one reporter.

To get inside the business, he angled for a leadership role in the Grand Avenue Base Ball Club, a team that played on days when the Brown Stockings did not need the park. Von der Ahe obtained a place on its board of directors in 1876, when he was twenty-seven, possibly with the help of the club's president, Eleventh Ward City Councilman J. B. Woestman, a fellow Prussian immigrant, former grocer, and rising flour manufacturer who lived near Von der Ahe on Grand Avenue. (When Woestman was implicated in a bribery scandal that spring, Von der Ahe provided security for his $2,000 bond.) The directors pledged to put a good team on the field, promising that "none but the best amateur players would be engaged, and that honesty would outweigh skill." Von der Ahe immersed himself in the operation, and before the start of the second season, he was elected vice president. From that post, he secured the concession at Grand Avenue Park for selling beer by the mug and whiskey by the shot, including during National League games played there.

But Von der Ahe had to wonder how much longer that concession would be worth anything. All over the country, it had become an open question whether professional baseball could even survive. Spectators were abandoning the sport, which seemed destined to wilt away, another American fad on its way to oblivion. If he wanted to make more money, Von der Ahe would have to find a way to make baseball popular again.

———◄◦►———

AMERICA WAS IN THE GRIP OF A TERRIBLE DEPRESSION FOR MUCH of the 1870s, and professional baseball was barely surviving as the decade drew to a close. The sport's reputation had been blackened by dishonest and drunken players whose dubious performances on the field led many paying customers to quit wasting their money on the game. The first professional league, the National Association of Professional Base Ball Players, founded in 1871, had staggered through five seasons, damaged not only by its crooks and boozers, but also by uncompetitive and poorly financed teams from minor markets as well as the boring dominance of one club, the Boston Red Stockings. The National Association could hardly be called a league—it was more a loose structure designed to award a pennant—since there was no fixed schedule, and any club could enter by paying a $10 membership fee, paltry even then. By the summer of 1875, William Ambrose Hulbert, the resolute president of the Chicago White Stockings (today's Cubs), had endured enough of such nonsense. He staged a coup, drawing the richest clubs of the West out of the National Association and compelling the best teams of the East to join them in a smaller, more exclusive new circuit, the National League of Professional Base Ball *Clubs*, with the emphasis on giving club management control over players. It survives to this day as the National League.

From the owners' standpoint, Hulbert's league—with a fixed schedule and solid teams in baseball's biggest markets—was a decided improvement over the chaotic National Association. Even so, gamblers still swarmed over ballparks, and betting fueled much of the public's interest in the game. The huge amounts of money at stake inevitably spurred attempts to fix games. Sure enough, in late 1877, four members of the first-place

Louisville Grays—including their superb pitcher, Jim Devlin—were implicated in throwing the National League pennant, blowing games to let Boston capture the flag. And since some of the players, including Devlin, had already signed to play for the St. Louis Brown Stockings in 1878, that team, too, got coated with the slime of their corruption.

The Brown Stockings could hardly afford this latest stain. They had already been soiled by a long series of gambling scandals. There was strong, if not quite actionable, evidence, for instance, that at least two St. Louis players were working for the notorious Chicago gambler Mike McDonald to throw games. Moreover, an explosive newspaper exposé charged that Brown Stockings manager George "Burtie" McManus, in cahoots with his captain, the shady Mike McGeary, attempted to buy Louisville-based umpire Daniel Devinney for $250 to shade calls in St. Louis's favor. Disgusted with these developments, much of St. Louis simply gave up on baseball. The civic leaders who ran the Brown Stockings, having lost the services of Devlin and other stars who might have helped erase the organization's debt, dropped their plans to build a new park downtown and instead folded the club. After years of top-drawer professional baseball, St. Louis had no major-league team for 1878.

This was grim news for two brothers who were sportswriters at competing St. Louis newspapers, Alfred H. Spink of the *Missouri Republican* and William Spink of the *St. Louis Globe-Democrat*. Recognizing that their jobs were not long for this world without baseball, they helped cobble together a semipro team, gave it the old name of Brown Stockings, and scheduled a series of games. "But the baseball-loving public, disgusted at the way they had lost the splendid team they had hoped for, would have none of it," Alfred recounted. The new club played to mostly empty stands at Grand Avenue Park and the smaller Compton Avenue Grounds. When the Spink brothers lured the National League's celebrated Indianapolis Browns to visit St. Louis in 1878, the home club failed to collect enough gate money even to fund the visitors' trip back to the hotel down on the bob-tail horsecars.

By mid-1879, St. Louis seemed to have sworn off baseball. Even a heavily advertised game in June drew only a smattering of spectators, who, in the words of the *St. Louis Globe-Democrat*, "gazed at the beggarly array of empty benches, and thought of the olden time when 'standing room only' was the general rule." The Brown Stockings limped on into 1879 and 1880 under their intrepid player-manager Ned Cuthbert, a former and future major leaguer. He and his players divided up the receipts after each game, giving about one-quarter of the take to the man who ran the grounds, Solari. The money was pitiful, though, and the neglected park was rapidly becoming shabby.

Into this situation stepped Von der Ahe. Cuthbert, who knew the German from his beer sales at Grand Avenue Park, recognized that this prosperous neighborhood burgher and rising civic leader was an ideal candidate to bankroll St. Louis's return to the big time, which meant in the National League. At first, Von der Ahe was reluctant to risk his money on the scheme. "It was 'Eddie' who talked me into baseball," Von der Ahe revealed late in life. "He picked me out, and, for months, he talked league baseball, until he convinced me that there was something in it." By late 1880, Von der Ahe had come around to seeing what many American investors could not—that the business of baseball did not have to die; indeed, it might merely be in its infancy. American-born men who knew the game well had repeatedly tried to make a go of St. Louis baseball and failed, but the German immigrant formed the conviction that he could earn a fortune. He had a vision of making a day at the park a more exciting experience than ever before, with cheap tickets, booming beer sales, and big crowds adorned by beautiful women. What's more, he saw a revitalized ballpark as the centerpiece of West End development and believed it would boost his business and his real-estate investments.

Such a vision required a great deal of imagination. Under the management of the exhausted Solari, Grand Avenue Park had deteriorated into a dump that, according to Al Spink, "contained a weather beaten grandstand and a lot of rotten benches." A two-story building, part of which Solari evidently used as his home, stood in right field, fenced off from play, only 285 feet down the line. Von der Ahe persuaded Solari to drop the lease on the ballpark and then, to his old neighbor's apparent surprise, forced him out of the building. Von der Ahe intended to rip down the stands and replace them with a fresh new wooden grandstand. He would build an upper deck and bleachers on the side, making the new park "the most commodious in the country." That project would cost at least $2,500, a substantial investment, particularly at a time when baseball was considered close to death. Von der Ahe was undeterred. He cofounded a new organization to pick up the lease and run the grounds, the Sportsman's Park and Club Association. Other men were involved, but Von der Ahe boldly bought up most of the stock, reportedly sinking his life's savings of $1,800 into the scheme. That was a significant amount of money in an era when the average factory worker earned less than $500 a year.

Displaying a spirit of innovation well ahead of his time, Von der Ahe envisioned his new park as a multipurpose entertainment complex with "a cricket field . . . a base ball diamond, cinder paths for 'sprinters,' a hand ball court, bowling alleys and everything of that sort." By one account, sportsmen who were passionately devoted to wing shooting contributed to the new facility, intending to hold weekly shooting events at the grounds under the auspices of the St. Louis Gun Club (which may help explain the new name of the Grand Avenue grounds, rechristened Sportsman's Park). Von der Ahe also made plans to use Solari's house as a beer garden, setting chairs and tables out in deep right field, literally in play.

But readmission to the National League—which the Browns' backers thought was key to their financial hopes—went nowhere. "The owners of its clubs had no use for us," Al Spink recalled. Gambling scandals had given St. Louis "a black eye in baseball circles the country over." And, surely, years of poor attendance at St. Louis games, and Von der Ahe's intention to sell oceans of beer, did not help, either. At that point, no one outside the immediate circle of investors seemed to have the slightest faith that Von der Ahe could turn it all around. But the National League's snub was just as well, since Von der Ahe had a different vision.

The National League, with its fifty-cent tickets and ban on Sunday ball, marketed the game only to the rich, or at least the upper middle class—the lawyers, accountants, and businessmen who had the freedom to take a break late in the afternoon and go out to the ballpark. Von der Ahe had another idea: to welcome working men and fellow immigrants, those who toiled all week and could not break free from their jobs to attend a game. These men had only Sundays available for something like baseball. They could not easily afford the National League's admission price of fifty cents, but they could come up with twenty-five cents for a ticket. With this insight, Von der Ahe made baseball a much more inclusive game; in a sense, he helped make it the American game.

It took guts—some thought reckless stupidity—to invest in baseball in 1880, particularly in St. Louis. "When [Von der Ahe] pulled out of the savings bank the most of his hard earnings and invested it in resurrecting the national game in St. Louis, he knew as much about baseball as a porker does about theology," sportswriter Harry Weldon claimed. "Chris had no experience then but was plucky and game enough to risk the money in the venture when no one else would touch it with a pair of tongs." That was a bit of an exaggeration, since Von der Ahe had been involved peripherally with the game for a number of years. But, however little or much he knew about baseball, the immigrant grocer knew this: to make a dollar in America, a man had to take a chance. "If it sells beer, I'm all for it," he told his fellow baseball investors.

In the early spring of 1881, a group of players sat on the field in front of Von der Ahe's splendid new grandstand, talking about the upcoming season. Although they were barely eking out a living, the players were solid professionals. Most of them either had major-league experience already or would someday. "It was agreed as we all sat there on the green sward that we would work together to build up the sport," Al Spink recalled three decades later. "Each player promised to be prompt at each game, to do his level best at all times and to take for his pay just as small a percentage of the gate receipts as the general welfare of the park and its owners would allow."

Lost in the golden glow of Spink's memory was a bitter wrangle that led up to that serene gathering, a fight between the players and Von der Ahe over dividing up the proceeds. The new owner, determined to recoup his investment, announced plans to boost his share of the gate and slash the players'. That spurred threats of a walkout. The players' leader, William Spink, received a cut of the gate for his efforts and had no interest in seeing it reduced. He insisted that the Browns would be better off abandoning the truculent Von der Ahe and his spiffy Sportsman's Park and going off to play at the smaller, shabbier Compton Avenue Grounds. Had William swayed the players, he might well have left Von der Ahe with an expensive new ballpark and no team. But Von der Ahe shrewdly outflanked Spink, quashing the rebellion by offering two star players, Bill and Jack Gleason, an extra $100 each to stay with him. He also promised to use his political connections to secure them patronage jobs in the city's fire department. In the end, Ned Cuthbert and other key players decided to remain, too, realizing it made little financial sense to abandon their big new ballpark. Frozen out after fighting to restore baseball's popularity, William Spink felt betrayed by the mercenary Gleason brothers. He refused to speak a word to either of them until his death in 1885. "Had they remained with Spink, Von der Ahe would probably have never been heard of in connection with base ball," noted one reporter. Chris's gutsy move dramatically increased his power over baseball in St. Louis.

Among those who stayed with Von der Ahe was William's own brother, Al. Despite the new park and a willingness of players and management to work together, the outlook still "seemed cold and bleak," Al recalled, for one glaring reason: the Brown Stockings, who played in no organized league, could not easily find opponents. "It was up to me to fill the breach," he said. Al proposed a clever idea to a fellow baseball writer, Oliver Perry Caylor of the *Cincinnati Enquirer*, in another heavily German, lager-loving city that had lost its slot in the National League. He urged Caylor to round up whatever professional players were still lurking in town, slap on them the nostalgic name of Cincinnati Reds, and bring them to St. Louis for a three-game, Saturday-through-Monday series in late May 1881. It proved a brilliant scheme. Thousands of people thronged Sportsman's Park. "The names St. Louis Browns and Cincinnati Reds proved magic in so far as reawakening interest in the game in this city was concerned," Spink recalled. At the end of the game, Von der Ahe, "happier, apparently, than any of the rest," grasped Spink by the hand. "What a fine big crowd! But the game, Al, the game. How was it? Was it a pretty good game? You know I know nothing about it."

Hoping to keep the crowds pouring in all summer, Spink arranged visits from the "prairie nines" operating in the Midwest, semipro clubs at best. Fortunately, they were willing to come "just for the fun of playing," receiving nothing beyond expenses—railroad travel to St. Louis in cheap cars, a stay in a second-rate hotel, and a trip on the horsecars to and from the park. "There was of course no discipline, no order, no anything, each player coming and going as he pleased," Spink remembered. One team, the Chicago Eckfords, arrived with only seven men, minus the two most important players—catcher and pitcher. Spink managed to salvage the game when, en route to the park, he spied two youngsters playing on a lot in North St. Louis and hauled them along—catcher Kid Baldwin and pitcher Henry Overbeck, both of whom later had professional careers, Baldwin in the major leagues.

As the city's passion for baseball reignited, the *Globe-Democrat* passed along a joke that was making the rounds: "Base Ball is old in the world, as is proven by the very first line in Genesis: 'In the big inning,' etc." And Sunday after Sunday, spectators who had attended morning religious services drained kegs of Von der Ahe's beer in the afternoon. "He took no interest in the game, but stood over his bartenders, watching the dimes and quarters that the crowd showered over the bar," player Tom Brown recalled. "Hear dem shouding out dare," Von der Ahe supposedly said, looking over the crowd. "Tree tousand tem fools and one vise man, and the vise man is me, me Chris Won der Ahe!"

By midsummer 1881, the wise man's investment was paying off handsomely, to the astonishment of poor Solari, whose previous management of the same property "was not," in the words of the *St. Louis Globe-Democrat*, "an overpowering success." Driven by jealousy, or perhaps a sense that the German had hoodwinked him, Solari became so resentful that he "resorted to some means of ruffling the feathers of the club at large and Von der Ahe in particular." For starters, he challenged Von der Ahe's liquor license. Solari lost that one, but he and other citizens, worried about bullets flying in a residential neighborhood, managed to persuade local authorities to revoke shooting privileges at the park. "As a final piece of spitework," Solari erected a high fence in front of Von der Ahe's house, obstructing the family's view of the park. Not content with that, he had Von der Ahe arrested on charges, quickly dismissed, of making false affidavits about the park's neighbors. Three months later, someone managed to get Von der Ahe hauled before the Second District Police Court for exhibiting "Base ball, cricket, etc., without [a] license." The court continued the case until a later date. It never again made the papers. Perhaps Von der Ahe called on his political connections or paid a bribe to make the problem disappear. In any event, Solari's harassment failed to slow him down. Von der Ahe was determined to make this venture work.

Professional clubs began to take note of the huge crowds Von der Ahe's Browns were drawing on Sundays. No longer did St. Louis have to rely on seven-man teams for opponents. The outstanding Akrons of Ohio, as well as such famous unaffiliated eastern clubs as the Athletics of Philadelphia and the Atlantics of Brooklyn, were now interested in coming to get a share of Von der Ahe's gate. When they arrived that fall, the turnout was so strong that Von der Ahe and his fellow independent baseball entrepreneurs reached the obvious conclusion: to hell with the National League. It was time to start their own major league. The old league's response to these upstarts, it turned out, would be anything but pleasant.

2

THE BEER AND
WHISKEY CIRCUIT

ITTING AT HIS DESK IN HIS WELL-APPOINTED HOME ON 1334 40TH
Street in Chicago, National League President William A. Hulbert
took his pen in hand to compose one of his famously blunt letters.
Hulbert was fiercely proud of his reputation as the iron-willed leader who
had rescued professional baseball—even if he had failed to make it terribly popular—and he intended to defend that legacy as long as he drew
breath. He had always greeted the world as a no-nonsense man, strong
and decisive, posing for his photograph with a firm demeanor and a scowl
of skepticism. But on this cold, windy Tuesday of November 8, 1881, the
portly forty-nine-year-old businessman was weakening. His chest hurt,
he was short of breath, and he was getting seriously worried about what
was happening to the game he loved. The nefarious characters who, six
days earlier, had founded a new league, the American Association, rival
to his six-year-old National League, seemed determined to ruin his life's
work. He hoped to speak reason to them. His eyes smoldering, he dipped

his pen into the ink and started scratching out a letter to the American Association's new president.

Hulbert was a shrewd, pugnacious man in the mold of his adopted city of Chicago, which, in his view, was the epicenter and epitome of can-do America. "I'd rather be a lamppost in Chicago," he was fond of saying, "than a millionaire in any other city." Born in Burlington Flats, Otsego County, New York—not far from Cooperstown—in 1832, he had come to Chicago as a child with his parents, who were among the earliest settlers of what was then a muddy frontier outpost. His father, a farmer named Eri Baker Hulbert, set off for Chicago a year ahead of his wife and child to take over a general store there in 1836. His initial trip, which by the time his son had reached adulthood would be a reasonably quick railroad journey, took Eri a miserable sixteen days. He traveled for twenty-four hours on the canal packet from Utica to Buffalo, endured a rough voyage to Detroit, and went the rest of the way "tramping on foot, with the mud up to [his] knees," or riding in an old wagon with nothing to protect him from the elements. His son inherited his dogged persistence. Educated at Beloit College, William married the daughter of a grocer, took over her father's business, and turned it into a thriving coal delivery operation. He became a prominent member of the Chicago Board of Trade, where he was known "as a clear-headed, farsighted, and successful operator." At the same time, he rose to the presidency of the Chicago White Stockings baseball club and, from that perch, founded the National League and took over *its* presidency. As the de facto czar of professional baseball, he fought hard for the game's integrity, insisting on strong management power over players—and his own authority over wayward owners.

As early as 1876, Hulbert taught his fellow owners that he was not to be trifled with. After the League's very first season, he expelled both the New York Mutuals and the Philadelphia Athletics, even though the clubs represented the two biggest cities in America. They had failed to play out their full schedules, something he considered an unpardonable breach of the rules, despite the fact that there were extenuating circumstances. The Athletics' owner confronted Hulbert in his hotel room during the League's annual meeting that winter and tearfully pleaded for a second chance. "I beg of you not to expel us; we will enter into any bonds; we will do anything," he said. Hulbert's response was merciless: "No, we are going to expel you." Although New York and Philadelphia were longtime baseball hotbeds, Hulbert believed that the credibility of the game and the reliability of the National League schedule came first.

Similarly, Hulbert refused to budge on his edict of lifetime expulsions for the four crooks from Louisville who had thrown the 1877 pennant. Many in baseball pleaded for clemency, noting that pitcher Jim Devlin, in particular, was destitute, had a family to feed, and had been treated badly by the Louisville club. The ill-educated Devlin, struggling to spell common words, was driven to write a pathetic letter to influential and kindhearted Boston manager Harry Wright, begging him for help: "I am living from hand to mouth all winter I have not got a Stich of Clothing or has my wife and child You Dont Know how I am Situated for I Know if you did you woed do Something for me I am honest Harry you need not Be Afraid the Louisville People have made me what I am to day a Beggar . . . I am Dumb Harry I dont Know how to go about it So I Trust you will answer this and do all you Can for me."

Devlin later showed up at Hulbert's office in a threadbare jacket on a cold winter day and literally got down on his knees to plead forgiveness. "I heard him entreat, not on his own account—he acknowledged himself unworthy of consideration—but for the sake of his wife and child. I beheld the agony of humiliation depicted on his features as he confessed his guilt and begged for mercy," recalled Hulbert's lieutenant, Albert G. Spalding. Hulbert trembled as he struggled to control his emotions, and he pulled fifty dollars from his wallet. "That's what I think of you, personally," Hulbert said, "but, damn you, Devlin, you are dishonest; you have sold a game, and I can't trust you. Now go; and let me never see your face again; for your act will not be condoned so long as I live."

In Hulbert's view, the game could not afford excessive sympathy for players. He oversaw the imposition of the essential, if blatantly unfair, reserve clause—which bound players to their teams even after their contracts expired, effectively eliminating any opportunity for them to become free agents and sell their services to the highest bidder. Hulbert and his fellow owners contended that clubs could not retain value if the players they nurtured could simply pick up and leave. Their argument held sway over major-league baseball for nearly a hundred years, and even now players in their first several seasons in the big leagues are tied to the reserve clause before they can become free agents.

The owners felt they needed strong controls because players tended to be hard-drinking, self-serving, sometimes dishonest young men who were out to make a buck any way they could, and not especially good at keeping their promises. These unruly men emerged from an America where there was far less opportunity for higher education than today, a land of harsh working conditions without much of a social safety net, other than niggling charity from religious institutions. Professional baseball offered at least a temporary escape from stifling, dangerous mines or factories or dreary hard labor on farms. Though not even remotely as wealthy as today's multimillionaires, major-league players of the time were reasonably well off. They were paid two to three times what many of their fellow Americans earned toiling ten to twelve hours a day, six days a week.

Still, playing professional baseball was anything but an easy life. The sport was filled with agony and injury. It was played bare-handed—gloves for most of the fielders were not prevalent until the late 1880s—which meant pain and frequent broken fingers. Catchers did have some minimal protection. They wore gloves on both hands with the fingers sheared off so that they could grip the ball, wore chest protectors, and had primitive wire face masks (dubbed "bird cages"). But foul tips could smash through the wire of those masks or split catchers' fingers, sometimes exposing bloody bone and sinew. And the lack of shin guards led to agonizing bruises and injuries. Owners, operating on small profit margins or losing money, only paid for twelve or thirteen men per team. Everyone was expected to work hard. When a man got injured, his pay often stopped— no play, no pay. Rules did not permit substitutions during games except in the event of injuries or illnesses so acute that the player clearly could not go on. (The umpire decided whether that was the case, often provoking bitter arguments with managers.) As a result, men played in pain, sometimes aggravating their injuries. Careers tended to be short.

Those extra players who were not in the starting lineup were expected to help out by working the gates in their street clothes, collecting tickets. Baseballs themselves were pricy items, and owners preferred to use only one per game, instead of the one-hundred-plus used today. They were as hard as modern baseballs, and the same size and weight, but had a rubber center rather than a cork one, which made them more difficult to drive for distance. (Even so, professional sluggers could knock them over the fence.) If fouled off into the crowd, or even out of the park, the balls had to be fetched and returned to the field. By the end of the game, as the sun set on parks without lights, the ball had become stained with dirt and tobacco juice, making it extremely difficult for a batter to see. Often, it was mushy; sometimes, the stitching—which was black rather than red, and sewed closer together than on today's balls—would come loose.

Modern fans would find the early game different in other ways as well. For decades, foul balls caught on the bounce were outs. The National League eliminated the "foul-bound catch" in 1883, but the American Association retained this play until June 1885, making for mad dashes into foul territory by the fielders. Batters had an advantage under the rules in being able to choose either a "high" (between letters and belt) or "low" (between belt and knees) pitch zone when they came to the plate, and the umpire had to adjust. Foul balls were not yet strikes, and skilled hitters, such as Arlie Latham, could foul off pitch after pitch, tiring the hurler without losing ground in the pitch count. But there was no rule yet giving a batter his base if he was hit by a pitch—and competitive and hardhearted pitchers ruthlessly took advantage of that, driving batters off the plate and, not infrequently, stinging them with fastballs.

Making all this scarier was how close pitchers seemed. The pitcher's mound had not yet been invented; pitchers worked in a level, rectangular, four-by-six-foot box with six-inch-square iron plates affixed to each corner, its front edge only fifty feet from home plate. Inside that box, pitchers could take a kind of run and hop to more swiftly propel the ball. Batters, wearing only cloth caps rather than today's protective helmets, had little time to react.

It was a fast-paced and dangerous game, and Hulbert harbored no illusions about the character of the men who played it. In one letter, he voiced his disgust to a Worcester official about one particularly mercurial outfielder. "Lipman Pike has for many years been notorious as a shirk, fraud and brat," Hulbert wrote. "He is a conspicuous example of the worthless, ungrateful, low-lived whelps that the League will do well to publicly throw overboard by means of a published *black list*." Hulbert got his blacklist, then promptly denied ten men their livelihood in baseball, not only barring League clubs from hiring them, but prohibiting lucrative exhibition games against any club that *did*. That made it all but impossible for the banished men to find work. In a highly publicized "Address to Players," Hulbert warned that the League was imposing "stricter accountability" on those inclined to drink to excess. Hereafter, he declared, the organization would not "permit or tolerate drunkenness or bummerism" by players. No longer could a ballplayer "disgrace his club and his avocation by scandalous and disreputable practices."

Controlling these young men was only part of Hulbert's agenda. At the core of his plan to set baseball on a road to economic salvation was a campaign to attract upper-middle-class customers and their families. Many such customers had given up on baseball in the 1870s, disgusted by the gamblers, boozers, thugs, and painted strumpets who had infiltrated ballparks. Hulbert hoped to lure back the middle class through a Puritan agenda of no Sunday ball, no beer sales, no gambling on the grounds, and a fifty-cent admission price, high enough to keep the riffraff out.

In 1880, the owners of the Cincinnati Reds had incurred Hulbert's wrath by selling beer on their grounds and renting the park out for Sunday non-League games—something the organization depended on to make ends meet, given their bum players and the League's high admission price. Like St. Louis, Cincinnati was loaded with German immigrants who had come to expect such civilized pleasures. The dispute came to a head at the League's fall 1880 meeting, when Cincinnati Reds President W. H. Kennett refused to sign a pledge against beer and Sunday ball, pleading that his stockholders could not condone a pact that would be tantamount to financial suicide. "Beer and Sunday amusements have become a popular necessity," O. P. Caylor of the *Cincinnati Enquirer* tried to explain to the puritanical owners back East. "We drink beer in Cincinnati as freely as you used to drink milk, and it is not a mark of disgrace either." But two days after Kennett refused to sign the pledge, Hulbert and his fellow owners gave Cincinnati the boot, as they had New York and Philadelphia. Caylor found it hypocritical in the extreme. "We respectfully suggest, that while the League is in the missionary field, they turn their attention to Chicago and prohibit the admission to the Lake Street grounds of the great number of prostitutes who patronize the game up there."

O. P. Caylor,
New York Clipper, *October 29, 1881*
(Library of Congress)

By the fall of 1881, it was clear that Hulbert's stout leadership had forced owners and players into line. But his struggle had come at a great cost: Some of the best markets in baseball were now deprived of a presence in the League, and Hulbert had managed to drain a good deal of fun out of baseball in the process. To his dismay, ambitious men in cities that the League had abandoned decided to fight back.

On November 2, 1881, they gathered at Cincinnati's plush Gibson House hotel to talk about forming a less repressive league of their own. The delegation was top-heavy with liquor interests—not only the beer-selling Chris Von der Ahe, but also J. H. Pank of Louisville's mammoth Kentucky Malt Company and Cincinnati officials who represented brewer-investors. Von der Ahe's passion and drive made an instant impression with the group. Harmer Denny McKnight, chief executive of Pittsburgh's Allegheny Club, suggested that Von der Ahe run the meeting as chairman, but the German politely demurred, returning the compliment by nominating the more articulate McKnight to serve in that difficult and time-consuming role. Then they got down to business.

The delegates formed a new league called the American Association, quickly admitting the St. Louis Browns, Cincinnati Reds, Louisville Eclipse, Brooklyn Atlantics, and Pittsburgh Alleghenys as members. The

Association owners voted to give visiting clubs a puny rate of $65 per game, rather than the League's 40 percent of the gate. This had the effect of making it harder for the poorer Association clubs to sponge off the richer ones; each club had to stand on its own, making the bulk of its profits from its own home games. (The $65 guarantee was one reason a wary Brooklyn pulled out before the start of the 1882 season, ceding its place to the Baltimore club owned by Harry Vonderhorst, another brewer who wanted to push his beer at the games.) On such holidays as Decoration Day or the Fourth of July, however, when huge crowds tended to flock to the park, gate receipts would be divided evenly.

There was still a question of placing teams in America's biggest cities, Philadelphia and New York. Two delegations from Philly had arrived; the Association gave the Athletics club the nod because it already had a ballpark lined up. New York proved thornier. The flamboyant manager of the independent New York Metropolitans, "Truthful Jim" Mutrie, was on hand, but seemingly more as an observer than participant—and, probably, as a double agent. (His nickname, needless to say, was ironic.) Mutrie and his partner, John Day, had made piles of money from the National League by pitting their Metropolitan Club against visiting League teams, and neither seemed terribly eager to put that revenue stream at risk. Indeed, Mutrie declined even to enter the meeting room, saying he wanted to learn the policies of the new league before committing his club to anything. And, immediately after the meeting, he caught a train to Chicago, where he sat down with Hulbert behind closed doors. He emerged only to announce that the Mets would not be joining the Association.

But, with or without New York, a new major league was born. Although the Association patterned its constitution after the League's, it prided itself on more "liberal" policies than its stodgy competitor. Reflecting the strong beliefs of Von der Ahe, Association ticket prices would be half the League's, at twenty-five cents apiece, and Sunday baseball would be permitted. Surprisingly, given the predominance of liquor interests in the owners' ranks, the Association initially barred the sale of hard liquor and beer at games. When Von der Ahe and officials from Cincinnati protested that the closing of their ballpark bars would cost each franchise $4,000 to $5,000 in pure profit for the season, their fellow owners rescinded the rule. Louisville initially declined to run a ballpark bar, but after "mushroom beer stands" sprang up just outside Eclipse Park in 1882, run by "two very smart citizens who will make a fortune if they live long enough," according to one newspaper, the franchise reconsidered before the 1883 season.

All in all, this would be a league that catered to every class of spectator, from laborers to wealthy gentlemen, a league that would make it possible for a workingman to enjoy a beer at the ballpark with his wife or girlfriend on his one day of the week free from toil. The Association pointed away from Hulbert's puritanism to the modern idea of enjoyment at the game. But critics were disgusted with this freewheeling operation and the liquor interests that backed it, dubbing it "the Beer and Whiskey Circuit."

Although the new Association vowed to keep its hands off crooked and dishonest players blacklisted by the League, it flirted with the idea of signing those whose sins were a little less clear. One was Charley Jones, who could serve as a poster child for the League's haughty treatment of players. A flamboyant, muscular slugger from North Carolina with a handsome waxed handlebar mustache, Jones quarreled with his club, the Boston Red Stockings, about late pay during the 1880 season. In those days, club officials were wary of hauling around too much cash on the road, since they did not want to become targets of hotel thieves or armed robbers. Thus, they typically held off giving players their full pay packets (which the men were due to receive twice a month) until they got back home. In the meantime, clubs advanced the players small sums to help them get by. The proud Jones, a bit of a prima donna, was unhappy with this arrangement. He flatly refused to play during one road trip until he was paid in full what Boston owed him, which had climbed to the then-significant sum of $378, when star players typically earned much less than $2,000 a year. Boston management, outraged at Jones's gall, expelled him and, with Hulbert's help, barred him from organized baseball for the rest of the year and the following season—even after a judge ordered Boston to pay Jones his back salary. The Cincinnati Reds, however, hoped to hire him for 1882, in violation of the League's orders.

Hulbert instantly recognized the threat posed by the American Association—not only to the business interests of the National League but also to his own ability to keep an iron grip on players and owners. Soon after meeting with Mutrie, he sat down to write his letter of warning to McKnight. Hulbert might have had trouble communicating with the liquor interests who seemed so eager to stain baseball's reputation, especially that fellow from St. Louis who seemed little more than a German bumpkin grocer. But McKnight, a college-educated bookkeeper who had founded an iron manufacturing company, struck Hulbert as a man of substance. He might listen to reason—or veiled threats.

"The sole purpose of the League (outside the business aspect) is to promote and elevate the game; make it worthy the patronage support and respect of the best class of people," Hulbert explained to McKnight. "The League will never recognize an Association of clubs by fraternizing with it, or any club members of it, which prostitutes itself by becoming a sanctuary for the League's disqualified players." In other words, the Association could not count on any remunerative exhibition games against League clubs unless it gave up on the idea of grabbing people like Charley Jones. That player, Hulbert insisted, deserved no forgiveness. He had "deserted the club, refused to perform service, abstained himself from their team when it was on a trip." Overlooking such behavior "would set a most pernicious example" that would surely haunt the Association. Hulbert further warned against selling liquor, pointing out that ticket sales improved at the Chicago grounds after it was banned in 1877. As for Sunday

William Hulbert
(*Transcendental Graphics*/theruckerarchive.com;
reprinted with permission)

games, the big crowds on the Lord's Day would merely drain attendance from weekday games. Finally, in defense of his own personality, he added, rather unpersuasively, "I am not the bulldozer I am painted."

By then, Hulbert was fighting for more than his legacy; he was fighting for his life. Years of stress as a hard-driving Chicago business executive and leader of an endangered professional game, combined with a powerful appetite that was revealed in his stocky physique and double chin, had taken a severe toll on his heart. He was growing weaker from the ravages of cardiac disease. "More than a month, I have been ailing," he confessed in a second letter to McKnight, ten days after the first. "My doctors have let me out a few hours in the middle of pleasant days, but active attention to business is positively interdicted." The tension he felt over the American Association's descent into booze, cheap prices, and Sunday baseball surely did not help any. Still, he mustered the strength to make one last impassioned plea in a tone approaching desperation. "You cannot afford to bid for the patronage of the degraded; if you are to be successful, you must secure recognition by the respectable. A Sunday playing club, that is at the same time accessory to beer hawking, is beyond doubt, a curse to any community. The youth of the land are everywhere crazy about base ball. You should not help build up an Assn of clubs that will permit such things."

AT FIRST, IT APPEARED THE TWO CIRCUITS MIGHT LIVE IN HIGHLY profitable peace. Perhaps in response to Hulbert's pleas, the Association's Cincinnati Reds did back off from their plans to sign Charley Jones, leaving the National League's precious blacklist intact. In April 1882, clubs from the rival leagues met in twenty-one crowd-pleasing exhibition games. The League won all twenty-one, settling rather decisively any debate over which circuit was better, but the contests nonetheless drew thousands of paying customers. One of the most notable attendees was Oscar Wilde, the flamboyant British poet, playwright, and all-around wag, who saw the League's Cleveland club beat the Alleghenys during his much-publicized tour of America. "He admired the game very much," one reporter noted, "but the uniforms were not quite to his aesthetic taste."

The appearance of peace and goodwill was highly misleading, however. The already tense relationship between the two leagues had frayed to the point of snapping. Rumors circulated that National League owners had contributed to a secret war chest, to be used to bribe back any player who jumped to the American Association. Certainly, something turned around infielders Dasher Troy and Sam Wise, who, after signing perfectly valid contracts with the American Association, abruptly returned to the National League. "That men should be so devoid of all sense of honor as to ignore their own signatures, and thus bring certain disgrace upon themselves, seems beyond understanding," O. P. Caylor sputtered in the *Cincinnati Enquirer*. Ballplayers had whined ad nauseam about the "tyrannical rules" of the League, but as soon as a new organization emerged, ready to advance their interests, they had promptly stabbed it in the back. "After these exhibitions of the mental weakness of professionals we have no hesitation in corroborating the oft-expressed opinion of President Hulbert of the League," Caylor wrote. "It is to the effect that although there are white men among the players the majority are ignorant and uncontrollable men, who have not the least idea of honor; that they should be treated as such, and that in dealing with them there should be no mercy or leniency shown them. . . . People may talk all they please about the iron rules of the League, but they are not half so rigid as they ought to be."

Hoping to preserve the peace between the leagues, McKnight pleaded with Hulbert to return Troy and Wise before it was too late. Stubborn to the last, Hulbert declared in an interview that he saw no need to respect Association contracts, or even to recognize the Association's existence: "I don't care to go into the question of the League's attitude toward the so-called American Association further than to say it is not likely the League will be awake nights bothering its head about how to protect a body in which it has no earthly interest, and which voluntarily assumed a position of hostility toward the League." League teams, meanwhile, began trying to make off with the Association's biggest stars. "I thank you kindly for your generous offer to [Pete] Browning," Louisville Eclipse President J. H. Pank wrote in a sarcastic telegram to William G. Thompson, the mayor of Detroit and president of that city's National League club. "It grieves me to say to you that he will play in Louisville next season. Perhaps you can get him the following season. In the meantime, you miserable reprobate, farewell."

Hulbert raised another ruckus when he barred League teams from playing against the American Association's Philadelphia Athletics. From now on, he ruled, League clubs would have to play all their Philadelphia exhibition games against the Phillies, an independent team that had sworn to respect League contracts and was being groomed for full membership. Athletics boosters had never forgotten that it was Hulbert who, five years earlier, banished their club from the League. The fact that he was yet again undermining the beloved Athletics was almost too much to bear for John P. Campbell, baseball editor of the *Philadelphia Item*. Hulbert's "brains seems to have run to his paunch," Campbell steamed. Since League clubs had cleared $9,000 playing exhibition games against the Athletics in 1881, Hulbert was apparently willing to damage his own teams for the sake of bearing a grudge. "We wish to be understood as declaring an open and unrelenting war on League practices as exemplified by Hurlbert [*sic*]," Campbell wrote, "and we hope to have the pleasure of writing at no distant day the obituary of a man who has done more to kill off the game in this country than any man living." The young reporter may well have known that Hulbert wasn't expected to live much longer. If so, his vindictiveness was a fair sample of the sentiment in the Association camp. "The League has tried to smother us and refused our friendship," wrote McKnight. "They will find too late that we can stand it better than they."

Hulbert died on April 10, 1882, just before the start of the regular season. A friend and Chicago lawyer named W. I. Culver who was "present at Mr. Hulbert's bedside during the weary nights of his long and fated illness" noted that he bore his agony with characteristic fortitude. "Though impatient of suffering and of the restraint of his daily increasing weakness, he was bold and manly to the last; certain that his days were numbered, hopeless of cure, writhing in times in pain, he awaited the liberator death, with as much composure as he would have greeted a friend. He lived and died a man." American Association officials seemed less tender toward his legacy. Within weeks of Hulbert's death, McKnight ordered a halt to all exhibition games against League clubs, planning to hit his adversary where it hurt—in the purse.

The American Association's twenty-five-cent price of admission proved immensely popular in 1882. Vastly bigger crowds turned out for its games than for the League's with its fifty-cent tariff. Sunday baseball was also a hit. Von der Ahe's Browns took part in the first major-league game ever played on a Sunday, on May 7, 1882. That game was played in Louisville, but as soon as the Browns were at home, they played Sunday after Sunday, drawing many people who never attended National League games, just as Von der Ahe had predicted. Immigrants, in particular, turned to baseball. It gave them a way to learn what America was all about: a quarter, carefully saved, could get them into the splendid spectacle of an American Association game, and they could even go on Sundays, the one day of the week they did not have to work. Inside the park, they could see in the grandstand well-dressed and well-fed people—people who were living the American life to which they aspired—and, on the field, tough, ambitious players who were not all that far above the working poor.

A less upscale, freely drinking crowd could be a mixed blessing, of course. Association crowds tended to be not only bigger than the League's, but also rowdier and cruder. Returning from a Sunday game in Louisville in May, a dedicated St. Louis Browns rooter named John Cooney complained that "some 500 hoodlums" had positioned themselves behind home plate, where they "rent the air with blackguard words and hoots of disapprobation at every move made by the Browns." Such obnoxious behavior, the *St. Louis Globe-Democrat* ventured, would never pass muster in classier League parks. "In the League cities the crowds attending the ball games are made to behave, and any blackguard conduct results in prompt ejectment from the ground. In the cities where the American Association is represented, notably Louisville and Cincinnati, the hoodlums appear to rule the roost." That being the case, the paper suggested to supporters that "when they visit these two places they take along with them shot-guns as well as their ball clubs, and use the former when too hard pressed."

Numbers on the backs of uniforms had not yet been invented, and to help spectators identify players the Association embarked on a novel scheme to dress each man differently based on the position he played. That was dropped early in the season when both the public and the players found the look more laughable than helpful. But even after that, the players in this raucous new league were lax about keeping their uniforms clean and in good repair—or even uniform. "The Alleghenys in the early part of the season were neat," one critic noted, "but when last here one man in their nine wore brown instead of blue stockings, while some wore blue, some gray and some white caps. The regular uniform shirt was not worn by all the players, two or three coming out in tights." Baltimore wore "trampish-looking suits," while the St. Louis Browns were among the worst offenders: "Comisky [*sic*] has a weakness for wearing a cap different in color from that worn by his colleagues. First it was a gray that he wore, then a light blue; now he eschews caps altogether and comes out in a white turban. Sullivan seldom wears the same cap twice. Dorr very often wears a pair of breeches that look as though they were made to fit the Cardiff Giant," a reference to the ten-foot-tall "petrified" nude man that had been dug up in 1869 in Cardiff, New York, and put on display by P. T. Barnum—a colossal hoax, naturally. "McGinnis' failing is in always wearing a common undershirt instead of the regulation garment." It all contributed to the fledgling league's general air of seediness.

Meanwhile, on July 4, Louisville hosted balloon rides at Eclipse Park, but had to cancel them abruptly when the balloon caught fire during one ride before reaching the level of the press box above the grandstand. Tom Brown, an outfielder for the Baltimore club, later recalled the Association's funhouse spirit. "Can you imagine the difference between a Philadelphia Sunday and a Sabbath day at gay Coney Island?" That was "about the difference" between baseball as it was played in the sober, proper National League and the loose, "rough-and-ready" American Association.

Outfits and safety concerns aside, the new league was reminding Americans why they so loved the game. Something about baseball captured the national spirit, its striving, impatient, rebellious nature superimposed over a love of pastoral beauty, justice, and order. Moreover, baseball seemed to epitomize the American interplay between communal effort and something more essential: brilliant individual achievement. The 1880s version was particularly fast-paced and action-packed. Batters did not drag out the time between pitches by incessantly stepping out of the box, taking extra swings, adjusting their uniforms, or scratching themselves; they stood ready to hit, while pitchers stood ready to throw. Since there was no broadcast advertising, there were no delays between innings. Games raced along, rarely lasting longer than two hours, and often taking no more than ninety minutes. Like America itself, baseball demanded initiative and guts, and the men playing it sometimes resorted to guile and even violence as well as skill to get the better of their fellow man.

In 1884, the *Sporting Life* listed examples of the "low trickery" professionals employed to hold and defend their advantage, such as "slyly cutting the ball to have it changed, tripping up base runners, willfully colliding with fielders to make them commit errors, hiding the ball, and other specially mean tricks of the kind characteristic of corner lot loafers in their ball games." Mark Twain described the game as a perfect image of his America: "the very symbol, the outward and visible expression of the drive, and push, and rush and struggle of the raging, tearing, booming nineteenth century!"

Though the Association offered no real pennant race—the Cincinnati Reds finished eleven and a half games ahead of the second-place Philadelphia Athletics—paying customers poured into Association parks throughout the summer in numbers that dwarfed the turnout at games of the far superior National League, which featured a great championship fight. By the *Cleveland Leader*'s count, five of the Association's six teams outdrew the National League's mighty Chicago White Stockings—and Chicago had pulled in three times more people than any of the other seven League clubs. All that business meant that Association clubs were flush with cash as the 1882 season neared a close—and were thus in a strong position to steal the National League's best players for 1883, putting that older league at dire risk.

In a panic, the Hulbert-less owners of the League's clubs convened an emergency meeting on September 22, 1882, at Philadelphia's Continental Hotel to figure out how to fight back. William G. Thompson, president of the Detroit Wolverines, set the tone with a speech he delivered in his room after dinner, drinks, and cigars. "You cannot afford to sneer at the American Association and call it the abortion of the League," the mayor told his fellow owners. "The American Association clubs have all made money this season, and the aggregate population of the cities in which they play far exceeds that of the League cities. . . . No, gentlemen, you cannot afford to sneer at the Association. They are taking our players because they can afford to pay higher salaries."

The League's answer was to toss aside Hulbert's stern principles— his refusal to cater to the big markets and his stubborn loyalty to his faithful franchises, no matter how small. It was time to face reality. The owners voted to chuck out Worcester and Troy, though the small-city franchises had broken no rules, and replace them with clubs in the two biggest markets: the Philadelphia Phillies and a new team that Mutrie and Day planned to create in New York. They also fought to recover players who had absconded to the Association, bribing them to return to the fold or threatening them with lifetime expulsion. By the time American Association executives held their own special meeting on October 23 in Columbus, Ohio, they were, in the words of the *Cincinnati Enquirer's* O. P. Caylor, "worked up to a fever-heat, and they arrived here cocked and primed . . . to show the bullying League that from now out it was war to the knife." Their major order of business that day was to expand by two teams, ushering in the Columbus Buckeyes and the famous New York Metropolitans, Day and Mutrie having decided to field a club in *both* leagues. That raised the total to eight clubs, the same as the National League.

Then, having proclaimed the Association's parity with the League, the owners shoved a dagger into the heart of Hulbert's blacklist. The executives passed a resolution proclaiming open season on the League's proscribed players, with the exception of the four Louisville crooks. This was a declaration of unlimited war against the League, which had considered its blacklist a strong protection against crooked and unruly players, and a powerful weapon during contract negotiations. Chris Von der Ahe, his impetuous anger roused by his enemies' tactics, told a reporter that he thought the action "was a splendid one. The League thought they could sit upon us, and take our players as they wished, even if we did expel them. Why can not we, who are on a paying basis, do the same?"

Both leagues, it was now clear, were advancing rapidly beyond the final outposts of negotiation and compromise. An ugly fight for players and patronage loomed, and it seemed possible—even likely—the war would rage until one of these two leagues was destroyed. Von der Ahe predicted it would be the National League. "I think that in 1884 Chicago, New York and Philadelphia will be the only surviving members of the League. Then they will have to come to us," he said. Vengeance was decidedly in the air. "Next season it will be war to the knife," McKnight vowed in an interview. "We will ask for no quarter." As one war measure, McKnight banned lucrative postseason games with the National League during that autumn of 1882.

The Cincinnati Reds went ahead and played some anyway, using a lawyerly evasion to pretend they were not violating McKnight's prohibition. In early October, the Reds formally discharged their players for the season. The players then reformed as an independent team for the month of October and boldly scheduled games against the League's Cleveland, Chicago, and Providence clubs. McKnight was furious at this attempt to end-run his embargo. But Cincinnati played on. And, because it did, the champions of two major leagues clashed in October for the first time in baseball history.

Some have labeled the Cincinnati Reds–Chicago White Stockings games of October 1882 the original World Series. But they were considerably less than that: just a couple of exhibitions. Mike Kelly didn't even bother to accompany his Chicago teammates to Cincinnati, "being at home singing lullabys and loving ditties to his new wife." Still, the idea of a postseason faceoff between the league champions appealed to Americans from the start. Despite an admission charge of fifty cents, twice the regular-season rate, the first of the two games at Cincinnati's Bank Street Grounds drew 2,700 Reds fanatics, a crowd full of more enthusiasm "than young America is with plum-pudding after the Christmas dinner." The White Stockings were bigger, literally and figuratively, than the Reds—taller and more muscular, with three straight National League pennants under their belts. But the Cincinnati crowd—including "large numbers of our country cousins, their uncles and their sisters' 'fellers'" from rural Ohio and Kentucky—helped even things out, making it a point "to bubble forth in yells that must have awakened the sleeping heroes of the Revolution, if there were any within several leagues of the grounds." Their shouts of "Ya-ha! Yi ki! Rip, rah," drowned out blaring calliopes and the scream of locomotive whistles nearby.

The crowd had reason to shout. Reds pitcher Will White, the first major leaguer to wear spectacles, held the League champions to eight scattered hits, beating the heavily favored White Stockings, 4–0. One hillbilly from "across the river" in Kentucky summed it up succinctly: "them yar little fellers licking them big 'uns." An even bigger crowd of 3,500 turned out the following afternoon. This time, Chicago's little Larry Corcoran silenced the mob and restored the natural order of baseball by mowing down them little fellers, 2–0, surrendering only three singles. Still, even one win by an Association nine against baseball's best team put an exclamation point on a memorable debut season for the new league.

Even so, McKnight was furious when he learned that Cincinnati had betrayed him. Before Chicago came to town, he had issued a stern warning to Reds manager Pop Snyder: Play one more game against the National League, and "you and any of your players who participate . . . will be expelled." Two weeks later, at the Association's annual meeting, McKnight tried to make good on his promise. After hours of debate, two of the owners, the more radical McKnight and Von der Ahe, voted to summarily kick Cincinnati out. But the cooler moderates in the room, Lew Simmons of the Philadelphia Athletics and J. H. Pank of the Louisville Eclipse, opposed the measure, no doubt recalling that the Association owed its very existence to such heavy-handed decisions by the League to abandon good baseball cities. When the tie vote effectively blocked expulsion, the delegates agreed on a significantly less draconian punishment: a formal reprimand and a fine of $100. McKnight's threatening telegram became the basis of a moldy legend that he interrupted baseball's first World Series in midplay and forced its cancellation, as if a modern set of seven games had been under way. In fact, Chicago had never scheduled more than two.

As 1882 came to a close, the American Association was eight clubs strong, occupying some of America's best baseball cities and benefiting from low ticket prices, crowd-pleasing beer sales, and Sunday ball. But the Association faced its own dangers. Incessant warfare with the older league threatened to destroy its profits. Gamblers continued to do big business at ballparks, threatening to corrupt the game. Owners had invested heavily to put a better brand of baseball on the field, and they had to wonder whether that would pay off in sufficiently bigger crowds or they had disastrously overspent. Could the owners somehow reach a peaceful accommodation, maximizing their profits instead of ruinously fighting? The coming season of 1883 could well determine whether baseball would make its comeback or turn back onto the path to oblivion.

3

THE MINSTREL STAR

I N THE 1880 CENSUS, PHILADELPHIA—WITH 847,170 PEOPLE TO
New York's 1.2 million—was America's second biggest metropolis, a
booming center of trade and manufacturing, one observer wrote, "with
the inexhaustible coal and iron fields of Pennsylvania at its back." Loaded
with wealth, it offered all the amenities of a bustling city filled with proud
and civic-minded people—hospitals, museums, libraries, markets, parks,
theaters, a zoo, academies and colleges, churches, concert halls, busy
wharfs, printing houses and newspapers, excellent waterworks and sew-
erage, 61 public drinking fountains, 2,000 miles of streets—of which 900
were paved—and 1,300 streetcars pulled by 8,000 horses (fare, five cents).
No less than eight railroads provided transportation to the outside world.
By the standards of nineteenth-century America, cleanliness was a local
obsession: according to Philadelphia's Board of Health, of 145,000 buildings in the city, 26,000 had water closets, or toilets, and many more had
piped-in water. An "unbounded supply of fresh water and its universal
use for bathing and cleansing purposes" helped give the city an excellent
mortality rate. "The smallest and cheapest house has its bathroom, and

the incessant washing of sidewalks and doorsteps is a grievance complained of by strangers who are trying to see the city on foot," observed
one writer. That such a modern, lively, cultured city would lack a top professional baseball team seemed unthinkable to Lew Simmons, a local
baseball fanatic who had won national fame in another nineteenth-century entertainment fad, Negro minstrelsy.

Born on August 27, 1838, in New Castle, near the western border of
Pennsylvania, Simmons had loved to show off and win applause from
an early age. At some point he found he could get laughs by imitating
the jokes and songs of the traveling minstrel troupes that rolled through
the region. At the tender age of eleven, he made his way to Warren,
Ohio, 30 miles west of his hometown, to perform in blackface, mimicking black dialect, singing comic tunes, and strumming his beloved banjo
in a town hall lit by candles. Three years later, the boy ran away from
home to join the circus. In those days, circuses welcomed young, cheap
performers, including boys who could sing tunes and cavort as clowns.

Lew Simmons and his banjo,
Lew Simmons' Songster *(author's collection)*

Simmons spent the rest of his life virtually on the road, most notably on the minstrel stage, crooning comic and sentimental tunes and performing as a "tambo"—a figure who made witty quips, often at the expense of the white master of ceremonies, punctuating his jokes with a shake of the tambourine.

A few years into his budding career, the question that the minstrel shows implicitly raised—whether black Americans really were fully human—ignited the Civil War. Simmons, who was twenty-two years old when the firing on Fort Sumter plunged America into war, successfully avoided service. But he contributed to the cause on stage, helping to popularize the stirring new battle song "When Johnny Comes Marching Home." In 1864, he joined the famous Carncross and Dixey's Minstrels in Philadelphia, and by the end of the war, he was one of America's greatest minstrel stars.

A seventy-two-page paperback book, *Lew Simmons' Songster* (1868), celebrated his fame. It included pictures of his act—some disturbingly racist—and lyrics to his hit songs, including "The Base Ball Fever," "Conducting a City Car," "Going Out a Skating," and, poking fun at German immigrants, "De Man Vat Likes de Lager Beer." In 1870, he boldly formed his own his minstrel company, Simmons and Slocum, and built a handsome opera house at 1003 Arch Street in Philadelphia that was still in existence in the twenty-first century as the Trocadero Theatre. Simmons traveled the world, performing in blackface in Turkey, England, China, and South America. He spent one winter as the proprietor of a minstrel troupe at Cape Town, South Africa, catering to British soldiers fighting in the Zulu War.

During his off-hours, Simmons indulged himself in skating and baseball, demonstrating an athlete's grace and coordination in both sports. Over the winter of 1866–1867, Lew made headlines by combining the two skills, playing baseball on ice in one of those silly exhibitions that seemed to delight the nineteenth-century mind. In warmer weather, when the theaters tended to be shut down, Simmons was a good enough ballplayer to take the field for the Philadelphia Athletics, already one of the best teams in the country. Highly regarded for his heavy batting, he scored ten runs in a single game on July 30, 1866, as the Athletic and Philadelphia clubs inaugurated Oakdale Park, at Eleventh and Huntington streets. The

Title page,
Lew Simmons' Songster (*author's collection*)

following spring, the club awarded him a gold-headed cane "as a slight appreciation of his efforts on behalf of Philadelphia's favorite team."

Simmons's performing career was too profitable for him to play baseball full-time, yet he never stopped loving the game. He got out to the ballpark whenever he could, and his piping cry of "pretty work!" was a familiar sound in the grandstand for years. But, just as in St. Louis, baseball in Philadelphia had withered by the late 1870s, rotted out by gambling corruption and the loss of a place in the National League. In 1881, two Philadelphia men—Billy Sharsig, a theatrical manager, and Charlie Mason, a former professional ballplayer who now owned a cigar store, and who was known as more of a devotee of "highball" cocktails than of baseball—decided to make a stab at reviving baseball in their city. They formed a partnership to field an independent, gate-splitting team named after the once mighty Athletics. According to Al Spink, "Sharsig's capital consisted of a stocking of gold, the life savings of his old mother which he had borrowed." They brought Simmons on as an experienced theatrical manager and diehard baseball lover. He would serve as their business manager.

For a time, it appeared that Sharsig had squandered his aged mother's nest egg. "When I went around among the newspaper offices and asked them to publish some baseball matter," he recalled, "they said: 'Billy, get out. We have no time to talk about a dead crow.'" Sharsig found he had to bribe editors to put squibs about the Athletics into the papers. Perhaps this, from the *Philadelphia Item* in June 1881, was one of them: "Baseball is destined to be as popular as ever in the city. The Athletics were the entering wedge to this return of enthusiasm over the game."

Oddly enough, though, the prediction started to come true as summer wore on. The players seemed to be honest, the games were exciting, and the owners knew how to entertain crowds. Late in the year, Sharsig and Mason offered second baseman Chick Fulmer an ownership stake for $200; when he balked, Simmons jumped in as the third financier. He caught a train to Cincinnati in November 1881 to help found the new American Association, with his Athletics as a charter member. It proved to be an exceedingly astute investment. When the Athletics finished in second place in the circuit's inaugural season, attendance exploded. The three owners, who "kept no books but divided the receipts after each game," began taking home bags stuffed full of cash. Serving as ticket collectors themselves to spare the cost of hiring staff, the triumvirate reportedly pocketed $22,000 in clear profit for 1882. Once he saw the money pour in, Simmons abruptly reversed his career direction. He dropped his remaining minstrel work to pursue baseball full-time.

In a flowery statement sent out to prospective season ticket holders in April 1883, Simmons, Sharsig, and Mason boasted that they had revived baseball's "old-time popularity" in the city by ridding the grandstand of gamblers and ruffians and presenting an honest contest on the field. "Conducted on business principles, and freed from the demoralizing influences which had for several years alienated its most worthy patrons, [baseball] has, Phoenix-like, arisen with former prestige restored and rejuvenated," their announcement asserted. Using language designed to appeal to

Philadelphia's wealthy Protestant establishment—the ones who could afford season tickets—the owners stressed that people of quality could once again attend Athletics games without revulsion. "Those whose education and refinement had for a time sought suitable companionship only at cricket matches found again last year congeniality and enjoyment among the throngs that witnessed the skillful and exciting games of baseball played on our grounds."

Hoping to attract more such customers, the owners announced that each Thursday home game in 1883 would be "Ladies Day." Any woman who was accompanied by a ticket holder would be granted free admission. Women not only drew men to the park, they tended to keep the crowd under control, since men limited their swearing and violence around the fairer sex. The *National Police Gazette* joked that there was another reason why Mason was behind the concept, "as there is not a greater ladies' man in the United States than Charley. He is extremely handsome, has winning manners, is a great society man, and a pet among all the ladies. When Charley comes about all the mashers crawl into their holes." In any event, the owners pledged that the public's nasty experiences at ballparks infested with rowdies, drunks, gamblers, and their like were a thing of the past. The owners vowed:

> Ladies and gentlemen will be protected from the annoyance of distasteful expressions and spectacles by the rigid enforcement of our rules, which are that rowdies, drunkards or other objectionable characters will not be admitted under any pretense. The price of their tickets, if presented, will be refunded. Pool-selling or open betting will not be allowed. Respect for the umpire's decisions, however distasteful, will be enforced. Profanity, obscenity or other disorderly conduct among the audience will not be tolerated. The presence of a sufficient number of uniformed officers will guarantee the execution of the above rules, and the summary ejection of their transgressors.

Such promises were easier to make than to keep in the raucous American Association, especially in Philadelphia.

Of course, a well-regulated park and Ladies Days could accomplish only so much. To draw really big crowds, Simmons and his mates would have to field a champion team. Much like Von der Ahe, they resolved to buy a pennant. "This year, we decided to get solid players, regardless of salary," Simmons explained to a reporter. The buzz about Simmons's rebuilding effort had the desired effect: Philadelphians who had shrugged off baseball for years could now hardly wait for the new season to begin. "All of the Athletics' season tickets have been sold, and double the number could have been disposed of if necessary," the *Item* reported on January 21.

The Athletics would be playing in a handsomely rebuilt ballpark, though not by choice. After the owners of the team had gone to considerable expense renovating shabby Oakdale Park in 1882, they found the grounds sold out from under them during the off-season to a housing developer. The club had to hustle to sign a lease on a large city-owned vacant lot. Bounded by Twenty-fifth and Twenty-seventh streets in one direction and Master and Jefferson streets in the other, it was a busy location served by five horsecar lines—the very spot used by the old Athletics in 1864 and 1871 through 1877, and, incidentally, the site of the first game in National League history, on April 22, 1876. To be sure, these hallowed grounds had not been perfectly preserved during the five years that pro baseball had been gone. The deep outfield was now covered with buildings, though the *New York Clipper* reassured readers that the remainder was "large enough for all practical purposes."

As soon as the winter broke, "landscape gardeners" quickly went to work, making the field "almost as level as the bed of a billiard table." By mid-April, the playing field was still an expanse of dirt, but it had been "plowed and harrowed and sowed heavily with lawn-grass seed." The club erected a lovely new grandstand, "handsomely ornamented with fancy cornice-work" and painted white, at relatively little cost, by recycling the lumber from the dismantled fences and grandstand at Oakdale Park. The new grandstand featured 1,600 arm-chairs, with room for 400 more. On the upper deck sat the press box, which could accommodate twelve reporters, as well as thirty-two private boxes, each with five chairs. Large bleachers stretched out along the foul lines, making the park's total seating capacity about 6,000. The players' dressing rooms were placed under the grandstand, and the club's business offices had been built near the left-field corner. "Although not yet completed," the *Clipper* reported that April, "enough has been done to show it will be one of the finest baseball grounds in the country."

When the unfinished park formally opened on April 7, 1883, four thousand hardy Philadelphians shivered in the cold to welcome back baseball. The exhibition game featured the Yale University squad, the best college team in the country, which had garnered fame largely on the strength of its wonderful pitcher, Dan Jones. The beefed-up Athletics crushed their amateur opponents 12–0, with the club's new slugger, Harry Stovey, "[leading] off with a three-bagger, which would have been a home run if the field had not been soft," and then scoring the first (and winning) run. Bobby Mathews, the Athletics' new pitcher, threw a four-hit shutout, letting only one Yale runner reach third.

It was not college ball, though, that most paying customers wanted to see in the spring. They yearned for hard-fought interleague games, which in those days took place only in the spring or fall, not during the regular season. Association President Denny McKnight had banned those in October 1882. But an astonishing truce in the bitter war between the National League and American Association had suddenly made them possible in the spring of 1883.

⎯⎯⎯◦⎯⎯⎯

ABRAHAM GILBERT MILLS HAD BETTER THINGS TO DO WITH HIS life than to bicker with the saloon owners, beer manufacturers, minstrel stars, and sportswriters who seemed to run the American Association. In January 1883, the corporate attorney from Chicago had started a new, high-pressured job in New York City as vice president of Otis Brothers, the manufacturer of a hot high-technology product—the elevator, essential to the steel-reinforced skyscrapers that were suddenly going up all over the country. It was only out of love for the game and respect for the late William Hulbert that Mills had agreed in late 1882 to add to his already heavy workload by taking on a tough, time-consuming volunteer position that paid nothing: the presidency of the National League. He took over for the interim president, Boston Red Stockings owner Arthur H. Soden.

Mills was a brave and honorable man. As a youth in 1861, he had quit the Brooklyn Atlantics to serve with the 5th New York Volunteer Infantry

Regiment, known as Duryea's Zouaves, and had fought in some of the fiercest battles of the Civil War. But he tended to view matters less moralistically and more pragmatically than Hulbert. By the time Mills took the job of League president, he was resolved to do everything in his power to end the war between the top two professional baseball leagues. "We seem to be drifting in the direction which nearly ruined baseball many years ago, when contracts were disregarded and players employed on the basis of their skill—without regard for the odium their past conduct had brought upon the game," he wrote in a private letter. He did not share the belief that the time for talk had passed, and that President McKnight's threatened "war to the knife" was inevitable. "I take it," he wrote, "that these associations are run by full-grown men, and whatever the faults of the past may have been," these men should be able to "honor each other's contracts and return the good opinion of the public, which we are equally liable otherwise to lose."

Mills was far from the only influential voice demanding a halt to the rival leagues' internecine war. "It requires no keen sight to perceive that such a course must result disastrously to the pecuniary interests of both associations," Henry Chadwick wrote in the *New York Clipper*. The leagues simply had to stop their "Kilkenny fight" and work together if they hoped to root out corrupt players and keep salaries under control. The League's terrified owners, fearing the Association was about to crush them, were only too happy to pursue peace, and Cleveland's new manager, Frank Bancroft, was ecstatic about the renewed prospect of games between the two circuits. "If they can play together, it will put thousands of dollars in the pockets of both," he wrote to a friend. Bancroft believed "the representatives of the two associations are able and honorable gentlemen" and that all would go well "if the cool-headed men are in the majority."

It turned out that they were. President McKnight, tired of seeing players sign agreements only to bolt, stressed to his fellow Association owners that, "although his club has suffered as badly as any from violated contracts, he was willing to let that pass, rather than to bring about a worse complication of troubles." Lew Simmons, declaring that he had "slept on the matter," swung around and supported peace. In the end, only one of the Association's eight owners opposed the peace movement: the stubborn

Chris Von der Ahe of the St. Louis Browns. He argued, to no avail, that the Association, with its bigger crowds and profits from liquor sales, would win a war of attrition if the owners only had the guts to wage it.

The lawyer Mills drew up a "Tripartite Agreement"—the third signatory being the minor Northwestern League—that made perfect sense: the three leagues would agree to respect the contracts now in place; honor the reserve clause; and forget about the players they had lost, no matter how strong their claim, setting aside "narrow-minded views and personal vindictiveness," as Chadwick put it. Each club, except those in Philadelphia and New York, would own a monopoly on baseball in its city. In the interest of peace, the National League would also shrink its blacklist, springing some talented players from the dungeon of unemployment and shame. Although League owners themselves refused to take back three former stars whom they held in particular contempt—Joe Gerhardt, Charley Jones, and Phil Baker—they would no longer block the way if American Association clubs wanted them.

Through their teams of negotiators—the prominent figure from the American Association being Cincinnati journalist O. P. Caylor, who served as secretary—the two leagues finally met on February 17, 1883, at the Fifth Avenue Hotel in New York City. There, they reached a peace accord. It was a landmark day for baseball. Later called the National Agreement, Mills's deal became the framework for organized baseball down to this day. "If Hulbert made the National League possible," historian Lee Allen observed, "Mills made organized baseball possible." Wisely, the deal said nothing about Sunday games and beer. Even John P. Campbell of the *Philadelphia Item*, who had fumed for years at Hulbert's confrontational tactics and had even wished him dead, was delighted to see peace. "It may be said to have started the game on a new career that will prove highly advantageous to all concerned," he predicted. More than 130 years later, it is clear that Campbell's prophecy was a wild understatement.

———

THE DEAL CERTAINLY PROVED HIGHLY ADVANTAGEOUS IN Philadelphia. On April 14, the first truly beautiful spring day of 1883, some ten thousand people stuffed themselves into the new Athletic Park for the initial interleague clash between the Association's Athletics and the League's Philadelphia Phillies. It was the biggest baseball crowd in Philadelphia since the halcyon years of the early 1870s, when the rivalry between the Athletics and the Brooklyn Atlantics drew thousands. Henry Chadwick, writing in the *New York Clipper*, viewed that afternoon as a turning point in baseball history—the golden day when it became clear that the "Philadelphia public's confidence in the integrity of play of the professional clubs of the city has been restored, and it is to be hoped permanently."

The Phillies had been a rush job, thrown into the National League on short notice in 1883 to give the senior circuit a presence in a crucial baseball market. Nobody expected much. They were only a slightly upgraded version the 1882 Phillies, a low-salaried independent club that won only sixteen of its sixty-five exhibition games against National League teams. Betting men thought Lew Simmons's highly touted Athletics would easily walk away the winners of this first clash, the *Clipper* noted, "and their money talked to the tune of 100 to 80, and in some instances greater odds offered, and these were not eagerly taken." Even the Phillies shared that opinion. "They hoped for the best—a close fight—but were prepared for the worst," observed the *Clipper*. By contrast, "it was all-important for the Athletics to win this first game, not only to show the improved strength of the new team, but to inspire confidence in their ability to win the American pennant-race."

Although the game would not start until 3:30 P.M., a crowd began to form around the main entrance at Athletic Park at noon, and it grew to a thousand by 1 P.M. The nostalgic Chadwick loved the scene. "On squeezing through the narrow portal of the entrance we saw the veterans of the old-time Athletics Tom Pratt and Al Reach on hand attending to 'biz,' and Manager Lew Simmons and Superintendent Ryan up to their ears in preparatory work." Co-owner Mason, a man renowned for his "genial disposition, attentiveness and politeness," spotted the dean of baseball writers and led him upstairs to the press box, "from whence a splendid view of the extensive grounds and capitally-prepared field was obtainable. . . . It was a sight to see the rush." Every seat was taken by 3 P.M. Philadelphians who came later were herded onto the field, where they stood six deep in front of the outfield fences. Latecomers, stunned to find the game sold out, offered "fancy prices" for tickets "without avail."

The owners of the Athletics were caught unprepared for baseball fever of this intensity. Chadwick, noting how long it took the mob to exit after the game, urged the Athletics to build several more gates; "otherwise it will become a general resort for pickpockets to ply their trade." Another irritant was the constant stream of visitors permitted to enter the press box and distract working journalists with their inane chatter. But the revived passion for baseball on display was the most important impression of the day.

To almost everyone's surprise, the much-despised Phillies walked off with an easy 6–1 victory over the vaunted A's. "The defeat won't do the team any harm," Chadwick reassured the Athletics' followers. "They were too confident before. They now see that they have work to do, and they will do it." But they didn't do it, at least not right away. Despite the resumption of that April's miserable weather, six thousand Philadelphia baseball lovers came out for the rematch. In a cold, drizzling rain, the Phillies out-hit their opponents. The Athletics' fumbling in the field was "unworthy of an amateur club." The Phillies won 8–1. Five days later, Phillies pitcher Hardie Henderson carried a no-hitter into the eighth inning, leading his men to a 3–1 win over the Athletics, their third straight victory. "Simmons has become quite gray and has lost 50 pounds of flesh since the Athletic-Philadelphia series of championship games commenced," the *National Police Gazette* chuckled. "He has learned an awful lot about baseball in the past few weeks."

But on April 26, just five days before the start of the regular season, the Athletics finally came around, clubbing the Phillies 10–2. Two days later, the Athletics did it again, winning 10–3. And on April 30, the eve of opening day, another massive crowd of ten thousand turned out to watch the final battle of spring training between the two Philadelphia clubs. They packed the grandstand and bleachers at Athletic Park, while the overflow spilled out into right field. For the third straight time, the Athletics pummeled the Phillies, winning 9–4. That tied the city series, leaving the question of superiority until the clubs would be able to meet again more than five months later—in the postseason contests already planned for October.

Lew Simmons and his fellow owners could not have been terribly disappointed with the results. American Association clubs won only four of thirty-one games against League teams that April, and their Athletics owned three of those four victories. More important, the crowds were all that the triumvirate could have dreamed of. An astounding fifty thousand tickets were sold for the six Athletics-Phillies games, the equivalent of a full season's attendance for many professional clubs during the late 1870s and early 1880s. None of this would have happened had the trio not boldly invested in baseball. Or had Mills and a handful of coolheaded owners—Simmons included—neglected to force a peace on baseball, one that arguably saved the game.

The one man who had clamored for war to the end, the bitterly competitive Chris Von der Ahe, had no choice in the matter. He would now have to turn his ire from the National League to his American Association rivals and outsmart them to capture the pennant.

4
❦

The Moses of St. Louis

PRIL 1 IN ST. LOUIS WAS MISTY, GLOOMY, AND RAW—"ALMOST wintry at the ball park and thoroughly cheerless," said one observer. The hundreds of men pouring in to see the game pulled their coats closer, rubbed their hands together, and blew on their fingers for warmth. But a short Irishman taking in the scene had cause to smile as he saw the grandstand and bleachers start to fill up. He knew the boss would be pleased. In spite of the weather, there was going to be a big crowd today— very big, for a mere exhibition game. And Mr. Von der Ahe would surely know whom to thank.

Timothy Paul "Ted" Sullivan, a peppery little fellow with a bushy mustache, had been working hard toward this day. He was an immigrant from County Clare in the old country. Born thirty-two years earlier, during the Great Famine that had claimed 1 million lives in Ireland, he had escaped to America at the age of ten with his parents. Blessed with an Irishman's gift for talk, Sullivan had been putting it to good use for months in the service of his new employer, the St. Louis Browns. He had cajoled some of the nation's best ballplayers into joining him in St. Louis in 1883. Then he had regaled local sportswriters, touting his dazzling lineup. Sullivan's Browns had become a hot topic in local offices, barbershops, smoke shops, clubs, and saloons—wherever men gathered.

And now, one month before the regular season's May 1 opening, the baseball aficionados of St. Louis were coming out by the thousands to see for themselves, shivering a bit in their winter coats and hats, but chattering with excitement, their breath making clouds in the frigid air. By game time, the stands, still fragrant with new wood and fresh paint, were packed solid.

A gong sounded, and some six thousand pairs of eyes turned to see the players march crisply out of Solari's old place in the right-field corner. To the spectators' amazement, the once disheveled Browns formed a straight line, in order of height, "in military precision, and not like stragglers." The crowd roared its approval of the drill work, "which told that the efforts of the management in seeking to lift the game out of the rut were duly appreciated." At another stroke of the gong, the men marched toward first base. Then, separating, they jogged "double-quick" to their positions and tossed the ball around, getting loose. The symbolism of that entrance by Sullivan's men could not have been clearer: this year's Browns would stress excellence.

Even their uniforms helped to make the point. The Browns' mismatched apparel of 1882 was no more: "The old and slovenly uniforms had vanished along with the cripples, and the neatly attired players looked as bright as new dollars and full of life," the *St. Louis Globe-Democrat* said. To the surprise of many spectators, the Browns had even traded in their traditional brown stockings, caps, and trimmings, without trading in the nickname many used for the team. They were now wearing scarlet, the color of their bitter Midwestern rivals, the Cincinnati Reds, the American Association's defending champions—and the color that would later stick to the team when it became the St. Louis Cardinals. One customer grumbled, "When St. Louis plays Cincinnati there will be some sad mixing up. Better to have stuck to the brown." But the roars drowned out the catcalls. St. Louis was ready for a winner, in any color.

A beefy, red-cheeked young man surveyed the park with twinkling eyes. Von der Ahe loved the crisp new uniforms, and he loved showing off what he could buy with his fattened purse. He had made piles of money in 1882, as workingmen and their families responded warmly to his Sunday games and twenty-five-cent tickets. But his team's performance had embarrassed him. Back on September 16, 1882, as the season entered its final three weeks, St. Louis languished in next to last place:

	W	L	PCT.	GB
Cincinnati Reds	49	23	.681	—
Philadelphia Athletics	37	30	.552	9½
Louisville Eclipse	36	30	.545	10
Pittsburgh Alleghenys	36	35	.507	12½
St. Louis Browns	34	40	.459	16
Baltimore Orioles	16	50	.242	25

However little he knew about baseball's intricacies, Von der Ahe lacked the patience to endure repeated painful losses. Even before the schedule could be played out, he moved boldly to remake his club. And to lift the Browns to the next level, he had felt compelled to double-cross a loyal ally, his baseball adviser and player-manager, Ned Cuthbert.

For years, the Philadelphia-born Cuthbert had been the de facto leader of professional baseball in St. Louis, patiently rebuilding the game as head of the independent, gate-sharing St. Louis Browns teams. He was regarded as something of a hotdog—he "played to the grandstand," the *Sporting News* alleged, positioning himself deep in the outfield and swooping in for crowd-pleasing shoestring catches of routine fly balls—but he was well loved in St. Louis for his drive and dedication. After Von der Ahe had fended off the players' short-lived rebellion in 1881, he had relied on Cuthbert's judgment to assemble the team on the field—both in 1881, when Cuthbert led the Browns to an outstanding 35–15 record, playing against some of the finest independent clubs in America, and in 1882, when the Browns entered the new American Association, and the players signed season contracts rather than split the gate. In a moment of high hopes, Von der Ahe had promised his old friend a $1,000 bonus if he captured the Association's first pennant.

By September 1882, Von der Ahe had lost faith in the man. He needed a sharper baseball mind working with him, and he was prepared to discard Cuthbert as ruthlessly as he had William Spink and Augustus Solari, with the same effect: demonstrating who really controlled professional baseball in St. Louis. Blithely undercutting Cuthbert's authority, the owner began openly seeking a replacement late in the season, even asking the players for advice. Some touted Ted Sullivan, a former minor-league manager who had a knack for organizing teams and developing great players. At the moment, Sullivan was hidden away in Dubuque, Iowa, running a profitable business hustling newspapers and snacks on train runs in the Midwest. But baseball remained his true love. He had managed an independent professional baseball team in Milwaukee, in 1876, and more famously, the 1879 Dubuque Rabbits, champions of the Northwestern League, a club he had loaded with future stars—among them Old Hoss Radbourn, the greatest pitcher of his era, and an ambitious nineteen-year-old named Charlie Comiskey, son of a Chicago councilman.

The elder Comiskey, frustrated over his son's obsession with baseball and poor performance in school, had shipped Charlie off to St. Mary's College in the hopes he would shape up. Instead of buckling down, the teenager met Ted Sullivan, who instantly recognized his talent and shifted him from the freshman to the senior team—"his first promotion," Sullivan recalled, "and I dare say his most cherished one." The father became incensed when Sullivan turned the lad into a professional player, bringing him along to Milwaukee, and then to Dubuque. Sullivan coached his lanky protégé in a style of playing first base that dated back to the 1860s—standing well off the bag, where he could roam for grounders, counting on his long legs to get him back in time to take the throw if the ball went to another fielder. That strategy had gone out of fashion in the 1870s when the "fair-foul" hit came to dominate the game, as great batters like Ross Barnes learned how to plunk a ball in the infield, only to have it spin off into foul territory beyond the reach of fielders. The fair-foul hit had been eliminated before the 1877 season, the rules mandating that any ball that landed in fair territory but went foul before passing first or third base was, in fact, foul. First basemen who had previously been forced to hug the line could now roam, and Sullivan coached the lanky Comiskey to take advantage of that freedom.

In 1881, Sullivan arranged to bring the Dubuque club to St. Louis for an exhibition game, showing off the resolute, sure-handed Comiskey. He later wrote to Von der Ahe, urging him to hire the first baseman for the

1882 season before some other club grabbed him. St. Louis was interested, but was willing to pay Comiskey only a paltry $75 a month, which
was less than the $125 he was earning in Sullivan's train business. But
Sullivan offered his protégé some sage advice: The "baseball tide had
come in" for him, and Comiskey should sail his boat, because nobody
knew in 1882 if it would ever return. "If you intend to play ball in the back
woods of America, two hundred dollars would not be enough, as you
would never be heard or seen—it would be time lost. St. Louis is the
proper market to show your goods." If he shone there, the Browns would
later reward him handsomely. Comiskey duly signed on for little more
than what Von der Ahe paid the German-speaking deliverymen at his grocery. Still, when Charlie's first payday came around, an appreciative Von
der Ahe handed him $125, tacking on $50 more than the amount negotiated. It was a gesture the young ballplayer never forgot. Comiskey hit a
feeble .243 with one home run in seventy-eight games that year, but he
impressed Von der Ahe as a steady, hard-working, and intelligent young
man who might someday become a leader. And when Comiskey spoke
highly of Sullivan during the 1882 season, Von der Ahe listened.

Al Spink, who also had Von der Ahe's ear, was another Sullivan man.
"To me he is today and always has been plain Ted Sullivan, the best judge
of a ball player in America, the man of widest vision in the baseball world,
who predicted much for the National game years ago, and whose predic-
tions have all come true," Spink recalled years later. Though small, Sullivan stood out in any gathering. He had "a face and eyes that beam
intelligence," Spink noted, "and a head which reflects nothing so much
as the wide awake, go-ahead and aggressive spirit of the owner." Von der
Ahe had heard enough. Making clear that he was interested in a manager
"who had a mind of his own," he invited Sullivan to a face-to-face interview on neutral ground—Chicago.

Von der Ahe poured on the charm. "He perfumed my atmosphere
with the fragrance of the many bouquets he threw at me," Sullivan recalled. Von der Ahe called him "his long-looked-for Moses," the man who
would lead the Browns out of the wilderness to the Promised Land. It is
not clear whether Sullivan had qualms about Von der Ahe's impulsivity,
his tendency to insert himself into baseball management decisions, and
his dismissive treatment of underlings, all qualities he had surely heard

about from his former Dubuque players. The fusion of these two fiery "alpha males"—something like the volatile mixture of New York Yankees boss George Steinbrenner and manager Billy Martin a century later—was bound to set off an explosion at some point. But, charmed by Von der Ahe's passionate faith in him and St. Louis baseball, eager to manage a top ball club, and no doubt convinced that he—rather than this clueless grocer—would be making the baseball decisions, Sullivan accepted the offer. In his words, he agreed "to enter the gilded cavern of professional baseball."

With six American Association games still left for the Browns under Cuthbert, the St. Louis Globe-Democrat reported on September 20, 1882, that "Ted Sullivan, the little man who organized and managed the once famous Dubuque team, is to have charge of the St. Louis nine in 1883." On September 24, Sullivan was spotted at Sportsman's Park, watching the Browns beat the Nationals of East St. Louis, 6–0, in an exhibition game, and contemplating how he would tear apart the team and put it back together again.

Wasting little time, Sullivan set out in the autumn of 1882 to buy a championship team for the man the papers called "Der Boss President." In Boston, Sullivan won over Jim Whitney, perhaps the swiftest pitcher in the game, and Pat Deasley, his brave and long-suffering catcher, who had played in thirty-eight successive games with two broken fingers because no one else could stop Whitney's bullets. At the eleventh hour, Boston tried to lure Deasley back by offering his wife a diamond ring, but the catcher declined. In Providence, Sullivan won pledges from the Grays' superb third baseman, Jerry Denny, and the brilliant Old Hoss Radbourn, Sullivan's former pitcher at Dubuque, who wanted to play closer to his home in Bloomington, Illinois. From the Chicago White Stockings came five-foot-four right-fielder Hugh Nicol, soon to be a favorite with St. Louis urchins because he was the player who most closely approximated their size. Sullivan stripped the Philadelphia Phillies of infielder Arlie Latham, who was destined to be one of the era's most colorful and talented stars. Sullivan brought in his crony Tom Loftus from Dubuque, a shrewd baseball strategist, to serve as his new center fielder and captain. "Loftus on the field captains his men with the coolness of a Grant, and never becomes discouraged," the Dubuque Daily Times had observed in 1879, comparing him to the stubborn Civil War general. "A better captain never walked the diamond."

As it turned out, not all of these fine players actually made it to St. Louis. The peace agreement struck between the two leagues forced the Browns to return Whitney, Radbourn, and Denny to their National League clubs. One of the big reasons that Von der Ahe had wanted to keep the war going was precisely to keep the Association clubs free from heeding the League's reserve clause, so that he might keep these players. However disappointing to St. Louis, the loss of the three may have been a blessing in disguise, since they would surely have made the Browns far too dominant, ruining the competitive balance that produces crowd-pleasing pennant fights.

Pat Deasley
(Library of Congress)

Even without those stars, Sullivan built the nucleus of a club that would win four pennants and a world championship in short order. Von der Ahe's long-looked-for Moses also weeded out the worst players from the team, including the unfortunate Cuthbert. Although Cuthbert had once been among the fastest men in baseball, "now an ice wagon would have to be handicapped in a race with him," the *Cincinnati Enquirer* jabbed. Such decisions incurred the wrath of some veterans and their advocates in the press, who hotly disagreed with his evaluations. "I had to cut and slash in the building up and beginning of that famous team," Sullivan later recalled. "The grouches of the old fellows were not at all easy to wear down."

One of the worst grouches was David L. Reid, the prominent baseball writer for the *Missouri Republican* who was, in defiance of the obvious conflict of interest, also the secretary of the Browns, acting as a kind of business manager. Reid had been associated with various forms of the St. Louis Browns since 1875 and had accompanied Von der Ahe to the founding meeting of the American Association in November 1881. Having hoped to get the job that was now going to Sullivan, the wounded Reid promptly set to work criticizing the interloper's every move. Reid thought it was a mistake to sign Loftus and Nicol while letting other players go, and he objected to the change in club colors from brown to scarlet.

During the winter, Henry Chadwick, baseball editor of the *New York Clipper*, took up the cause of his fellow sportswriter. "Very much of the remarkable financial success attained by the Browns last season was due to his executive tact and ability," Chadwick declared. Since then, Reid had been a "strong and open opponent" of Sullivan, asserting "that the team engaged for 1883 is not nearly as strong as St. Louis could and should have placed in the field." Finding Sullivan and Von der Ahe deaf to these concerns, Reid severed his formal connection with the Browns in February 1883. But all season long, he maintained a withering flank fire at Sullivan on the pages of the *Missouri Republican*. He continued to whisper in the ear of an all-too-receptive Von der Ahe about all the things the new manager was supposedly doing wrong. Von der Ahe felt so bad about the writer's precipitous resignation that he arranged for the club to present Reid "a magnificent walnut and mahogany writing desk" as an expression of gratitude for his services.

While Reid grumbled, Sullivan continued his brilliant campaign of acquisitions, robbing the American Association's Louisville Eclipse club of the marvelous pitcher Tony Mullane. A combative Irishman himself who came to America at the age of five, Mullane was nicknamed "The Count" and "The Apollo of the Box" for his good looks and prodigious talent, even if he was on the small and slender side. Paid just $115 a month by Louisville, he won thirty games in 1882, the second most in the league, and threw the Association's first no-hitter on September 11. But his preening ego and selfishness offended many in Kentucky, and the *Louisville Argus* insisted that Mullane would not be missed. "Ever since his engagement with the club he has given the management trouble, and with due appreciation of his ability as a pitcher, we do most cheerfully congratulate ourselves upon his decision to go away to St. Louis and to establish himself there as the big boss of all the blusterers," the paper said.

Hitters, though, knew that the pitcher had much to be conceited about: a blazing fastball and a perplexing curve, delivered illegally over the shoulder. At the plate, he was a switch hitter. More remarkably, he could throw his pitches with both arms—something he demonstrated in a July 1882 game against Baltimore. When three left-handed batters came to the plate, Mullane "changed his delivery from right hand to left, and puzzled the batters considerably." He could not keep it up for long, given his conditioning to use his right arm, "but it was very effective while it lasted." Even more effective was his cold and calculated viciousness; he seemed willing to strike men down—even maim them—if they crowded the plate and made it harder for him to sneak across strikes. "Watch me polish his buttons," Mullane said about good hitters he faced.

Tony Mullane
(Library of Congress)

Tony was "a great hand at frightening the batters," Von der Ahe recalled. "He would throw the ball right at the batter sometimes, particularly if he was a strong batter." He wasn't playing around: Mullane had a widowed mother, two sisters, and two young brothers back home in Erie, Pennsylvania, who were depending on him for support, and he had to be successful to maximize his earnings. The fiercely competitive pitcher had even overcome a deadly attack of malaria during the winter. He showed up in the spring somewhat weak and thin, and when he saw one tall, robust pitcher, he mused out loud: "If only I had that chap's heft." But he rapidly put on weight in April and May. "Tony does not 'kill' as easily as some people," one reporter observed. Sullivan faced the daunting task of turning him into a team player.

While the manager radically rebuilt the club, Von der Ahe spiffed up the plant. By March, Sportsman's Park no longer looked much like its 1882 incarnation. The bleachers along the first-base line, "which gave many a one a roasting last year," were roofed over now, like the grandstand. In left field, the open bleachers had been extended all the way to the outfield fence; these cheap seats would become the new "stamping ground" for St. Louis "hooters." Dirt walkways, which had often turned soupy with Missouri mud on rainy days, were now attractively covered over with gravel. Four ticket booths had been constructed to help serve crowds "on red-letter days." The press box was to be enclosed, sparing reporters the constant irritation of visits from various grandstand "experts." Responding to customer complaints, Von der Ahe banned the sale of refreshments in the park's small upper deck, ensuring that "the lively waiter will no longer obstruct the view of the spectator in that section."

In the outfield, Von der Ahe ordered the construction of "an immense blackboard" that would carry the progress, via telegraph, of the other games taking place in the American Association—a feature sure to attract many customers who bet on baseball and desired instant results from around the league. In the park's renovated dressing rooms, each player was "provided with a compartment of his own, in which to stow away uniforms, bats, balls, etc."—lockers, in other words, a novelty at the time. As a finishing touch, Von der Ahe installed some high technology, a rare telephone line to the club's headquarters at the corner of Sixth and Pine downtown, so that the progress of games could be instantly "bulletined" to baseball lovers there. And now that his struggling neighbor, Augustus Solari, had stopped harassing him, Von der Ahe generously hired him as his groundskeeper, making good use of his expertise in maintaining the old Grand Avenue Park. In mid-March, Solari spent a week running a 4,000-pound roller drawn by four horses over the bumpy field, smoothing out the rough spots. He kept the horses from tearing up the field by wrapping their hooves in old carpet.

———◇———

ON ST. PATRICK'S DAY, A REPORTER FOR THE ST. LOUIS GLOBE-Democrat snuck into the renovated park to get a glimpse of Sullivan's new men. He found catcher Deasley "sending the ball around like a shot from a rifle." Out in right field, Nicol seemed "very small, but he is quick as a cat, and picks up and throws to the infield with great speed." Out at first base, "taking everything sent that way," was fleet-footed Comiskey.

The left side of the infield was particularly impressive. At shortstop was Bill Gleason, another one of Sullivan's Dubuque players. A supple, strong St. Louis firefighter, Gleason played baseball without pity for anyone who got in his way. He had caused a furor in 1882 when, attempting to score, he closed his two "brawny fists" across his chest and slammed them into Philadelphia Athletics catcher Jack O'Brien, knocking him senseless. The *Philadelphia Item* called him a "brute" and urged spectators to "mark him" for their opprobrium when he came to Philadelphia. "If he should some day break a limb or his neck, not a ball player in the American Association would feel the slightest regret," the *Sporting Life* contended. In another collision at home plate that season, he snapped the wrist of Cincinnati catcher Phil Powers, forcing him to sit out for six weeks. Gleason was a mighty tough customer, even by the standards of a game filled with them.

At third base was the "lithe and spry" Arlie Latham. The *Globe-Democrat* man noted that "he picks up and throws like lightning" and "is a strong batsman and a splendid base-runner." (In admiring Arlie's speed, Von der Ahe later observed: "Dot poy Latham . . . can run like a cantelope.") The infielder, who had just turned twenty-four that week, also had a reputation for savagely mocking and heckling opponents, throwing them off their game. "Latham is the mouth of the St. Louis club, Comiskey the head. Each is valuable in his place," the *Sporting News* maintained. Latham took a special pleasure in ridiculing his own employer behind his back, brilliantly mimicking Von der Ahe's swaggering walk as the Browns paraded from the railroad depot to their hotel. According to one oft-told story, when a street crowd roared at Latham's act, an annoyed Von der Ahe asked, "Why do they laff at us? Ve ain't funny. Ve lick der stuffings out of every team in baseball."

In time, Latham would be dubbed "The Freshest Man on Earth" after a popular song—fresh, in this sense, meaning rude, audacious, and insolent. He was certainly fresh with the ladies. Carefully parting his slicked hair fashionably down the middle, he engaged in several publicized romances, including one with a "St. Louis blonde." His wife, Emma Latham, back home in Massachusetts with their three-year-old son, Clifford, later complained bitterly that Latham failed to provide any money for their support and that he beat her "because she refused to submit to the gratification of unnatural desires." In bringing him to St. Louis, Ted Sullivan "little thought what havoc Latham would create. . . . From his first appearance he had the reputation of being the idol of the younger ladies," the *Sporting News* laughed. But Sullivan seemed to have little interest in the nocturnal habits of his men, preferring to focus on their efforts on the field. The manager tested his new infield by trying to knock ground balls between Gleason and Latham. The two stopped almost everything.

On March 20, Von der Ahe gathered the Browns for his first clubhouse speech of the season. He welcomed the new men and "had a good word for the old players," the few who had survived the manager's scythe. Then he made it clear that there would be only one leader of the club in 1883: "From that time forward, they were under the sole management of Mr. Sullivan," who "would hold them responsible for their actions both on and off the field." To encourage good behavior, the owner offered a handsome bonus of $100 to each man who could get through the season without being fined—not bad money, considering that some players earned that for a full month's work. "It is a generous offer, but is hardly likely that one man will run the gauntlet with Sullivan manager," the *National Police Gazette* observed (rather erroneously, since Von der Ahe was far more liable than Sullivan to punish wayward players). Then Von der

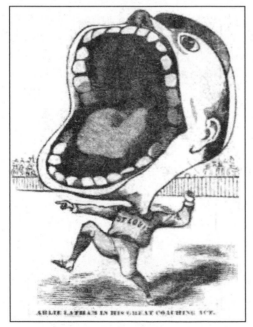

Arlie Latham,
Sporting News, *June 18, 1887*
(Library of Congress)

Ahe turned the meeting over to Sullivan. The new manager "remarked that he hoped to see the team at the top of the heap and winners of the pennant, but that [in] all events he trusted they would be nearer the top than the bottom." A new era had begun.

On that cold April 1, Sullivan finally got to show the public what the new Browns looked like. George "Jumbo" McGinnis, a tall, big-chested twenty-nine-year-old from North St. Louis who worked as a glassblower, did the pitching. Surely happy to be teaming up with a first-class veteran catcher in Deasley, McGinnis threw a one-hit shutout, handily beating the Grand Avenues. But it was Latham who charmed the crowd, becoming "an immediate favorite," said the *Missouri Republican*. "His neat, rapid style, clean handling and throwing prove him to be a natural ballplayer in all that that means." Early in the game, the club's new field captain, Loftus, "commenced to whoop up his men," admirably performing the duties of his post, which included calling out the name of the player who should take a fly ball as well as telling fielders where to throw the ball.

The *Globe-Democrat* was impressed: "He is always on deck coaching his men, and when they are not at bat his voice, calling to this man or that from the out field, sounds clear, and is always obeyed." In 1882, by contrast, Cuthbert had been "seldom heard above that of the others, and there was always more or less confusion." That change was significant, the paper explained. "The strength of the Chicago club has always been in their 'coach.' [Cap] Anson's stentorian tones have often rattled the opposing team when defeat seemed assured. . . . If there is any position in the world where a man cannot be too boisterous, it is that which places him in command of a professional base ball nine."

The denizens of St. Louis, who had been just about ready to give up on the game four years earlier, were now mad for baseball. One week after the grand opening of the spring exhibition season, eight thousand paying customers showed up, overwhelming even the capacity of the renovated Sportsman's Park. Every seat was taken, and the crowd was so dense near a low fence surrounding the outfield that it broke it into pieces, "letting the eager sightseers into the field." Only weeks after renovating his park, Von der Ahe had to send carpenters back to make repairs and construct new open bleachers in front of the deep outfield fences. Sullivan's men throttled the minor-league Reds from Springfield,

Illinois, 12–0. The St. Louis men wore "their new red jackets yesterday and looked gorgeous," the *Globe-Democrat* enthused. One Browns supporter suggested they switch from white to red shirts—a rather modern uniform idea—since the jackets looked so good.

The following Sunday, before a throng of hollering kids taking advantage of specially reduced ten-cent tickets, the Browns drubbed the Northwestern League's Ft. Wayne Golden Eagles, who were adorned in bright gray uniforms with black stockings and different colored caps. This time, the Browns won with the help of a "decidedly unprofessional" trick. In the second inning, team captain Tom Loftus, filling in at second base, caught a pop fly, walked to the pitcher's box, and, to all appearances, handed Jumbo McGinnis the ball. When McGinnis started to pitch, the Ft. Wayne runner edged off the bag. Suddenly, Loftus dived at him and tagged him out. For an instant, the crowd did not understand what had happened; then, when it dawned on the spectators that Loftus had pulled off a hidden-ball trick, their laughter filled the park. The *Globe-Democrat*, striking a moralistic tone, chided Loftus, concluding that "fair-minded spectators do not favor that style of ball-playing." It was becoming increasingly clear, however, that these Browns did not particularly care about fairness; they came to win.

St. Louis crowds were being treated to a new brand of baseball, highlighted by the best base-running they had ever seen. "It is bold, dashing[,] and the men are not afraid to slide or dive if there is any chance of making their bases," said the *Missouri Republican*. The boys in the stands had already adopted Hugh "Little Nick" Nicol as their hero, offering high-pitched cheers every time he stepped to the plate. "Right field has never been filled in this city as Nick is filling it," the *Republican* applauded. One local team even named itself the "Little Nicols." Hugh's on-field theatrics, reprised by a later St. Louis star named Ozzie Smith, only boosted his popularity. After scoring during one spring training game, Nicol "tumbled and bounced about, turning somersaults and cart-wheels in a manner which would have done credit to one of Cole's Arabs," a popular circus act, the *Republican* reported. Looking better and better, the Browns won their last three preseason games, all against professional clubs, by a combined score of 47–0.

Knowing the Browns would face tougher competition in the regular season, Ted Sullivan tried to tamp down raging expectations. "It is not the first or the last installment of games that will win the championship. It is a steady and honest pull that counts," he stressed. "We will rely on that to land us there, and if we fail of success our campaign will have pleased the people of this city, for I guarantee that it will be an honorable and manly one." The snarky Dave Reid refused to accept such a watered-down definition of success: "St. Louis calls for something more than 'honest and manly play,'" he said. "It wants a winning team, and cannot afford to accept anything else."

By then, the Browns' revival had led to the invention of a new word to describe the team's passionate supporters. According to Sullivan, on off-days that April, the new manager found baseball addicts suddenly hounding him at the club's headquarters downtown. It was there that players relaxed while men dropped in to purchase tickets, buy a drink, study the schedule, or talk to one of their heroes. One day, Sullivan recalled, a man came in and "commenced to ply me with questions about baseball in general." The visitor "knew every player in the country with a record of 90 in the shade and 1,000 in the sun. He gave his opinion on all matters pertaining to ball. There was no player but he had a personal acquaintance with." Finally, someone took pity on Sullivan and called the pompous know-it-all outside. "What name could you apply to such a fiend as that?" Sullivan sighed when the man was gone. "He is a fanatic," Charlie Comiskey noted. Sullivan, smiling, decided to shorten the word to "fan." "So, when he was ever seen around headquarters, the boys would say, 'the fan' was around again," Sullivan wrote. (That, at least, was *one* version of the story Sullivan told of the invention; there were at least three, all of them widely differing in detail, and agreeing only that the coinage of the word "fan" was his.) By the turn of the century, the term was in widespread use. In 1883, however, "crank" and "fanatic" continued to be preferred.

The cranks greatly irritated Sullivan, but their dollars—amounting to thousands per game—made his boss a supremely happy fellow. When Sullivan arrived at work on the sunny Wednesday morning of April 4, Sullivan recalled, "Chris whispered in my ear that he thought there was something in a plush box for me at his office." The manager hastened to see what it was. "When I opened the box there was a handsome gold watch and a chain contained therein." Von der Ahe had inscribed the gift with Sullivan's name and the date. The owner beamed as an astonished Sullivan looked it over.

At that moment, Sullivan felt a wave of affection for his clumsy boss, who obviously recognized the hard work the Dubuque man had put in for the sake of the team. In spite of all the warnings he had heard about Von der Ahe's overbearing nature and constant interference, here was a powerful sign of respect. And the owner had promised, in front of all the players, that Sullivan would be the man in charge. As Von der Ahe's long-awaited Moses, Sullivan just had to remember to keep on winning, leading the Browns ever closer to the land of milk and honey.

5

THE SHRIMP

I T WAS INSANITY. BOBBY MATHEWS, THE VETERAN PITCHER OF the Philadelphia Athletics, already had an aching arm, a sore ear, and a pounding headache after being slammed in the skull by a baseball the day before. Now, he had to fight his way through mobbed streets in downtown Philadelphia on a steamy Memorial Day afternoon to get back into the ballpark and do his job. The whole city, it seemed, had gone crazy.

The A's had already won one game that morning, beating Columbus 8–5. But when Mathews arrived for the Athletics' second holiday game, set to start at 4 P.M., thousands of people blocked his way to Athletic Park. What's worse, the gates had been locked shut. The little wooden ballpark was already stuffed with fanatics, eager to see the soaring Athletics take on the defending American Association champions, the Cincinnati Reds, in one of the most intensely anticipated match-ups of the young season. The Athletics had been forced to suspend ticket sales at 3:15 P.M., forty-five minutes before game time, leaving thousands out of the action. Every seat had been sold, small boys lined the tops of all the fences, and thousands of people stood on the rooftops and filled the windows surrounding

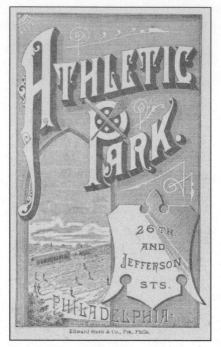

Athletic Park, 1883 scorecard
(Robert Edward Auctions; reprinted with permission)

the park. And still, every horsecar of every railway line arrived crammed full of baseball enthusiasts, with twenty more people clinging to the roof who were trying not to tumble off.

Confronting locked gates and *SOLD OUT* signs, many disappointed Philadelphians gave up and walked a few blocks away to Recreation Park, grudgingly purchasing tickets to see the National League's wretched, cellar-dwelling Philadelphia Phillies, who were already on their way to one of the worst seasons that any major-league club would ever have. (One sports-writer, learning that Boston players had discovered a lucky horseshoe in the dust marked "O. Winn," joked that if the Phillies had found one, theirs would have been stamped "O. Hell.") But thousands more remained at the Athletics' ballpark, milling around, desperately seeking some way in. In their frenzy, hundreds of sweating men pressed against the locked gate of the Twenty-sixth Street entrance until it gave way with a loud crack.

The mob rushed for the gate, and nearly one thousand people poured in before club-wielding policemen barricaded the entrance. The throng burst onto the field, where thousands of others had already gathered. Many got in only after their clothes were torn or their hats mashed.

The owners now feared that someone might get trampled in a bloody stampede if they opened the gates even a sliver to admit late-arriving season ticket holders—or the players themselves. They had to call for ladders to be placed against the outside fence. Under tense police guard, Bobby Mathews and his teammates climbed up and over the fence into their place of work. It was clear that a mania for baseball was gripping the country. Everywhere that there was a game, the stands were stuffed, the crowds overflowed onto the field, and more buses were on the way, all loaded to the rooftops with fanatics. Browns owner Von der Ahe, traveling with his team (after promising to keep his distance), could hardly believe the explosion of interest that he had helped to ignite. "I thought St. Louis had it pretty bad, but it is worse, if anything, elsewhere," he told reporters. "At Baltimore the crowds are enormous, six and seven thousand people going to the grounds. The club has made more money than St. Louis and has $7,000 in the bank ahead of its season. In Philadelphia the grounds are not big enough to hold the people, and so it goes."

But, while this sudden spurt of baseball madness delighted owners, its display on Memorial Day appalled many Americans. This was a day that had been set aside not for sporting events, but to remember the hundreds of thousands of young men who had lost their lives in the Civil War, North and South. A writer for the *Pittsburgh Dispatch* touched on the guilt some felt that afternoon at Exposition Park: "All day long momentous storm clouds hung over the city like omens of disaster, and at frequent intervals showers of rain would come pelting down like reproaches on the heads of pleasure-seekers for the solemnity of a day made sacred by the memories of the nation's dead." Even so, eight thousand people attended the doubleheader there—the biggest crowds in Pittsburgh baseball history to that point—and the ballpark rocked with "the most tumultuous applause ever heard on a Pittsburg[h] ball field."

The *Providence Press* defended the fans, arguing that it was unrealistic to expect the harried, hardworking younger generation to care as much about America's searing tragedy as did older folks who had suffered through it. "Americans have so few breathing spells and live in such a hurry and rush at all other times, that it is not surprising to find that, as memories of the war grow less vivid, and new generations are coming on, to whom the great civil strife is only history, the day has less solemnity and more of general pleasure-seeking for the masses," the paper said. It was useless to complain that the younger generation failed to appreciate the sacrifices of those who bled and died in the Civil War: "It is impossible that the intense feeling of the actual experience should be aroused in mere listeners, and working people need all the holidays and pleasure-seeking they can get." The *New York Herald*, noting the mobs of happy people on the streets and in the ballparks, shared that view, pointing out that "Americans have none too many holidays . . . so this newest excuse for a general getting-out-of-doors cannot be too carefully cherished." In any event, the *Providence Press* said, "it was a great day for base ball, and proved that the national game is losing none of its popularity."

To say the least. In Philadelphia, the chaos on the field inside Athletic Park that Memorial Day was almost as bad as the mob scene out on the street. Fifteen minutes before the scheduled starting time, the Athletics pushed their way out of the dressing room into a swarm of people. Grown men gawked at them, one reporter observed, the way children stared at Jumbo, the celebrated giant African bush elephant that P. T. Barnum had purchased two years earlier from the London Zoo for $10,000. Mathews, accompanied by catcher Jack O'Brien, tried to find an opening in the crowd so he could warm up, but the spectators jammed around them eight or ten deep, barely giving the pitcher room enough to swing his arm. Losing patience, Mathews barked at them so fiercely that they backed off, though he was smaller than many of them.

At five-feet-five-inches and a scant 140 pounds, Bobby Mathews was only about an inch shorter than the average American male in 1883. But he was small for a professional athlete, a fact that reporters liked to stress. The *National Police Gazette*, with a characteristic sneer, called him a "little shrimp." But though he was diminutive, the Baltimore native was a stubborn competitor, a gnarled veteran of well over a decade in professional baseball. In the days before reconstructive arm surgeries and careful conditioning, only a handful of pitchers managed to survive so long, and Mathews paid for it in constant pain and physical deterioration. He had

Bobby Mathews
(Robert Edward Auctions;
reprinted with permission)

started his long, hard career at age sixteen, with the Maryland Juniors, and moved up quickly, joining the professional Marylands and then the Kekionga Club of Fort Wayne, which was in the first all-professional league, the National Association.

He pitched and won what some consider the very first major-league game, beating Cleveland with a five-hit, six-strikeout, 2–0 shutout on May 4, 1871, a stunning performance in the days when run totals regularly soared into the 20s. (Shutouts became much more common in the 1870s as a deader ball came into use and top professionals improved overall fielding.) Moving on to the Baltimore Canaries, New York Mutuals, and Cincinnati Reds, Mathews found his arm worn down by constant use. When no National League team would sign him in 1878, he had to rebuild his career with the Worcester Live Oaks in the minor-league International Association. But, though he was expelled for drunkenness—the team hired a black pitcher, John "Bud" Fowler, to replace him—Mathews fought his way back to the big-time. Now he had begun an incredible run of three magnificent seasons.

By 1883, he looked much older than his thirty-one years, his face lined, weather-beaten, and stress-worn—at least the part of it that could be seen behind his shaggy mustache. But as scrawny and battle-worn as he appeared, Mathews was still a master at making skilled batters look foolish flailing at his junk pitches. Like Old Hoss Radbourn, a former teammate at Providence, Mathews brought a keen mind to his craft. "He had the most remarkable memory for a batter's weaknesses of any pitcher who ever lived," baseball executive James Hart told the *Chicago Tribune*. "He was quick to size up a batsman. . . . He had perfect control, and this enabled him to put them up just where a fellow didn't want 'em. . . . Another thing about Mathews, he could pick up tricks of other pitchers quicker than anybody you ever saw. And there wasn't any trick of pitching that he couldn't pick up. If he saw you doing something new one day he would be doing it the next—that is, if he wasn't doing it the same day. He was one of the really great pitchers of the profession." One of the first men in baseball to throw a curve, Mathews had learned the art by standing behind home plate and studying how rival Candy Cummings held the ball and let it go. Within a short time, he could make his own pitches break much better than Candy's. As it turned out, Cummings won a plaque in the Hall of Fame as the reputed inventor of the pitch, while Mathews, who developed its potential and used it to vastly greater effect, got left out.

Before coming over to Philadelphia, Mathews had won nearly 200 major-league games: 131 of them in the old National Association—42 in 1874 alone, with the New York Mutuals—and another 61 in the National League, helping to propel the Providence Grays to their pennant in 1879. Simmons and his ownership team had to spend a good deal of money to lure him away from the superior league and the Boston Red Stockings—$2,200 a season, making him the highest paid member of the Athletics. (Billy Sharsig recalled that he met Mathews in New York's Bingham House during the 1882 season and slipped him a $1,000 advance to seal the deal.) The Athletics even signed Mathews's catcher with the Red Stockings, Ed Rowen, to make sure the pitcher would feel comfortable in Philadelphia. They had staked a lot on the little man's arm.

At the start of the 1883 season, the *Sporting Life*, a Philadelphia-based weekly, advised the Athletics to send Mathews out to pitch every game, instead of following the newfangled practice of rotating the top man every other game with a lesser pitcher to spare the ace's arm. "Bobby is tough and can stand the work," the writer promised. That was easy for him to say. In reality, expanding schedules were making life excruciating for pitchers. There were fourteen more games on each team's schedule in the National League in 1883 than in 1882, and eighteen more in the American Association. Adding to the strain was a rules change that allowed—in effect, compelled—pitchers to throw much harder. Early baseball rules required the ball to be pitched underhand; now, in 1883, pitchers merely had to release it anywhere below the shoulder, though many cheated, sneaking in overhand throws. And under the dray-horse standards of the time, pitchers worked an astonishing number of innings, finishing almost every game they started. The great Pud Galvin, for example, who hailed from the St. Louis Irish neighborhood known as the Kerry Patch, led the National League that year with 656 1/3 innings pitched—about *three times* more than the season leaders in modern ball. But, as tough as pitchers were in the 1880s, few men's arms could endure the punishment of throwing hard curves every game without a break, especially after more than a decade of wear and tear.

Mathews tried to do it, at least for the first few weeks of the season, because the Athletics had no sound number-two pitcher. Like most players of that era, he seemed to bear pain with remarkable fortitude. On May 29, the afternoon before the Memorial Day doubleheader, a ball glanced off his bat and slammed into his unprotected ear; batting helmets had yet to be invented. Two physicians in the stands rushed onto the field as soon as they saw Mathews crumple and fall. But after a short delay, Mathews shook off his wooziness and returned to the batter's box. Then he resumed his place in the pitcher's box and defeated the Reds 2–1, striking out the side in order in the ninth.

Less than twenty-four hours later, the little shrimp was back to try again—but whether the holiday crowd would let him was another matter. The Athletics had to halt their batting practice almost as soon as they started for fear of killing one of the many fans milling around them. Meanwhile, the thousands who had come early enough to obtain seats were clearly enjoying their day off at the ballpark. When a few drops of rain fell, one man pulled a handkerchief out of his pocket to brush the dust off his hat before it could make a permanent stain. Suddenly, ten thousand handkerchiefs appeared, the laughing owners slapping away at their garments, while five thousand more fluttered their handkerchiefs for the fun of it.

But good-natured as it was, the crowd posed serious logistical problems. At 4 P.M., when the game was supposed to begin, thousands were still clogging the field, many forming a square around the infield two to five people deep—and they weren't budging. The few Philadelphia policemen on the grounds proved useless. Lew Simmons appeared and bawled at the crowd with a voice trained to be heard in the back row of opera houses. But his pleas had no effect. He'd have to figure out another way to move the mob so that the game could begin. Even so, his impatience was tinged with amusement. This was his beloved team, and he was having enormous fun making more money than he had ever imagined possible.

THE CROWDS OBVIOUSLY LOVED WHAT THE FORMER MINSTREL STAR had done with the Athletics. He had begun his shopping spree many months earlier with a brilliant acquisition: the superb Harry Stovey, who was then languishing with the National League's soon-to-be-defunct Worcester club. Stovey, only twenty-five at the time, was a born ballplayer. Tall and slender, fond of wearing his cap at a jaunty angle, he was a triple threat: a swift runner, a graceful fielder, and a hard hitter. During the deadball decade of the 1880s, he blasted more home runs than any other player in the major leagues, most of them long line drives that shot past outfielders while he galloped around the bases. Although early records are hopelessly incomplete or misleading on this score, Stovey was also probably the greatest base-stealer of his age. His left hip became so bruised and lacerated from sliding into the bases that he invented his own sliding pad, possibly the first ever used. Al Spink marveled at his aggressive running, noting that Stovey slid hard feet-first into a base "and, rebounding, he would come to a standing position fully prepared to continue his chase around the bases in case the throw was not right on the mark."

In leaving Worcester behind for Philadelphia, Stovey was returning to the place he had once called home, the city of his birth and youth, the scene of his first amateur triumphs in baseball—triumphs that he had tried to hide from his family. A direct descendant of the man who recast the Liberty Bell, he was born Harold Duffield Stow, but had played under the invented name of Stovey to keep his less-than-respectable career a secret from his mother. To lure him back to Philadelphia, Simmons reportedly promised him a handsome salary of $2,000, fully 60 percent more than he was earning with Worcester—the kind of big money that the Association's business model and large crowds made possible.

And there were still more National Leaguers in Simmons's clutches. Rhode Islander Fred Corey, obtained from Worcester, could play infield and pitch. The Athletics' suave new captain, Philadelphia-born right fielder Lon Knight, came from the Detroit club. He had risen from a tough childhood: born Alonzo Letti, he was nine when his father succumbed to typhoid fever. Lon was sent to Girard College, a private school in a bucolic setting on the outskirts of Philadelphia that had been founded in 1848 with a bequest by Philadelphia financier Stephen Girard to help fatherless boys escape a life of destitution and crime. There, his name was changed to Knight, perhaps because of the ethnic hostility that persisted against Italians. The Athletics' new shortstop, the hard-hitting, redheaded, Chicago-born Mike Moynahan, was another former National Leaguer, and a tough customer to boot. In 1882, a thrown ball shattered the forefinger of his left hand, which was unprotected, since fielders' gloves were not yet in use. Ignoring the pain, Moynahan picked up the ball and threw a runner out at third base before leaving the field. Later, the hopelessly mangled finger had to be amputated at the first joint. Yet Moynahan kept on playing ball. All this talent from the first-rate National League instantly made the Athletics a top contender for the 1883 Association flag.

Simmons discarded most of the members of the 1882 Athletics, retaining only the four young men he considered the best of the lot. One was twenty-two-year-old catcher Jack O'Brien, the top hitter on the 1882 squad, author of three of the club's four home runs, and the gutsy man who had been smashed in the chest by Bill Gleason. In Henry Chadwick's opinion, O'Brien had "but few equals for pluck and coolness in his position." He described the catcher as "a swift and accurate thrower, clever in judging and catching foul balls, and expert in watching the bases." Another survivor was John "Cub" Stricker, a twenty-three-year-old who would prove himself one of the finest second basemen of his generation. Determined to focus entirely on his professional career, the young man set aside his milk delivery route during the winter of 1882–1883 to devote his full attention to hard practice. "Stricker says he is not going to allow anyone to outplay him at second base next season," the *Item* noted. "He has got so he can catch bullets shot out of a rifle."

———◇———

IT WAS A GOOD ENOUGH TEAM TO BURST OUT OF THE STARTING gate, rushing to first place, winning eighteen of twenty-one games in May and building up a five-and-a-half-game lead in the American Association. But Simmons didn't stop there. He could see that Mathews, as tough as he was, would not survive the season without pitching help. He set out in early May to get him some—and price was no object. "The man who stops to question the cost of a thing that will benefit the club or please the public is an idiot and will soon find himself left," explained Simmons, who was used to spending big dollars on stars to make money as a minstrel entrepreneur. Unfortunately, finding a good pitcher at this point wouldn't be easy at any price. An unprecedented number of professional teams—thirty-two of them in the major and top-tier minor leagues—had already combed through the nation's amateur and lower professional ranks for talent.

Even so, one battered veteran turned up in May who was available to the highest bidder. George Washington Bradley was a name pitcher and a "sharp, hard hitter," a fierce competitor who was not above using violence to win, and one of the greats of early professional baseball. In 1876, pitching for the St. Louis Brown Stockings, he was nothing short of brilliant, winning forty-five games, posting the National League's lowest earned run average, throwing the first no-hitter in League history—and coming within one out of throwing the second. Granted, he may have owed at least some of his success to knavery: before many games, Bradley reportedly met secretly with his catcher, and the two softened the game balls by slamming them with a bat against a stone slab, carefully covering them first with a cloth so that they would not be stained. Such deadened baseballs, of course, were harder to drive for distance.

The *Chicago Tribune* wondered about the "putty ball" that Bradley's team used, remarking that "instead of responding with a click when hit, it simply gave a dull thud like a chunk of mud." When umpires finally caught on, and the League began requiring that game balls be taken only from sealed boxes, after being wrapped in foil, Bradley lost his edge and began spending more time at third base than in the pitcher's box. He earned the nickname "Grin" for the ugly, even fiendish, expression that seemed frozen on his face. "No one before ever had such a tantalizing smirk," one reporter recalled in 1892, "and none of the modern detachment has given evidence that they can successfully imitate it." Given his fierce competitiveness, rampant cheating, and nasty bickering with umpires, some considered him little better than a thug. In April 1882, the *Cincinnati Commercial Gazette* quipped: "That portrait alongside the baseball column was generally mistaken for a likeness of George Bradley. It was, however, an excellent photograph of the dead outlaw and desperado Jesse James. Bradley still survives." O. P. Caylor complained that Bradley—"he, of the ungodly grin"—was as "successful at making himself obnoxious to the crowd" as he was at pitching. "But he can grin and kick and spout billingsgate," added another reporter. "In those things his average is No. 1."

By 1883, he was a thirty-year-old on the down slope of his career, working mostly as an infielder, but struggling to keep his job with the National League's Cleveland club by showing off some new pitches during spring training. His manager, Frank Bancroft, was not impressed. Though the club was paying Bradley the not-inconsiderable salary of $175 per month, Bancroft dropped him from the regular team, condemning him to the reserve squad, and was prepared to grant him his release. Bradley began writing to other managers, letting them know he was available. Caylor, for one, thought the veteran was washed up: "Bradley is not a pitcher; has not been for years; his [more suitable] position is on a railroad, section hand, eighty-five cents a day." Still, even though Bradley was not the hurler he once was, he didn't have to wait long for a response from talent-starved professional clubs.

Bradley quickly shook hands on a deal with the Association's Pittsburgh Alleghenys, who had lost their number-one starter and desperately needed help. But before he could arrive, Pittsburgh fans were shocked to learn that Bradley had broken his word and jilted the Alleghenys for a better deal from the Philadelphia Athletics, who wished to use him at third base as well as in the pitcher's box. "Moral: Never count on a ball player until you have him signed and locked up past the possibility of escape," the *Pittsburgh Dispatch* observed bitterly. Philadelphia supporters, of course, were delighted. "Bradley's ascension to the Athletic club has greatly strengthened the nine in its weakest point," one reporter gloated. "Now let the Western clubs come on, and, in the language of Macbeth, 'd—d be he who first cries hold, enough!'"

The Alleghenys, run by Association President Denny McKnight, were not inclined to forgive and forget. Furious to be facing Bradley in his first Association appearance, the club lodged a formal protest, charging that he was ineligible to play because he had first pledged himself to Pittsburgh. The harsh feelings between the rivals threatened to fracture the Association. The owners convened an emergency meeting on June 5 in Cincinnati to try to resolve the dispute. Called to explain himself, Lew Simmons glibly reminded his fellow moguls that, although he may have violated the league's rules in wresting Bradley from the grasp of another club, "every other club in the association, with the exception of the Cincinnatis, was equally as guilty." The red-faced executives had to admit that Simmons had a point, and they went home without punishing anyone. Six weeks later, however, President McKnight was still barely speaking to Simmons, a man he now considered a scoundrel.

⊲◦▸

ON MEMORIAL DAY AFTERNOON, IT FINALLY TOOK THE MUSCULAR athletes of the Philadelphia and Cincinnati teams, "by dint of pushing, threats and persuasion," a full hour beyond the starting time, to enlarge the square of fans around the infield so the second match of the doubleheader could be played. The clubs quickly agreed to special ground rules: balls hit beyond the outfielders into the mob surrounding the field would be doubles, and runners would be limited to advancing one base after a passed ball.

Even so, the large crowd made it hard to play ball. In the fifth inning, spectators twice got in the way of Athletics catcher Jack O'Brien as he tried to fight his way through the mob to grab pop-ups. Handed two extra outs to work with, the Reds pushed across two runs that badly burned the Athletics. With a desperate burst, the Philadelphia team tied the game in the ninth, only to lose in the eleventh inning, 10–9. The crowd went home disappointed, though nevertheless buzzing with excitement. The owner of the Reds, Aaron S. Stern, boasted that his team was now on its way toward repeating as champions. "The Athletics will be second and the Metropolitans third," he predicted. "But, understand me, the fight will be a hot one."

Mathews massaged his aching right arm. That one got away, but there would be many more chances to win, if his wing could only hold out through September. The Cincinnati owner could shoot his mouth off all he wanted, but many observers knew that these Athletics, fortified by Bradley, could hold their own against anyone—the Reds, the New York Metropolitans, or even Ted Sullivan's vastly improved St. Louis Browns. And Mathews would spend the next four months doggedly, painfully, almost heroically trying to prove it.

6

WHO'S IN CHARGE?

HE BROWNS OPENED AWAY FROM HOME, IN CINCINNATI, ON
May 1, leaving most St. Louis fanatics, in those pre-television, pre-
radio days, unable to see or hear the game. But that did not deter
local baseball lovers from following the action. They formed crowds
around newspaper offices and the Browns' headquarters downtown,
where runners posted inning-by-inning results from Cincinnati, fresh off
the telegraph wire, in plate-glass windows. As it became apparent that a
great game was unfolding, more people crowded in, spilling over the sidewalks into the streets.

Three hundred miles to the east in Cincinnati, the afternoon "was
beautiful beyond compare—as perfect a May day as ever greeted the vi-
olets of spring," O. P. Caylor observed in the *Cincinnati Commercial
Gazette*. In the ticket booth outside the Bank Street Grounds, a foghorn
of a man named Charley Thompson sent his "sweet, silvery voice" floating
out over Millcreek Bottoms neighborhood "like incense from the altar,"
bawling: "Fe-orty and fee-fty cents in the she-ade, twen-ty-fe-ive cents in
the sun. Have your little piasters available, gentlemen!" Twenty-five cents,

in other words, got a spectator into the ballpark, to sit in the exposed bleachers; shade cost fifteen cents extra. Two backup Reds players, pitcher Ren Deagle and catcher Phil Powers, worked at a hectic pace collecting tickets at the turnstiles. Some 3,500 people filtered in, as vendors hawked the Reds' new "neat and pretty" scorecards, a nickel apiece, featuring on the back standings of both the American Association and the National League, to be updated on a daily basis. The *Enquirer* was delighted to see the Cincinnati management "making good use of everything"—including the center field fence, where gaudy advertisements were now splashed—to "turn a few honest pennies to defray expenses" and increase profits.

Profits would ultimately depend, of course, on how well the Reds defended their crown. For now, Cincinnatians were wild about their club. Fifteen minutes before the game, "a buzz of excitement" hummed through the sold-out ballpark. Prominent in the crowd was Browns owner Chris Von der Ahe, club director William F. Nolker, and their families, who had taken the Ohio and Mississippi Express to watch all three Browns games in "Porktown." Nolker was a typical Von der Ahe associate, a fellow immigrant from Westphalia who had made it big in St. Louis as a co-owner of the new brewery Brinckwirth & Nolker. Under a brilliant blue sky, the baseball lovers looked out over packed wooden stands and a well-groomed diamond, with thirty-six carriages and buggies "and two ladies on horseback" parked deep in the green outfield. O. P. Caylor noted with pleasure that the audience was "not only large in numbers, but was of a class which gives *tone* to the sport."

At exactly three o'clock, a gong rang out, and all eyes turned to the newly erected flagstaff north of the bleachers. Soon a massive, 9-by-18-foot pennant—"the price of so many hard-earned victories," the *Cincinnati Enquirer* observed—was hauled up the pole. Manufactured by Horstmann Brothers of Philadelphia, the famous textile company that had earned a fortune supplying uniforms during the Civil War, it was made of the "best quality white bunting," with a blue serrated border. "Champions 1883," the pennant read in big blue letters. Though the Reds had actually won the pennant in 1882, that was not an error; under the conventions of the time, the title would be Cincinnati's until the "1884" champions were crowned at the end of the 1883 season.

As the flag was being raised, the wind suddenly died down, and the pennant hung lifeless, "drooping down the staff," Caylor noted. Superstitious spectators instantly interpreted this as a dubious sign for the coming season. But just as the gong was rung a second time, summoning the Cincinnati Reds to the field, "the flag caught a passing breeze and proudly waved its graceful length before the 7,000 eyes that leveled at it." The crowd roared its approval and settled in to see whether ace Will White would pick up where he had left off. He had dominated the league in 1882 as its greatest pitcher, by far, with a 40–12 record and a 1.54 earned run average. Unfortunately, Will had woken up that morning with a wretchedly sore shoulder. He announced he "would pitch if desired, though he knew he could not do the work he would warm up to in a week or so." It was so desired.

As soon as the game began, the Browns' aggressive new captain, Tom Loftus, started up a steady chatter, trying to motivate his men and fluster the champions. Other St. Louis players joined in, jabbering away and taunting their opponents. That was standard practice for the Browns: Bill Gleason and Charlie Comiskey, while coaching the runners, liked to position themselves on either side of the enemy catcher "and comment on his personal habits, breeding [and] skill as a receiver, or rather lack of it." The *Commercial Gazette* insisted that all this noise was a waste of breath, arguing that the cool Reds veterans were above getting rattled. The contrast between St. Louis's prating and "the quiet, earnest, silent team work of the Cincinnatians was by no means creditable to St. Louis' team."

Cincinnati struck first, jumping to a 4–0 lead, and deceiving most of the crowd "into thinking that the game would be transposed into a general picnic," the *Enquirer* noted. But Browns starter Jumbo McGinnis recovered—in part by cheating, it seemed. From midgame on, the hefty pitcher "openly violated the pitching rules by throwing on a level with his head." By raising his arm above the legal limit of his shoulders, McGinnis got enough power behind his pitches to successfully shut down the Reds. Cincinnati captain Pop Snyder hotly and repeatedly complained to the umpire that McGinnis's overhand pitches were illegal, but the official "refused to enforce the rule."

While the Browns' pitcher began to throw a series of scoreless innings, the St. Louis man who was most effective at riding the enemy, Arlie

Latham, went to work trying to disrupt the rhythm of Will White. Latham's bench jockeying had been so extreme during spring training that even his manager had ordered him to shut up. "I told him he was too d—n fresh," Sullivan recalled. And for a while Latham tamped it down. But now that the games counted, he was back in form. "My dear Mr. White," Latham shouted at the pitcher, "we have been very courteous to you during the game, but as the Browns need a few runs we will have to be a little rude to you for a while." After one inning of Latham's nonstop needling, White, wiping the sweat from his spectacles, came over to Sullivan. "I think all your players are gentlemen except Latham," White groused. As Will got sorer, weaker, and angrier, the St. Louis boys rallied to tie the game in the eighth, 4–4, to loud applause, "their friends in the grand stand yelling themselves hoarse."

By then, the *Enquirer* noted, fans of both clubs were "worked up to a great pitch of excitement. Encouraging yells came from all sides to their respective favorites, and for a while it was perfect pandemonium." Back in St. Louis, outside the Browns' headquarters, a shout went up as a man posted the ninth-inning score, showing six successive goose eggs for Cincinnati. Tension mounted in the tenth, when he posted zeroes for both clubs. Delighted that the Browns were holding their own against the champions, the street crowd buzzed with "universal admiration . . . for the staying powers of the St. Louis boys in a game that so severely taxed their playing abilities." Latecomers crowded in around the window.

At the Bank Street Grounds in Cincinnati, "the excitement ran intense" as the small boy working the scoreboard ran up the number eleven. That inning would be a memorable one. The Browns' leadoff batter, Jack Gleason, could only manage to tap an easy grounder to the Reds' shortstop, but the crowd's grateful yell "died in its infancy" when Long John Reilly dropped the throw—an occupational hazard of bare-handed first basemen. McGinnis, next up, plopped the ball into shallow right field, only to see Joe Sommer scoop it up and nail Gleason at second base. The Browns' Hugh Nicol got a better piece of it, whacking a long drive over the head of left fielder Charley Jones, the handsome troublemaker with the handlebar mustache whom William Hulbert had tried to keep out of baseball. Jones raced back and leapt, but the ball skipped off his fingertips. While he raced to recover it, McGinnis sprinted home, finally giving St. Louis a 5–4 lead.

The problem now was holding it. The Reds' Sommer led off the bottom of the eleventh with a single, and twenty-five-year-old John Corkhill, nicknamed "Pop" because he was prematurely bald, came to the plate. He had been working as an off-season police officer in Philadelphia the previous November when Reds President Aaron Stern came looking for him, having heard about his prowess with the Phillies. Forced to search high and low through the streets of the officer's precinct, Stern at last located Corkhill. He complained that Pop was a hard man to track down. "Don't you know you can never find a policeman when you want one?" Corkhill deadpanned. On opening day, Stern must have been pleased that he had gone to all that trouble, because Corkhill drove home Sommer with a double, tying the score 5–5 and sending the crowd "wild with noble rage." After Snyder grounded out, Reds shortstop Chick Fulmer blasted a hard grounder between the shortstop and third baseman into left field. The Cincinnati crowd turned "stark mad" as Corkhill crossed home plate with the winning run in the 6–5 thriller.

However heartbreaking the defeat, many Browns loyalists took it as a moral victory. On the streets, it "was generally accepted as a big lift for St. Louis, playing so strong a game against the supposed heaviest team in the association." Ted Sullivan must have known better. Already, thanks to injuries in the preseason, his Browns had taken on the look of a "hospital nine," as the *Enquirer* put it. Catcher Pat Deasley, a crucial leader on the field, was out with a bad finger, jarred by a foul tip. Worse, handsome Tony Mullane, one-half of the Browns' two-man pitching rotation, was suffering a "severe attack of inflammatory rheumatism" that made it impossible for him to throw hard.

As a result, McGinnis, sore after pitching eleven innings on opening day, had to go out the very next afternoon and pitch all over again. Not surprisingly, he found it impossible to put anything on the ball. As Cincinnati batters slammed pitch after pitch, McGinnis became visibly angry, and he decided to go over his manager's head. At the end of the third inning, "tired of hearing the sharp whizz of the ball as it came past his ears from the heart of the Cincinnati 'sluggers,'" McGinnis walked over to the owner's box to protest. Whining that "his arm was not only sore but that he believed it to be permanently injured," McGinnis begged Von der Ahe to replace him with Mullane. Sticking up for Sullivan, Von der Ahe refused. McGinnis strode back to the pitcher's box and deliberately "tossed in easy ones to his opponents." By the fifth inning, Cincinnati was ahead 12–0. Finally, catcher Tom Dolan took over as pitcher and mercifully brought the game to a 12–1 conclusion. O. P. Caylor, still irritated by McGinnis's overhand throwing, was happy to report that, this time, the illegal delivery only "brought about disaster. Truly, virtue is its own reward."

While McGinnis was lobbing meatballs, at least one member of the Browns was still fighting hard to win—the insatiably aggressive Bill Gleason. On a bang-bang play at the plate, Gleason bowled over Reds catcher Phil Powers, who had just gotten over an illness that melted off twelve pounds and earned him the nickname of "Shadow." The local papers found nothing to admire in Gleason's combativeness. "This is the same player who ran into Powers last year and broke his wrist necessitating his retirement from the field for nearly six weeks," the *Enquirer* pointed out. "The collision was most likely purely unintentional on Gleason's part, but he should be more careful, and not let his zeal to win run away with his judgment."

Unfortunately, the zeal to win was in short supply among the Browns that week. The Reds completed the three-game sweep the following day, beating a St. Louis boy, Charlie Hodnett, a former apprentice printer who, in those days before massive scouting operations and farm teams, had been lifted off the city's sandlots and rushed in to fill the yawning gap in the Browns' pitching staff. Hodnett, about twenty-two, was so nervous that he walked the first two Reds batters before he was able to settle down. The rookie pitcher ended up losing only narrowly, 3–2. Caylor was impressed. "This young man is no slouch," he wrote. "He shows the makings of a fine future pitcher. His rising ball in particular is very deceptive." As it turned out, Hodnett would pitch only four games for the Browns, stepping aside as soon as Tony Mullane was able to throw hard again. (After pitching for St. Louis's club in the Union Association in 1884, Hodnett died of a crippling rheumatoid condition before his thirtieth birthday. He ended up a pauper in the St. Louis Poor House.) While waiting for his throwing arm to heal, Mullane earned his keep by playing in the outfield and contributing some hits. During the third straight loss to Cincinnati, he "looked anything else but a sick man as he trampled the grass in center field," the *Enquirer* noted. It was Mullane who made the longest hit of the day, a triple to right field. "His playing . . . would warrant any body in staking a few dollars that his chances for laying claim to his six feet of earth were very slim for a few days, at least."

But there was little else that seemed impressive about this team, the *Enquirer* gloated. From its perspective, the sweep had revealed critical flaws in Chris Von der Ahe's improved Browns. "If any member of the St. Louis base-ball nine, or any backer of the aggregation, has been troubled by the buzzing of the championship bee in his bonnet, he must be by this time thoroughly convinced that such a hope is the veriest delusion, only to be classed with the things of the past, and as impossible as the wild dreams of the enthusiastic inventor who is ready to announce he has solved the problem of perpetual motion." The taunt rang truer when St. Louis went on to Columbus and dropped two of its three games against the weak expansion club. "It is not probable that the St. Louis nine will be met by a delegation of enthusiastic citizens with a brass band on their return from this trip," the *Enquirer* laughed. Von der Ahe was at least as irritated and impatient as the club's most fanatical followers. Though he had pledged to leave club management to Sullivan, he wanted instant remedies through roster shakeups and changes in strategy. Even before the regular season began, Ted had been forced to fend off a report that Von der Ahe was prepared to shake up the outfield—"a statement as vicious as false," Sullivan snapped, one "calculated to create distrust among the players in those positions and to destroy their usefulness. Happily, however, they are men of good sense and judgment, and having confidence in the management, have gone on playing a good game notwithstanding the slurs aimed at them." For all of Ted's huffiness, the rumor was essentially true. Von der Ahe had been working behind the scenes already to undermine the manager's control.

Trouble erupted only a few days into the regular season, on May 5, when Sullivan telegraphed Von der Ahe his starting lineup for the game in Columbus. Against the owner's explicit instructions, Sullivan inserted his trusted captain, Tom Loftus, in center field. Von der Ahe immediately telegraphed orders to Sullivan to yank Loftus out of the starting lineup and replace him with utility man Tom Sullivan. Loftus had looked terrible at the plate—during the month of May, he could only muster a .182 average—

and Von der Ahe had concluded, perhaps egged on by Reid, that the new captain was simply not up to this level of play. All spring, Loftus had "not been enjoying his usual good health," Sullivan admitted, and it is doubtful Tom's well-being improved when, in a preseason game, a wild pitch struck him "full on the side of the head," the *Missouri Republican* reported, adding: "He staggered and fell—the blow was hard enough to break his neck." Loftus had struggled back onto his feet, and "after a moment or so he resumed his place at the bat and brought the run home." But, since then, he had looked pretty bad.

Mulling over his boss's direct order to sit Loftus down, Sullivan faced a dilemma. He knew players often came around after a tough start. If he permitted Von der Ahe to dictate his daily lineups, Ted would have little authority for the rest of the season. If he resisted—well, no one could say how the rash Von der Ahe would react. In the end, Sullivan ignored his boss's telegram and sent Loftus out as planned. The power struggle was on. Later that day, the Browns front office informed the press that Loftus and left fielder Jack Gleason were about to be released. That, in turn, prompted Bill Gleason to declare that he would quit, since his older brother's firing "was unwarranted by the circumstances and . . . he was merely being made a scapegoat for the short-comings of somebody else." Happy to see Ted Sullivan instantly plunged into a boiling cauldron of controversy, Dave Reid charged that the new manager had divided the team into competing cliques, with his new players and Iowa cronies on one side, and the veteran, pro-Cuthbert Browns on the other. "It is hoped, for the good of base ball interests in St. Louis, that the trouble will be found out and eliminated," Reid lectured. "Just at present the club can scarce stand any serious disaffection of the sort. . . . A day or two will probably bring matters to a climax."

Von der Ahe, worried that his high-priced team was collapsing and certain that he alone could set things right, impulsively "made preparation to start at once for Columbus to smooth out matters," Reid reported. But he arrived at the station too late to catch the train and had to postpone the trip. When the Browns trounced Columbus 9–1—with Loftus firmly ensconced in center field—victory seemed to release some of the tension. "Manager Sullivan was happy last night. He can now return to St. Louis with safety," the *Ohio State Journal* reported, half-jokingly.

In truth, Von der Ahe was far from satisfied. Having missed one train to Columbus, he intended to catch another to Louisville, the Browns' next stop. Rumors ran wild that he was heading to Kentucky to fire Sullivan for insubordination, less than two weeks into the season. Although Von der Ahe assured Reid that that was not his intention, Reid portrayed him as less than pleased with Sullivan. From here on out, Von der Ahe declared, he would be "watching matters more closely and would have his say in all that pertained to management in the future, with a view of making matters work in better harmony than they had been." Sullivan seemed to be on an exceedingly short leash—remarkably so, given Von der Ahe's extravagant gift of the watch and pronouncements about the manager's supposed authority a month earlier.

In Louisville, the owner forced Sullivan to accept that Der Boss President was the boss after all. As promised, Von der Ahe dumped both Jack Gleason and Loftus. A firefighter like his brother Bill, Jack was a brave man. He had been injured so severely battling a St. Louis blaze prior to the 1882 season that "for a time it was feared he would be permanently crippled." An alumnus, with his brother, of Sullivan's great Dubuque Rabbits in 1879, Jack was bitterly unhappy that Sullivan had moved him to the outfield in 1883 to make room for Arlie Latham at third base. He met privately with Von der Ahe to complain that "he could not do himself justice" playing out of position. Fortunately, Louisville quickly picked Jack up. Though Bill wanted to follow him out of St. Louis, he calmed down and stayed put. While he accepted Jack Gleason's departure, Sullivan must have been disappointed by the dismissal of Loftus, his handpicked, hard-driving captain from Dubuque who later enjoyed a lengthy career as a respected manager.

After firing Loftus, Von der Ahe tried to pacify Sullivan by seeking his advice for a new field captain. "Being a little angry at Loftus's release, I told him that I would suit myself, and I did not want any more of his dictating," the manager recalled, surely exaggerating his defiance. Sullivan chose a young player he knew well. In a Louisville hotel room, Sullivan called the men together and informed them that Charlie Comiskey would be the new captain. Then Sullivan told Von der Ahe that Comiskey wanted a $500 raise for the season for the extra work. "All right, Ted, if you think he is worth it," responded Von der Ahe, who, whatever his faults, was willing to invest in talent.

It soon became clear that both leaders had been right—Von der Ahe, in removing Loftus, and Sullivan, in turning to Comiskey. Watching Comiskey day after day with the Browns, Sullivan knew that his young pro-

tégé, though still maturing at age twenty-three, was a natural leader, able to tamp down disagreements and turn the team's focus to winning. A relentless competitor, "Commy" shifted nervously on the bench when watching the game and brooded over baseball during his off-hours. "He never went to sleep at night," his roommate Bill Gleason recalled, "until he had figured out how he was going to win the game the next day." Comiskey would go on to win 840 games as a big-league manager and then make millions in the risky business of founding the Chicago White Sox and the new American League. All that was "solely due to his aggressiveness and fearless spirit," Sullivan proudly noted. But it was Sullivan—and Von der Ahe—who put him on that path in 1883.

Charlie Comiskey
(*Library of Congress*)

WHILE VON DER AHE TUSSLED WITH HIS MANAGER, DEASLEY AND Mullane healed enough to play again. Mullane wasted little time reprising his well-known intimidation tactics. When Jack Leary of the Louisville Eclipse dared hit a home run off him on May 13, the "Apollo of the Box" promptly sent him a painful message. The next time Leary came to the plate, Mullane smoked his first pitch into the batter's right hand, "mashing two fingers and disabling him so that he will not be able to play for three or four weeks," the *Louisville Commercial* reported. Leary angrily swore that Mullane "threw the ball at him intentionally so as to cripple him," and few could honestly doubt it. Eleven days later, Mullane inflicted more shocking damage, slamming Louisville's tall, skinny captain, Joe Gerhardt, with a fastball in the ribs. "It sounded like a drum, and poor Joe staggered and fell, and stretched out unconscious with pain," said the *Missouri Republican*. "The poor fellow uttered a groan, dropped as a shot and stiffened out like a dead man. He was carried back to the players' bench and rallied in a few minutes, but was incapacitated for play," the *Globe-Democrat* added.

The *Louisville Courier-Journal's* baseball reporter, having watched Mullane pitch the season before, had no doubt of his evil intent. "It is a well-known fact that Mullane has shown throughout his career as a pitcher a desire to cripple any man who could bat him, and two of the best players in the club have become victims of this desire," he wrote. If it could be proved that Mullane had deliberately struck down Leary and Gerhardt, the writer argued, "he should be instantly expelled from the association." But it couldn't be proved. Mullane stayed on, brutalizing batters all season while professing innocence. "Some of these days Mullane will get his neck broken," warned the *Cincinnati Enquirer*, noting that "he kept up his practice of disabling batters by hitting Long John Reilly in the head during the last St. Louis Waterloo. John still carries a lump as big as a walnut under his hat." Mullane's hometown *Globe-Democrat* rallied to his defense, blaming the victim: Reilly "didn't dodge worth a cent when he got hit by that ball."

By the end of the road trip, the Browns had started to recover, winning two of three in Louisville to return with a 3–6 record. A beautiful sight awaited them in St. Louis. "The diamond and outfield at Sportsman's park have been mowed by Superintendent Solari," the *Republican* reported, "and looked as pretty as a huge sheet of green velvet yesterday." The Browns proceeded to reassert themselves, beating the Cincinnati Reds in the home opener and, healthier now, going 6–3 during the home stand to reach a .500 record. As April's exhibitions had suggested, this team was very different from the 1882 edition. They played hard under Sullivan, even violently. They grabbed and tripped enemy runners. When running the base paths, they slammed into their opponents, then broke for the next base while the flustered fielders fumbled with the ball. "It was well worth the price of admission yesterday to see Latham, Nicol and Comiskey profit by every opportunity to steal a base," the *St. Louis Globe-Democrat* enthused. "Daring work in this department leads to more fielding errors than any other branch of the game." Still, Von der Ahe was not satisfied. Just as the Browns were starting to click, he pulled another stunt that undermined and embarrassed his manager.

In late May, the owner decided to bring back, of all people, Ned Cuthbert—this time purely as a player, not as a manager, though no one could say what the future might hold. Dave Reid was delighted. "This is a little humiliating to the management, but shows wisdom," he gloated in the *Republican*. "His being shoved overboard by the club was a mistake in the first place." The signing had not come about easily. After Cuthbert's release, Reid explained, "personal troubles" had developed between him and Von der Ahe, "and it required considerable time to soften these down." Cuthbert had been ready to leave the city in a huff to manage a club in Quincy, Illinois, to the horror of his longtime St. Louis friends. "Finally, through the hard work and ministrations of a mutual friend," Roger A. Brown, who ran the club's headquarters, Reid noted, "matters were adjusted yesterday, and Ed is once more a member of the force on which he has done much good work in years gone by." St. Louis baseball lovers demonstrated how pleased they were with Cuthbert's return by presenting him with a floral "canopy with a base ball design in immortelles on the bases and Ed's initials." Betrayed by the man who ran his club headquarters, Sullivan was now saddled with a disgruntled, weak-hitting, thirty-seven-year-old outfielder—to turn thirty-eight in June—who was still popular with fans and angling for the manager's job.

Meanwhile, more than the club threatened to come apart. After a huge Sunday turnout of 12,200 on May 27, the upper deck of Sportsman's Park "swayed perceptibly" and "shook as if it would tumble to pieces" as customers made for the narrow staircase that served as the deck's only exit. Fortunately, no one panicked, but after the crowd got down, good citizens implored reporters to speak out about the danger before the structure collapsed and killed dozens of people. Such an accident "would be a death blow to base ball in St. Louis," the *Missouri Republican* warned. "It's dollars to doughnuts that the architect never suspected it would be used for such a purpose," the *Globe-Democrat* added. Von der Ahe got the hint. The owner called in German-born Edmund Jungenfeld, a prestigious St. Louis specialist in brewery architecture who had designed buildings at the Budweiser plant and the facility owned by club director Nolker. Jungenfeld strengthened and lengthened the roof while adding open seats on top of it.

The 1884 St. Louis Browns and the grandstand at Sportsman's Park
(*Transcendental Graphics*/thcruckcrarchive.com, *reprinted with permission*)

Von der Ahe was eager to cram all the paying customers he could inside his Sportsman's Park, which now had the hefty seating capacity of 11,000.

Somehow, in the midst of all this, Sullivan was able to turn his attention to the field as he led the Browns on their second road trip. After winning two out of three from the Allegheny Club in Pittsburgh, and sweeping the Orioles in three in Baltimore, St. Louis headed up to Philadelphia to take on the fearsome Athletics. Lew Simmons's men, with their torrid 19–4 record, .826 winning percentage, and full five-game lead over second-place Louisville, now seemed poised to run away with the pennant—unless someone stopped them.

———<o>———

GETTING INTO THE SPIRIT OF THE BIG SERIES, VON DER AHE boisterously declared that he would reward each of his men with a box of expensive cigars if they could capture at least two of the three games from the Athletics. The prospect of good smokes wasn't enough to prevent the boys from making a disastrous start in their opener in Philadelphia, on the cloudy Thursday afternoon of June 7, as they fell behind 7–1 in the first inning. Even so, Sullivan's men refused to become rattled. When rain started to fall, they shrewdly shifted tactics and began dragging their feet, blatantly trying to secure a rainout before the five innings could be played to make the game official. "They came in from the field as slowly as if each man had the rheumatism," said the *Philadelphia Press*. Deasley was typical. He went to the club bat bag and slowly pulled out nearly every one before finding one that suited him. "Then he had a little conversation with the umpire in regard to some point that he wanted settled, and after that he found considerable difficulty in getting planted in his position. He finally had to make a base hit." All the time the rain fell. When the Athletics came to bat, Browns hurler George McGinnis threw fat pitches straight over the plate, "the obvious intention being to give everybody a hit and put no one out, so that the inning could be protracted indefinitely."

The Athletics, catching on immediately, made an equally desperate effort to speed things up. The contest degenerated into a soggy farce. Athletics batter Jack O'Brien "adopted the counter tactic of trying to strike out," but catcher Deasley "was equal to the occasion, and failed to catch the ball. O'Brien then refused to run and thus compelled the umpire to declare him out." George "Grin" Bradley, next up, hit the ball but deliberately ran out of the baseline so that he would be called out. When another Athletics batter came to the plate, equally eager to make an out, Browns third baseman Arlie Latham called time and dashed off the field for his jacket. By then, the heavens had opened. "The umpire shouted after him in vain, and a moment later both teams followed him pell-mell to their room, while the crowd disappeared under the seats and the grand stand." After another thirty minutes of pouring rain, the umpire called the game. The Browns had scored a substantial psychological victory by dodging defeat.

The narrow escape became doubly important when St. Louis lost on the following day, a Friday afternoon game. But the Browns finally found their groove on Saturday. Comiskey, running the bases much as the demonic Ty Cobb would a generation later, kept one rally going when he dropped a bunt in front of home plate, sprinted down the line, and surreptitiously swatted the ball out of first baseman Harry Stovey's hand.

The illegal act, unseen by the umpire—only one man worked each game, making it easy to cheat—permitted Arlie Latham to scamper home from third. Comiskey promptly stole second base, then third, and scored on a ground ball, having manufactured a run from essentially nothing. The Browns won 3–0.

With the series locked at one victory apiece, the Browns looked even stronger during the final game, a Monday makeup for the rainout. Not that there weren't some stressful moments for the visitors. In the eighth inning, St. Louis led the Athletics by a seemingly insurmountable 9–4 when Philadelphia's Grin Bradley came up with the bases loaded. Bradley worked the pitch count to two strikes and six balls—the 1883 version of a full count—before driving a long fly ball past the outfielders, sending all three runners scurrying across home plate. At the last moment, Bradley decided to follow them, dashing home with visions of a grand slam, only to be cut down within a foot of the plate by a terrific relay throw. The Browns held on to win, 9–7, earning their fancy cigars, to the disgust of many Philadelphians. One local paper called the St. Louis men "about the toughest and roughest gang that ever struck this city. . . . Vile of speech, insolent in bearing, impatient of restraint, they set at defiance all rules. . . . The captain is an illiterate individual named Comiskey, whose sole claim to distinction rests upon his glib use of profane language." Rough or not, they went on to win ten of the eleven games on their road trip, a brilliant streak that thrust them into pennant contention.

They left New York at 7 P.M. on Thursday, June 13, and arrived in St. Louis on Saturday at 8 A.M. "Looking sunburned and warrior-like," the players found a beaming President Von der Ahe and a mob of "their near friends" waiting at Union Depot to tender them a hearty welcome home. The papers, which had been whipping up interest with telegraphed reports of the Browns' eastern exploits, promised a much larger crowd, a "monster gathering," at Sportsman's Park the following afternoon to greet the boys at their first home game in more than three weeks. With any luck, they might even capture first place during their home stand.

Although he was relieved that his team had turned its season around, Sullivan knew the Browns were still hampered by a serious lack of offensive production by the outfield, something he was trying to remedy. Von der Ahe was willing to open his pocketbook to buy better players, but

America's storehouse of baseball talent was nearly empty, thanks to the plethora of professional teams that had sprung up in 1883. At the same time, the leagues' new agreement to respect each other's contracts had limited the opportunities for raiding. "President Von der Ahe has offered fabulous sums to players, but the fact is that the market is run absolutely bare," the *Missouri Republican* lamented. American Association executives were swarming over even such weak semipro teams as the Chicago Dreadnoughts, elbowing each other aside to purchase anybody remotely worth having. "Every one of them went away empty-handed," explained Dreadnoughts Manager P. J. Norton, "for the team was drained early in spring of all the players worth having."

Sullivan, who had as good an eye for talent as anyone, told Von der Ahe he would keep looking. But in his frenzy for someone—anyone— who might hit, the owner, without bothering to consult Sullivan, went after the eighteen-year-old kid brother of the great Buck Ewing, the mighty catcher for the National League's New York Gothams, on little more than the naïve hope that talent might run in the family. Unlike his muscular sibling, John Ewing was "long, lean and about as big around as a bean pole." He had earned the sobriquet of "Ginger Ale John" for his solemn pledge to forever abstain from liquor. When Von der Ahe heard rumors that the Louisville Eclipse club was interested in Ewing's brother, Der Boss President made a beeline for Cincinnati in a panic and signed the teenager. Sullivan needed to watch him in only one game to form an estimation of both his talent and Von der Ahe's eye for it. Ginger Ale John went 0-for-5. "He was sent home the next day," the *Sporting News* noted, "and that was the last time Chris hired a man on the reputation of a relative."

Meanwhile, Sullivan had to give Von der Ahe's old friend Ned Cuthbert some playing time. The former player-manager appeared in twenty-one games, batted a wretched .169, and managed to produce exactly one extra-base hit, a double, before Sullivan could finally be rid of him. The search continued for hard-hitting outfielders who might lead the Browns to the American Association pennant, while Sullivan resisted the urge to strangle his insufferably "helpful" boss. But Von der Ahe was just starting, and a fight that would change the whole pennant race was coming.

7

THE $300 SPECIAL

T HE SUNDAY AFTERNOON OF JUNE 17, 1883, WAS LIKE MANY
sweltering days in St. Louis, the atmosphere almost unbearably
heavy with heat and moisture. At 2:30 P.M., the skies suddenly discharged their burden, letting loose torrents of drenching rain. Some of
the men and women who planned to watch the game that afternoon
rushed inside Solari's old place, the Grand Avenue saloon, which was
tucked into Sportsman's Park's right field. Thousands of people who were
already inside the park scurried under whatever roofing they could find.
Some two or three thousand more "who could find no shelter huddled
like kittens," the St. Louis Globe-Democrat reported. Sheets of water beat
down their umbrellas, "and two-thirds of those present were drenched to
the skin in five minutes' time." The playing field quickly became a lake,
while Grand Avenue turned into a rushing river. About a thousand people
thronging the sidewalk clamored "wildly and ineffectually" to be let inside
the park.

Suddenly, the rain stopped, and the sun burst through the clouds, glo-
riously illuminating the scene. "Then it was seen what kind of a base-ball

crowd St. Louis can turn out even with adverse elements," the *Globe-Democrat* said. The stands were packed. So were the new seats on the roof, which had been "loaded down with people until it became dangerous"—though there was no trembling this time. The open bleachers were filled, and people jammed the park's standing-room areas. "It was the biggest crowd that ever attended a ball game in St. Louis," the *Globe-Democrat* declared with amazement. At 3:30 P.M., a gallant nine of men in red caps, white shirts, white knickers, and red stockings appeared through thickets of fanatics and marched as a "platoon" to the center of the field. That was the signal for the crowd's first outburst of the day, a great roar of clapping, whistling, "hallooing," and pounding, perhaps the loudest cheer that had ever been unleashed for a ball club in St. Louis. "It was a grand ovation, a prolonged howl of triumph and welcome. It thrilled everybody who heard it," the paper said, and it did not let up until the platoon broke up and began to play catch, warming up. Next, the visiting New York Metropolitans appeared, each man carrying his own case with a bat in it. "They were a neat looking lot, not as heavy as the Browns, but supple and lithe-looking," though their uniforms seemed a tad dingy and soiled. "A few hours' practice in the laundry this morning would not do them any harm," Dave Reid quipped. Since the game either had to start by 4 P.M. or would have to be played as a pointless exhibition, the grounds crew raced to dump absorbent sawdust into the puddles along the base paths and the pitcher's box.

Though the people of St. Louis were only too happy to be enjoying the Lord's Day with beer, baseball, and joy, the Mets' star center fielder, John O'Rourke, refused to play because of his convictions as a devout Irish Catholic. John, the brother of an even better ballplayer (Jim, now in the Baseball Hall of Fame), was hardly a shirker. In an 1880 game, he had crashed so hard into the center-field fence at the Troy Ball Club Grounds that he had taken a five-inch gash in his throat and had needed to be carted off the field. But religion was a profoundly serious matter to many Americans in the 1880s, especially in the eastern cities, and not everyone shared the idea of Von der Ahe and his fellow Germans that Sundays were meant for fun.

From the start, the game was a tense affair, and the crowd "vigorously hissed" the ball and strike judgments of umpire Ormond Butler, twenty-eight, a former actor and manager of Ford's Opera House in Baltimore. The umpire, who showed up in his official Association uniform, may not have enhanced his aura of authority by removing his gold-buttoned blue jacket in the brutal heat, revealing a light summery "negligee" shirt. Dave Reid, for one, was disgusted. "One of the objects of the uniform was to give judicial gravity to the umpire," he lectured.

In the first inning, Charlie Comiskey launched the ball over the head of the Mets' Charlie Reipschlager, a catcher who had been conscripted to take over in center field for the more pious and talented O'Rourke. The titanic blow yielded a triple, driving home Hugh Nicol. Comiskey himself scored on a wild throw, producing a 2–0 lead and a burst of applause that lasted for a full minute. The Mets fought back to take a 4–3 lead, but the Browns would not lay down. In the eighth, Billy Gleason hit a two-strike blooper to left field for a single. Arlie Latham, next up, was hit hard by a pitch, which, under 1883 rules, did not award him first base. But he dusted himself off and clubbed a double into the gap, driving home Gleason with the tying run. Then, on an 0–2 count, Comiskey blasted the ball "as if from a cannon" over the hapless Reipschlager's head, yet again, for his second triple of the day, driving in the go-ahead run. In their final inning, with the Metropolitans loading the bases with two outs, Bill Holbert clubbed a drive toward the gap in right-center. "Nicol started for it amid a deathlike stillness," reported the *Globe-Democrat*. The game rested on Little Nick's catching it—bare-handed, of course. The crowd let out a loud roar, and the Browns ran off the field with a 7–5 victory.

There were some complaints after the game. Sam Boyd, the chief of city detectives, grumbled that Von der Ahe was "so blanked stingy" with his free passes that the mobbed park came close to being left without police protection. Even a reporter was blocked at the gate, unable to get in amid the throng of paying customers. He had to send a friend to hunt up Von der Ahe or the club secretary personally so he could gain entrance. Reid griped that the press box, which Von der Ahe had enclosed to spare the sportswriters annoying interactions with spectators, was "boarded up in winter style," blocking any breeze, "and the atmosphere was thick enough . . . to cut with a knife." But for all the kvetching, there was much to celebrate. Von der Ahe raked in nearly $3,000 for Sunday's game alone, and it was now clear that the team he had bought, with Ted Sullivan's painstaking guidance, was a splendid one. The Browns had clawed their way all the way back to second place, just behind the Philadelphia Athletics. And that afternoon, a beaming Von der Ahe distributed his box of superb cigars, as promised, to each of the men.

Over the unseasonably cool, bright, breezy days that followed Sunday's deluge, St. Louis struggled toward first place against an unyielding Metropolitan club. The tone of the game on Monday, June 18, was set early when Mets outfielder Chief Roseman boldly stretched a single into a double, and tried to score from second on a single. The ball was pegged perfectly to Browns catcher Tom Dolan, who held on, "just as Roseman came flying home, running with terrible force into him, doubling him up. It was a terrible collision." For a time it appeared the battered, woozy Dolan might have to leave the game, but the catcher toughed it out. St. Louis finally won the bitterly contested game in the tenth inning, 8–7. The Browns won again, 5–2, on Tuesday as the Athletics lost. For the first time in 1883, St. Louis was tied for first place.

After the Browns lost a thirteen-inning nail-biter on Thursday to the Metropolitans, 2–1, they swept the lowly Baltimore Orioles in three straight, thus earning fourteen victories in their last sixteen games. In honor of the Browns' impervious infield, named after Confederate General Thomas J. Jackson, the vendors at Sportsman's Park began selling "Stone-wall Sandwiches." Ted Sullivan declared that his players were "all anxious and willing to play," and he "never saw such eagerness" to get into the game. Dave Reid, for once sharing in the joyful mood, mused about the beauty of Sportsman's Park in a poetic passage that surely strikes a chord with anyone who loves baseball: The field, he wrote, "was sown in clover some weeks ago and is daily sprinkled and rolled. Some days ago it was mown from one end to the other, and, save where the brown and white marks of the diamond are traced, looks like a spread of emerald velvet. It is a sight one can gaze at for a long time without wearying."

Yet the umpiring continued to nettle. When the Mets' Chief Roseman tried to stretch a single into a double, and Browns second baseman George Strief appeared to tag him out two feet from the base, umpire Butler, "whose sight was like his judgment," called him safe. The disgust by St. Louis cranks got so bad that, when Butler suffered a terrific blow on the side of his head from a wild pitch, "a number of persons so forgot their humanity, good sense and decency as to cheer." It got worse. In late June, Von der Ahe would get so riled up about the umpiring that he made something of a national laughingstock of himself. But he was hardly alone in that era in despising and distrusting the men in blue.

———◇———

THIRTEEN MONTHS EARLIER, ON MAY 30, 1882, A YOUNG CLERK AT a store on Woodward Avenue in Detroit noticed a sheet of folded paper on the floor, a letter that must have dropped out of the pocket of some customer who had come and gone. When the clerk picked it up and began reading, he knew this was no ordinary note.

The letter was addressed to a well-known Detroit gambler named James Todd. The writer, who signed himself "Dick," explained to the gambler that he had to catch a train and would be unable to attend their prearranged meeting. But Dick left explicit instructions: Todd was to bet on the Providence Grays on Tuesday. On Wednesday, Todd was to bet on Detroit—unless he received a telegram that said, "Buy all the lumber you can," in which case he was to stick with Providence. "When you send me any money," Dick instructed Todd, "you can send check to me in care of Detroit B.B. club, and it will be all right." Here was explosive evidence that, even after all the angst of the late 1870s and William A. Hulbert's harsh punishments of transgressors, baseball at its highest level was still filthy.

The clerk promptly brought his discovery to William G. Thompson, president of the Detroit Base Ball Club and mayor of the city. No fool, Thompson instantly recognized that the letter would reopen concerns about the honesty of National League games. There was no escaping the grim reality: "Dick" had to be thirty-year-old Richard Higham, a well-liked, hard-hitting former outfielder who, though repeatedly suspected of being crooked as a player in the 1870s, had been allowed to become a League umpire after his retirement. He had worked most of Detroit's 1882 home games to that point.

Acting quickly, League directors convened an emergency hearing. Behind locked doors, three handwriting experts confirmed that the signature was indeed Higham's. Worcester manager Freeman Brown testified that he had seen the umpire in the company of a noted gambler in his city. Frank Bancroft, then managing the Detroit club, supplied additional details of suspicious behavior. The only witness in Higham's defense was the umpire himself, who vigorously protested his innocence. The directors, though, had heard enough. They voted unanimously to expel him from the game for life—making Higham the first and only big-league umpire drummed out for corruption. By that winter, Higham was reported to be in "congenial company," making his living as a professional gambler in Chicago's dens.

The National League had as good as asked for this disaster. It had recklessly clung to an antiquated system under which home clubs hired umpires on a per-game basis from a list of twenty-four men who had been preapproved by all eight League teams. The pay was $5 per game plus expenses, an amount so paltry that critics complained that no honest man of any intelligence or talent would even want the job. Inevitably, the list came to include the usual hard drinkers and ne'er-do-wells who were on the periphery of professional sports. "The only way to secure competent men is to pay them well," the venerable Harry Wright had warned, pleading with the National League for years to build a profes-sional umpire staff. The progressive-minded American Association had done just that in 1882, hiring four umpires on salary, monitoring their work, and assigning them to games. The system had generally worked well, somewhat reducing squabbles between clubs and building public confidence in the honesty of the sport. But many fans and journalists continued to believe that umpires, even at the major-league level, were stupid, incompetent, corrupt, or a toxic blend of all three.

After the Higham scandal, the National League followed the Amer-ican Association's lead and finally funded a full-time staff of four um-pires, paying each $200 a month. Association umps earned less—only $120 a month, plus travel expenses and a $3-per-day board allowance. As-sociation umpires also had to supply their own uniforms: a blue flannel, double-breasted jacket, with military cap, trimmed with gold cord and buttons. One St. Louis fan, getting a gander at the getup in May 1883, dryly remarked to another, "He only needs a whisk to look like a Pullman car man"—in other words, a railroad conductor aboard a fancy coach. As if on cue, the umpire "took one of the utensils from his pocket and began to dust off the home plate." It is remarkable—or perhaps a sign of how hard it was to earn a living in 1880s America—that so many good men were willing to endure the risks this job entailed for $120 a month.

Major-league umpiring was definitely not for the faint of heart. First of all, an umpire in those days faced the impossible task of trying to rule justly while working a game alone, since club owners were willing to fund only one umpire per game. A ballplayer who was good at cheating could easily exploit that, as Chicago White Stockings star Mike "King" Kelly amply demonstrated. He regularly cut from second base to home without ever getting near third, while the umpire's head was turned to follow a ball hit to the outfield. "Ball players are up to constant tricks, and nothing but the closest watch will keep us from being beaten by them," observed one of the toughest early umpires, former professional boxer Billy McLean. Yet parsimonious owners resisted the idea of even a two-man crew for nearly thirty years. When Hugh Nicol suggested that it made sense to post *three* umpires—one along each foul line, and one behind the plate—his proposal earned outright derision. "It is a wonder he doesn't think it would be beneficial to the health and comfort of the players to have nine beautiful young ladies on the field to face the players when they come in from the field," the *Sporting News* jeered. It wasn't until 1933 that the major leagues adopted the three-umpire system. In 1952, a four-man team was instituted for all regular-season major-league games.

The worst thing about working alone was the intimidation. It was no easy task to remain calm and impartial when two teams and thousands of fans were hooting and cursing at a man and challenging his manhood, if not threatening him with violence—threats on which they often made good. A number of players were experts at exploiting this intimidating situation, ferociously "kicking" at an umpire's decisions until he reversed his ruling, or was so shaken that he feared to make a tough call against the same club.

The men of Victorian America attacked umpires with a ferocity that seems incredible today. It may have been that, in a culture hemmed in by rigid rules of decorum, umpire bashing gratified a long-repressed urge to kick back at an authority figure. Much anger, admittedly, was anything but subconscious. Men who had bet their hard-earned money, particularly on the home team, felt justified in seeking revenge against anyone who had cheated them or their city. After a Browns victory in Philadelphia, umpire Ormond Butler had to flee to a nearby customhouse for safety. The mob waited hours for him to emerge. In the struggle that ensued, Arlie Latham got roughed up, while "the driver's lips were badly cut by a flying brick bat."

Marveling that so many police officers had to be diverted from their duties to escort umpires through angry mobs during the summer of 1883, sportswriter O. P. Caylor quipped that each ump should travel around the country with his own posse, or ask the governor of each state he visited to formally call out the militia for protection. "The umpire seems to be a b-a-d man," he wrote, "beside whom a Russian Nihilist is a seraph." Russian nihilists, needless to say, were anything but angels, given that one had succeeded two years earlier in blowing up Czar Alexander II, the man who had freed the serfs and sold Alaska to the United States.

"Mother, may I slug the umpire?" asked one poet in 1886, not so facetiously giving voice to the violent hatred the crowds felt for umpires:

> Let me clasp his throat, dear mother,
> In a dear, delightful grip
> With one hand, and with the other
> Bat him several on the lip.
> Let me climb his frame, dear mother,
> While the happy people shout,
> I'll not kill him dearest mother,
> I will only knock him out.
> Let me mop the ground up, Mother,
> With his person, dearest, do;
> If the ground can stand it, mother
> I don't see why you can't too.

Some good men cracked under the pressure, succumbing to the temptation to defend their honor. In 1884, Billy McLean, tormented by the "vile epithets" of louts in Philadelphia, angrily hurled a bat into the stands, striking an innocent man. Outraged, the crowd screamed "Kill him!" and jumped down onto the field. Police placed McLean under arrest for assault. The next day, he pleaded for compassion. "Goaded by uncalled for as well as unexpected taunts, I, for a moment, and but for a moment, forgot my position as an umpire and did what any man's nature would prompt if placed in a similar position." McLean called on club owners to eject hecklers. "Otherwise," he warned, "the death of an honest and manly game is in the near future."

As if mob assaults were not dangerous enough, umpires faced a constant risk of injury from hard-hit fouls. Most used no more protective gear than a mask, and some didn't even bother with that. John Daily of New York was working an Inter-State League game between Brooklyn and Harrisburg when a foul "almost drove the side of his face in," breaking his jaw in two places. The doctor who treated him noted that he would be able to consume only liquid food for several weeks.

The best of these Association umpires was Honest John Kelly, twenty-six, a profane, charming, witty, hard-drinking, hard-boiled New Yorker who had played some major-league ball as a catcher. He was that rarest of creatures: an 1880s umpire who won almost universal acclaim. Kelly became something of the dean of the profession, and when he quit after the 1888 season he held the record for the most games umpired in the majors, with 587. The *Louisville Commercial* called him "the best umpire in the country." O. P. Caylor went one better, contending that he was one of the best umpires ever to set foot on a ball field. "It is really refreshing to see Kelly umpire a game; he puts so much life into it," the *Ohio State Journal* observed. "He is all over the field, and seldom makes an error of judgment, because he is always right there to see how it is." Kelly asserted his authority without fear, and when fans failed to show him respect, it was they who got knocked in the next day's paper. The *Pittsburgh Dispatch* blasted a crowd of "howlers" for displaying a "most painful lack of breeding" during a series in June. "Kelly has won a reputation second to no umpire in the land for fairness and ability, and it is unfortunate that he should be made the victim of such an outrageous roasting as that of yesterday," said the *Dispatch*. Kicking rarely swayed Kelly. He kicked back. In May 1883, Kelly got into a screaming match with St. Louis Browns manager Ted Sullivan that created such a din it reportedly panicked a horse outside Sportsman's Park. The animal rampaged down the street until the buggy it had been pulling was "scattered in small fragments along Grand Avenue."

Some of the most effusive praise for Kelly that spring came from Chris Von der Ahe, of all people. Early in the season, when one St. Louis fanatic kept up a screaming tirade at Kelly, the umpire "coolly stopped the game," walked over to the offender, and demanded his removal from the grandstand. Von der Ahe stepped onto the field, in solidarity with Kelly, and ordered the police officer on the scene to do his duty. "Well, you will have to put me out too," warned a friend of the transgressor, as the crowd threatened to get out of control—"at which the officer dropped the first delinquent and collared the second. Assistance coming, both men were thrown out, but only the first was retained in custody." Von der Ahe announced that he would have him prosecuted for disturbing the peace.

Returning from the club's first road trip in May, Von der Ahe pronounced Kelly something special. Even in translation by Reid, who habitually turned the owner's idiosyncratic speech into something approaching Oxford English, the message came through: "I can candidly assert that never before in my life have I seen a better exhibition of umpiring than was given by Mr. Kelly. . . . His decisions were not only prompt but accurate, and he displayed a practical and scientific knowledge of the game seldom seen. His judgment was strikingly good, and his decisions rang with impartiality." Just a few weeks later, Von der Ahe would characteristically change his tune, concluding that this exemplar of umpiring perfection was rotten to the core.

———◇———

JUNE 28 WAS ANOTHER DAMP, CLOUDY DAY IN THE MIDWEST. DAYS of rain had swollen the great Mississippi and every stream in its vicinity, flooding fields and streets, but the main concern of men in and around St. Louis that morning seemed to be whether the great showdown between the Browns and the Athletics would take place. "All morning," the *Missouri Republican* reported, "the uncertain skies were watched anxiously from store, bank, office, factory and hotel." To the relief of all, the rain held off, and an atmosphere of pennant-race baseball prevailed at Sportsman's Park that afternoon. Despite the threatening weather, some six thousand people turned out, a big crowd for a Thursday—some thought the biggest ever for a weekday game in the city.

WELCOME VISITORS was painted on the grass in front of the pitcher's box, and the city meant it. The Athletics players had "carte blanche to do everything at Von der Ahe's expense," the *Philadelphia World* reported. "All who came to the grounds and said they were Philadelphians were given the best seats in the ground free." St. Louis baseball lovers who fondly recalled the 1876 Browns Stockings were happy to see that club's star pitcher, George Washington Bradley, back in town, taking the field once again. "It was the same old 'Brad,' grin and all, but a little stouter than of old," Dave Reid noted. Grin was stationed in center field. Bobby Mathews, who had pitched in 1876 for the New York Mutuals, took to the box once again. He was "only a little older than he was seven years ago, but sports a heavier mustache," wrote Reid. Considering the treatment that rowdy Philadelphians gave their Browns earlier that month, the St. Louis crowd was surprisingly gracious, giving the Athletics "a very cordial reception," the *New York Clipper* noted, "contrary to expectation." There were signs, though, that both clubs were starting to take this pennant race very seriously. Simmons and his fellow owners had canceled the Athletics' exhibition games during the western trip, a significant loss of money, but one they felt was worthwhile to keep the men fresh and limit their risk of injury.

The pitching matchup that day featured a "Jumbo" against a "Shrimp"— George McGinnis, five feet ten and 197 pounds, a hard-throwing right-hander who had won twenty-five games for the Browns in 1882, versus little Bobby Mathews, five inches shorter and 57 pounds lighter, who had won nineteen for the Boston Red Stockings. "It was virtually a battle between the two best pitchers in the American Association," the *Republican* contended. Mathews got in some trouble in the third, falling behind 1–0 when Bill Gleason drove home Tom Dolan with a double, but he was a puzzle to the Browns hitters from that point on. McGinnis was almost as good. Harry Stovey tied the game with a run-scoring double in the sixth, but the Athletics went ahead, 3–1, thanks to uncharacteristic errors by Gleason and Comiskey. In the fateful ninth inning, Bill Gleason broke Mathews's string of five straight hitless innings with a drive to center field. While Grin Bradley was chasing it, Gleason tore around first toward second. As the throw came in, A's second baseman Cub Stricker fumbled with the ball. But Gleason slid past the bag, and

Stricker managed to slap the tag on him while Gleason grabbed for the base. "Out!" umpire Kelly cried, killing any hopes the Browns had of winning. The call "provoked a perfect storm of hisses." As Kelly noted after the game, Gleason "hung onto the bag and played to the grand stand for sympathy," but the ump was having none of it. The crowd "cursed the umpire and expressed the belief he had sold the game," the *Globe-Democrat* reported.

The loss plunged St. Louis into mourning, noted an Athletics player, jotting down his impressions for the *Philadelphia Item*. Cub Stricker, returning to the hotel from an after-supper stroll that evening, "informs me that there is crepe all over the city," he wrote. The player described the Athletics at their ease that night, savoring victory. "The boys were objects of much interest about the hotel corridors in the evening, and were looked upon like a circus or some other curiosity. The boys are all seen at their best in the evenings, lounging in chairs in front of the hotel."

Von der Ahe spent the night in a far less placid mood. He was certain that this umpire Kelly, this man he had only recently so effusively praised, had thrown the game to the Athletics. An off day on Friday only gave the owner more time to fume, replaying in his head all the calls that went against the Browns. "The local baseball caldron was boiling and bubbling" all Friday morning, evening and night, "and is probably very hot this morning," the *Globe-Democrat* reported on Saturday. Someone had informed the easily enraged Von der Ahe that Kelly "had associated with the Eclipse and Athletic nines—a gross violation of the rules. But worse than all, he had played poker with members of the Eclipse nine." Von der Ahe made up his mind then and there: come what may, by God, that crook Kelly would not umpire the second game of the Browns-Athletics series.

On Friday, the owner wired American Association headquarters, demanding Kelly's replacement, throwing around his considerable weight, and threatening to "break up the American Association" unless he got his way. "That was a nice remark for him to make," huffed Charlie Mason, co-owner of the Athletics. "They say he does such things thoughtlessly, but that's no excuse." Mason offered $50 to anyone who could "produce reliable information that [Kelly] is crooked." There were no takers. Still, rather than risk losing one of his most lucrative franchises—there were already published reports that St. Louis intended to jump to the National League, should the Detroit club go under—American Association Secretary Jimmy Williams sheepishly ordered Kelly to trade places with Charley Daniels, who was umpiring in Louisville. Daniels was widely regarded as an "impartial, good humored and intelligent" umpire, the *New York Clipper* noted in a June 23 profile. "An atmosphere of glee surrounded" Von der Ahe when word came that Kelly had been yanked, and his followers proclaimed Saturday's game "already won."

Following orders, Kelly climbed aboard a 7 P.M. train on the Ohio & Mississippi Railroad that Friday night, bound from St. Louis for Louisville. "All went merrily until about 9 o'clock, when consternation spread through the camp," the *Globe-Democrat* reported. A telegram from Daniels informed the Browns that he had missed his train in Louisville, and there was no other train available to get him to St. Louis in time. Suddenly, the stunned Von der Ahe faced the prospect of a big Saturday game with nobody to umpire it. Without an official umpire on hand, it would have to be played as a meaningless exhibition, sure to infuriate his customers and decimate the turnout. Still convinced that he had been right to banish Kelly, Von der Ahe asked railroad officials how much it

John Kelly,
by John Reilly,
Cincinnati Commercial Gazette,
September 20, 1883 (Library of Congress)

would cost to hire a special train to transport Daniels to St. Louis. The answer came back from the Louisville & Nashville Railroad: $300—an enormous sum, about thirty times what an American Association umpire earned per game in salary. Still, it was cheaper than losing the gate from a Saturday game. "All right," said Von der Ahe. "Bring Daniels on." At about midnight, the arrangements were finalized.

His own manager, Ted Sullivan, was "struck dumb" when Von der Ahe came to him that Friday night at the club headquarters downtown to boast about his success in switching umpires. "Kelly was all right," Sullivan explained. "Why did you not speak to me about it?" Von der Ahe "began to realize at once that he had acted impolitic, which was characteristic of him," Sullivan recalled, "but he did not have it in his heart to tell me that he was such a fool as to pay $300 for a special for Daniels." Just then, a friend who served as an agent of the railroad came into the office to inform Von der Ahe that he had just received a telegram: Daniels had safely departed on a 10:40 P.M. special. "Three hundred dollars is pretty stiff, Chris, for changing umpires," the agent remarked. Blushing at being found out, Von der Ahe urged Sullivan to look on the bright side. "Ted, we will get it back at the gate tomorrow, as it will be a great ad, to see an umpire that was brought on a special train that cost $300 and it shows my power in the Association." In truth, a huge crowd the next day, buzzing about the newspaper coverage of Von der Ahe's stunt, paid the expense many times over. But the presence of umpire Daniels made little difference. The Browns fell 7–2, losing their second game in the four-game series to the Athletics. Back in Philadelphia, when the final result went up on the scoreboard during a dull Phillies game, boys in the bleachers amused themselves by whistling the "Dead March" and cheering.

On the next day, a scorching Sunday in St. Louis, some sixteen thousand people packed into Sportsman's Park, reminding one reporter of "a solid amphitheater of humanity gathered at some of the old Roman holiday entertainments." They got a classic battle between two great clubs that stretched into extra innings. With two men out in the bottom of the tenth inning, and Fred Corey pitching for the Athletics, Comiskey drove another one of his long flies past the center fielder for a double, then stole third base, just beating the throw. That brought up old Ned Cuthbert, "who shouldered his bat and looked determined" in spite of his feeble batting record. "Ned walked to the plate, rubbed a little bit of dirt on his hands from the home plate and then faced Corey," said the *Missouri Republican*. He swung at a pitch to his liking and sent "a puzzlesome bounding ball" past the pitcher. By the time second baseman Cub Stricker could get to the bouncing grounder, Cuthbert had reached first base and Comiskey had crossed home plate to give the Browns the 9–8 victory. The crowd, having waited for days for something to roar about, "went wild with delight. They broke over the field and sent up yell after yell of triumph." With a win on Monday, the Browns could salvage a split of the big series.

On that day, fierce heat roasted St. Louis again, a particular torment to Browns starter Jumbo McGinnis, "a very stout, fleshy man," according to the *Republican*. To the dismay of four thousand sweating fans, the "blue legs had no trouble at all hitting Mac," whose "pitching lacked force, speed[,] and was devoid of tactics." Some of his fat pitches looked "so lovely that the merest novices felt ambitious to be ball players so they could whack away at this beautiful delivery." The Browns' embarrassing 9–1 loss—the third in four games—dropped St. Louis two and a half games back in the standings. An infuriated Von der Ahe lashed out impulsively once again. He slapped a one-week suspension on the hefty McGinnis on the grounds that the pitcher had failed to take "proper care of himself." The *Republican*'s troublemaking Reid, who may have planted the bug in Von der Ahe's ear, applauded the hurler's punishment: "The plain truth is he is carrying so much flesh that he has no control of himself." The plainer truth was that, as the Browns struggled to remain in the pennant chase, Von der Ahe had deprived Ted Sullivan of one of his two starters—and one of the elite pitchers in the American Association. Despite sporadic soreness in his arm, McGinnis would win twenty-eight games that season, post the fourth lowest earned run average in the league, and lead the circuit with six shutouts.

Nobody had told Ted that working for Von der Ahe was going to be easy, but this was getting ridiculous.

8

BASE BALL MAD

W IIEN THE PHILADELPHIA ATHLETICS TOOK OVER FIRST PLACE in May and early June, they looked unstoppable. But then came the two losses to the Browns in Philadelphia—the ones that earned the St. Louis boys their premium cigars—followed by two losses to the Louisville Eclipse, including one on June 14 that was particularly painful. In the bottom of the ninth, Louisville's Jack Gleason stood at third with the club's best hitter, Louis Rogers "Pete" Browning, at the plate. The A's got out of a terrible jam when Browning hit a sharp grounder, and Gleason foolishly attempted to score, only to get thrown out at the plate. But the pesky Browning, taking first, immediately bolted for second in an attempted steal, and when A's catcher Jack O'Brien wildly heaved the ball over second base, it rolled right through the legs of Philadelphia's sleepy center fielder, Fred Corey. By the time Corey ran down the ball and returned it, Browning was crossing home plate with the winning run.

With the taste of that preposterous defeat in their mouths, the Athletics embarked in mid-June on their longest, most grueling road trip of the season. Before returning to Philadelphia more than a month later, they would play a total of twenty-four games in all seven of the other American Association cities—the kind of marathon that could quickly humble even a great team. Still, the owners preferred such endurance tests to more frequent excursions that ended up costing more money for train travel. In a world without television or radios, of course, the city's Athletics fanatics—so passionate that they had snapped the gates off their hinges on Memorial Day—were bereft of their team for weeks. The city's newspapers, battling for circulation, filled the void with extensive coverage of the trip by telegraph. Though papers of the time preferred using wire reports to the cost of sending a reporter on the road, the *Philadelphia Item* found a novel way to feed the craving. It hired a member of the club to file anonymous dispatches providing inside tidbits.

As the A's caught a westbound train, the American Association pennant race tightened into a four-team struggle involving baseball-crazed Philadelphia in the east as well as the Midwestern hotbeds of St. Louis, Cincinnati, and Louisville. But in all eight of its markets, the Association was transforming the public's perception of baseball itself, turning it from a fading game stained by corruption into a lively, affordable, fun-filled form of entertainment, the perfect two-hour escape from lives circumscribed by hard toil. In only its second season, the Association offered an array of colorful stars: Tony Mullane, Harry Stovey, Bobby Mathews, Pete Browning, Tim Keefe, Charlie Comiskey, Will White, Ed Swartwood, and Long John Reilly. Growing numbers of fanatics were obsessed with baseball, and they talked incessantly about players, acquisitions, injuries, and their favorite club's prospects. Even the National League perked up, having been forced by the American Association to enter bigger markets and compete for top players. "The whole country seems to be base ball mad!" the *Boston Globe* marveled in August.

The madness ignited by the Association was so intense that the Reverend H. C. Morrison, pastor of the Methodist Episcopal church on Chestnut Street in Louisville, felt compelled to deliver a Sunday sermon against it, warning that "in base-ball and all other games there is a tendency to run to extremes and subvert what was originally innocent amusements." The young were especially susceptible. "They absorb the mania for base ball, even to its worst features," which laid the foundation for a life of "sin and recklessness," in part through exposure to "obscene language and ribald oaths." Concerns about Sunday baseball were common to many homes. According to one account, a mother chided her boy Bobby for attending a game on the Lord's Day. "Think how grieved your father will be when I inform him of it," she said. "Oh, you needn't do that," Bobby said. "Oh, you told him, did you?" his mother asked. "No," replied Bobby, "he saw me there."

———◇———

THE ATHLETICS HEADED FIRST TO CINCINNATI, AMERICA'S EIGHTH largest city and home of the defending champions, for games on June 18, 19, 20, and 21. The Reds' quiet, workmanlike little second baseman, Bid McPhee, spent the night before the series opener under the care of a doctor, suffering agonizing stomach cramps, possibly from having consumed spoiled food or bacteria-laden water, a constant danger in 1880s America. But McPhee struggled out of bed in the morning to do his part, with the defending champions now only three and a half games behind. Nor could drenching rain all morning deter three thousand Cincinnatians from crowding into Bank Street Grounds in the afternoon. The field "looked like a young lake," the *Cincinnati Commercial Gazette* observed, but a grounds crew armed with brooms went to work on it, sweeping away the water, and a hot sun started to bake the muddy ground.

The Athletic club, shaking off the effects of jostling nineteenth-century train travel, stepped onto the field, and, according to the *Philadelphia Item* correspondent, turned in a sharp, brilliant practice. "This nerved us and there was not a member of the nine but that was confident of victory." One problem: they faced the Reds' lanky ace, Will White—a fearsome competitor, even if he did come across as a timid, rather professorial man, with his wire-rimmed spectacles, premature baldness, and formerly blond hair, which had turned white when he was just twenty-eight. Rather than blow his baseball money on women and drink, Will invested in a lucrative tea shop on Lower Market Street downtown, where hero-worshipping children turned out to watch him work behind the counter.

Will White at his tea shop, depicted
with a comically massive pitching arm,
Cincinnati Enquirer, *September 2, 1883*
(*Library of Congress*)

On this afternoon, battling the Reds' toughest adversary, White set
down the first thirteen Philadelphia batters in succession. The Reds third
baseman, Hick Carpenter, preserved the string with a phenomenal leaping catch of a Lon Knight line drive in the fourth inning, a play that made
spectators in the pavilion leap to their feet and wave their hats. It was not
until the fifth inning that the Athletics' Mike Moynahan broke up the no-
hitter by plunking the ball into left field. But by then, the game was essentially over. The Athletics scratched out only three more hits and lost
6–0, a most disappointing start to the road trip.

"We had made up our minds to wipe out the disgrace," the *Item's*
player-correspondent noted before game two, when the rubber-armed
Will White took the box for the second straight day. Incredibly, White
was even more dominant this time, winning 7–0 and holding the Athletics
to a sole hit. Later that night, Athletics second baseman Cub Stricker had
a strange dream: his club was on its way to Columbus, and although Harry
Stovey, the team's best hitter and most aggressive runner, managed to get
on board in the very last car, no matter how hard the rest of the Athletics

sprinted to catch up and climb on, they could get no closer. The train gradually pulled away without them, carrying only Stovey. The dream's uncanny pertinence to the pennant race would not be revealed for months. But the next morning, outfielder Bill Crowley, who had a friend who interpreted dreams, persuaded his teammates to buy a book on the subject. Catcher Ed Rowen studied the tome for a time and came up with an interpretation: in that afternoon's game, "one run would be made by the Athletics, and that would be by Stovey."

Sure enough, Stovey scored the Athletics' sole run that day. But, contrary to Rowen's reading, it was far from the winning run. Pitching his *third* game in three days, Will White allowed only four hits in the Athletics' third straight drubbing. Some 3,100 Cincinnati fans "howled themselves hoarse" in appreciation of the 11–1 flogging. The Athletics, the dominant team during the first seven weeks of the season, seemed to have run out of steam, while the Reds looked increasingly like the champions of the year before. In one of the great pitching feats of his era, a bespectacled tea merchant had thrown twenty-seven innings over three days and held the first-place Athletics to nine hits and one run. Suddenly, the A's had dropped seven of their last eight, and their lead was down to half a game. Meanwhile, the Reds made plans to rush in carpenters and expand their park by some 1,000 seats before July 4, "as the fever is growing with the crowds."

Something was bringing the boys from Philadelphia terrible luck, and the Cincinnati sportswriters thought they knew what it was. For more than a month, a yellow pup owned by Reds groundskeeper Charlie McNickel had been making his appearance on the field during games just before momentum swung Cincinnati's way. Clearly, the hound dog—dubbed "the yaller purp" by the local press—was some sort of good-luck charm. And charms were something that the deeply superstitious ballplayers of the time took terribly seriously. In the ninth inning of Will White's one-hitter, "to show his utter contempt for the Athletics' failure to bat," the yaller purp "walked up to their bat bag and deliberately insulted it in the presence of the vast crowd," eliciting great laughter.

Captain Lon Knight, having seen enough of the ineffective pitching of the tired Bobby Mathews and George Washington Bradley, gave the ball in the series' fourth and final game to utility man Fred Corey, who had previously pitched a little—mostly poorly—for Worcester in the National

League. No one could be sure what he would do now. "He sent in the balls with gunshot speed," the *Cincinnati Enquirer* reported, "and had a habit of tramping out of the [pitcher's box] and all over the grass like a nervous colt immediately after delivering the sphere." Nervous or not, Corey came through for the Athletics, surrendering only four hits, partly because Bradley made two brilliant catches in center field. The "fiend of the grin," as the *Enquirer* reporter called Bradley, also terrorized on the base paths, raising his arm and smashing Reds first baseman Long John Reilly in the mouth as he crossed the bag. "The blow might have been accidental, but it didn't look so to the spectators in the stands[,] and Bradley was hissed repeatedly," the paper said. Many in the audience thought Bradley should have been turned over to "the tender mercies of the coppers on the grounds." Meanwhile, the Reds played a listless game. "'Hick' Carpenter couldn't have stopped a part of the roof of the grand stand had it blown over his way," groused the *Enquirer*.

Hick Carpenter
(Library of Congress)

Freed from the curse of the yaller purp, who for an unknown reason "never once came out to smell . . . the visitors' bat bag" and lift a leg on it, the Athletics finally broke out of the doldrums, winning 14–5. The *Enquirer* urged management to hire a "cheap boy" to coax the dog across the field whenever the Reds were in danger of losing.

Despite salvaging that final game, the Athletics departed from Cincinnati in a state approaching shock. "We are alive and thankful for that," wrote the unknown player for the *Philadelphia Item*. "Another such week I never desire to pass through, and I simply voice the sentiment of the entire team when I say we are all broken up. . . . All we want is to get out of this Jonah town."

Their luck did indeed change once they left Porkopolis behind. The Athletics swept three in Columbus, took three out of four against their archrival St. Louis Browns—including the game umpired by Charley Daniels after his $300 train ride—and two out of three from the Eclipse. But their visit to the Association's southernmost outpost, roasting Kentucky, was simply hellacious. "In my lifetime I have struck some very hot weather and very hot places," the mystery player wrote, "but Louisville is entitled to the championship belt for the boss Hades on earth." In the morning half of the broiling Independence Day double-header there, the heat proved almost literally deadly: the Athletics' Jack O'Brien, wearing a stifling woolen uniform like everyone else, was behind home plate, slaving away as catcher and getting hotter and hotter, when he got dizzy and blacked out, felled by heatstroke. He was carried off the field, and doctors were immediately summoned. They did all they could for the unfortunate catcher, but he remained unconscious for hours, close to death. It was not O'Brien's first serious brush with mortality. A year earlier, on June 2, 1882, he had freakishly collided with the Reds' Bid McPhee, getting knocked senseless while the second baseman's spikes slashed his face. Fortunately, there was a doctor in the stands that day, "but for whose timely services O'Brien might have been past all suffering." His friends hoped his toughness would save him now in Louisville. The members of the Louisville Eclipse did all they could to help, and pitcher Sam Weaver sat by the bedside of his former catcher late into the night. Finally, hours after the game, O'Brien woke from his coma. He was forced out of action for a few days, but lucky to be alive.

The Athletics had no spare player available when O'Brien fell. Second baseman Cub Stricker took over the catcher's position, while Lon Knight filled second base. That left a hole in right field. Fortunately, co-owner Charlie Mason, a onetime Williams College pitcher who had later served with Philadelphia and Washington teams in the National Association, was sitting up in the grandstand. Mason clambered down, "threw off his silk hat, put aside his seer-sucker coat, rolled up his pants, and took Knight's position in right." Even in his street clothes, the thirty-year-old executive made no errors and slapped out a base hit—leaving him at the end of the

John O'Brien,
New York Clipper, *August 12, 1882*
(*Library of Congress*)

season leading the team both in batting (.500) and fielding (1.000), facts he was delighted to point out to the "real" players. For now, though, the Athletics faced a long pennant fight with an enfeebled catcher, a man who was almost as vital to the team as Bobby Mathews.

Unfortunately, the Louisville heat got worse. After the O'Brien scare, the captains of the two clubs, Lon Knight and Joe Gerhardt, met to discuss the situation. To the relief of both teams, they quickly agreed to postpone that Friday's game on account of the intolerable weather. But they would have to play on Saturday, come what may; neither team could afford to surrender the lucrative weekend gate take. As temperatures kept soaring, the Athletics' correspondent warned that there might be "nineteen grease spots on the field Saturday, representing all that is left of eighteen ball players and an umpire." Stranded in hellish heat, gasping for breath in those days before air conditioning, the exhausted Athletics lost their taste for nightlife and kept to their miserably hot, sticky hotel, or its porch, for the rest of the week. All the time, they looked forward to completing their trip in Pittsburgh and Baltimore, then heading home at the end of July. "I can assure you," the anonymous player wrote, "there will be a happy lot of boys when we once more put our feet on Philadelphia's streets."

ON THE AFTERNOON OF JUNE 30, MORE THAN A WEEK AFTER THE
Athletics had left town, Reds third baseman Hick Carpenter strode to
the plate with one man out and a runner on first. The Cincinnati crowd
broke into applause, hoping to inspire its hero to keep the rally going and
produce some runs against the New York Metropolitans. Alas, Carpenter
hit a sharp grounder straight at Mets shortstop Jack Nelson—a likely double play unless Hick could beat the throw to first. He didn't even try. As
soon as he saw Nelson flip the ball to second baseman Sam Crane, Carpenter abruptly stopped running, turned, and walked away—letting the
puzzled Crane lob the ball to first, easily completing the double play. The
Mets went on to win that afternoon, by a score of 9–5—dropping the Reds
further behind the first-place Philadelphia Athletics.

Confronted after the game, Carpenter made an embarrassing confes-
sion: he didn't run because he had lost count of the outs. He thought the
force at second base was the third out, ending the inning, not the second.
Such a lack of concentration by a well-paid professional was bad enough,
but in the heat of a pennant race it was unforgivable, thought O. P. Caylor,
a Reds shareholder and club secretary, who, blithely indifferent to the
conflict of interest, also covered their exploits for the *Cincinnati Commercial Gazette.* "It was pure carelessness, and inexcusable in any player,"
Caylor chided in the next day's paper. "Such slouchy work is calculated
to disgust spectators and demoralize a nine."

The lecture did little good. Only a few days later, Carpenter tapped a
ball down the line, then stupidly waited to see whether it would roll foul.
After a few seconds, it dawned on him that he had better sprint to first
base. But the fielder, seeing the befuddled Carpenter stall, snatched the
ball and threw him out by half a step. "His only excuse was that he *thought*
the ball was going foul," Caylor fumed, reminding readers that Carpenter
thought there were already two outs when he came to bat earlier in the
week. "A player has no right to *think* anything but that he has hit the ball
and he is wanted quick at first base."

Carpenter was a good player—almost certainly the best left-hander
to ever play third base in the major leagues. Southpaws in that position
are a rarity, since they have to pivot to make the throw to first. But his
mental lapses were all too typical of the 1883 Reds. That same week, Bid
McPhee misread a pick-off sign and got caught out of position. As a

result, an enemy batter was able to drive a grounder through his vacated spot on the right side of the infield to keep a rally alive. "This mistake cost three runs, and maybe more," Caylor complained. "There is no use disguising the fact, the team needs closer discipline. . . . It is running too loose for perfect success."

Still, Caylor was not seriously worried. Even as Cincinnati languished in fourth place in July, he was convinced that the club simply had too much talent to remain there. "If any one thinks the Cincinnatis' chances for the flag are any less than the other three he is much mistaken," Caylor asserted. "The Cincinnati team has men in its make-up who are bound to yet make the city feel proud of their work." That same week, Caylor quoted from a letter he had just received from Albert G. Spalding, president of the National League champion Chicago White Stockings, who were also struggling unexpectedly.

"We do not intend to lose the championship up here, do you?" Spalding wrote.

"Frankly, Al, we do not," Caylor responded. "The two champion clubs of '83 are great on pulling out in the end of the season."

WHILE THE REDS STRUGGLED TO FOCUS, LOUISVILLE SWEPT PAST them into third. During a four-week period, the Eclipse won thirteen of seventeen games, including a 14–0 demolition of the Pittsburgh Alleghenys. Kentucky crowds were enjoying the way the local sluggers ripped through enemy pitchers. But none of the batters delighted them more than Pete Browning, a quirky, homegrown boy who had been nicknamed "the Gladiator." He was a right-handed batter known far and wide for his savage line drives and obsessive interest in the art of hitting, one of the great new stars being showcased by the American Association.

The youngest of eight children, Browning was born in the modest Jefferson Street home that he would share nearly all his life with his mother, Mary. His father died in October 1874, when Pete was thirteen, succumbing to injuries sustained in one of the Midwest's terrifying tornadoes. The fatherless boy routinely skipped school, hiding his books beneath a doorstep at the home of his pal John Reccius, who himself would one day be a major leaguer. The one sport Browning didn't like was swimming,

because it hurt his ears too much. Browning suffered from an inflamma-
tion of the mastoid bone covering the inner ear, an ailment that rendered
him almost entirely deaf—and would drive him to drink throughout his
adulthood to numb the pain. His difficulty hearing may have contributed
to his aversion to school. He remained illiterate throughout his life, which
surely inhibited him socially. Longing for female companionship, he resorted to brothels—and, like Old Hoss Radbourn and Bobby Mathews,
he died of complications from syphilis.

Browning played baseball tirelessly as a teenager. He perfected his
skills as a member of local amateur and semipro teams, including the
Eclipse, which, like the Browns and Athletics, had earned a national reputation before the Association's founding. Twenty years old on opening
day in 1882, the tall, lean kid led the American Association with a .382 average while finishing among the leaders in total bases, home runs, doubles, and bases on balls. Browning did it while refusing to move up close
to the plate. Perhaps because of the pain in his ear, he lived in horror of
being hit by a pitch, a flaw that enemy pitchers naturally tried to exploit.
The Browns' Tony Mullane, of course, often threw at Browning, even
when the Gladiator had backed far off the plate. "Pete has a holy terror
of 'Tricky Tony,'" noted Harry Weldon of the *Cincinnati Enquirer*. But
Mullane could not seem to win the war of nerves. "Time and again Mullane has knocked off 'The Gladiator's' cap, or hit the bulge in his flannel
shirt, but has never been able to get a fair soak at the 'Pride of Louisville.'"

Weldon described Browning's remarkable powers of concentration: "He
stands erect, with his bat slung over his shoulder. He has a great 'eye' and
will not go after a bad one. The ball must come over the plate before he
will attempt to hit it. When he does select a ball, he steps forward in the
box, his bat whizzes through the air, and when it meets the sphere he throws
the weight of his body with the blow, and the ball leaves his bat with almost
the force of a rifle-shot." During the 1883 season, he would hit .336, third
best in the league, with an on-base average of .378, second highest.

Reporters loved him, for much the same reason they did Von der Ahe.
From the start of Browning's career, his escapades spiced up their stories.
Most amusing, perhaps, was his all-consuming devotion to baseball—and
his utter indifference to the world around him. In 1883, the *Cleveland
Leader* told the story of Browning's reaction to the death of President James

Garfield, who succumbed to infected wounds after an assassin's bullet tore into his back. The morning that the news broke to an anguished nation, a friend asked Browning if he was going to the ballpark that day.

"Yes," Pete answered.

"Why, don't you know that Garfield is dead?" asked his friend.

"No-o," replied Pete. "What position did he play?"

Harry Weldon believed that Browning was putting on an act. "Pete is not as stupid . . . as his talk would seem to suggest, and, with an eye to the main chance, he has turned these stories to his own advantage," Weldon wrote. "He is fond of seeing his name in print, and treasures every article that appears about him, no matter whether good, bad, or indifferent. He thinks they are a good advertisement, and Pete is a great believer in advertising." On road trips, for example, the Kentucky boy liked to get out of the train "at every little water-tank town and introduce himself to the few rustics he found on the platform," convinced such gestures would help him build a following, as indeed they did. According to one quirky tale, he carefully studied baseball's best hitter, the National League's Dan Brouthers, for pointers. Rather than pick up something about his batting stance, or his approach to certain pitchers, Browning noticed that Big Dan habitually dropped his pair of first basemen's gloves in foul territory beyond first base at the end of each inning. "Well, I don't play first base," Pete explained, "and I don't wear gloves, so I set myself to thinking what I could do to help my batting. I used to spend my time while in center-field trying to think of some good scheme. One day I was coming in from the field, and I happened to step on the third-base bag. Well, I made a hit. I stepped on it again going out and coming in, and got another. I got four in that game, and I have continued to step on that base ever since." That was a laughable lesson to draw, to be sure, though it is undeniable that great hitters have long used personal rituals to calm their jitters and help prepare them mentally to bat.

Browning was likewise fetishistic about his treasured bats, adorning each of them with the name of a character from the Bible. When he broke his favorite one in 1884, he went to an apprentice woodworker named Bud Hillerich for a replacement, which had to be made to his careful specifications. Armed with his new club, Browning went 3-for-3 the following afternoon, breaking a prolonged slump. From then on, he insisted that Hillerich make all his bats, and the famed "Louisville Slugger" was born. Eventually, Browning owned two hundred of the beauties. Soon, scores of major leaguers insisted on buying duplicates of the bats that Browning used, and the firm of Hillerich & Bradsby took off.

The bane of Browning's career, and an affliction that earned him greater name recognition than even he must have wanted, was his alcoholism. From his rookie season on, Browning imbibed heavily, making a public spectacle of himself and earning the nickname "the Prince of Bourbon." As early as August 1882, he appeared on the field visibly drunk. "His play and conduct were maudlin in the extreme and excited the laughter and derision of the crowd," said one game account. Though the reporter blasted Browning for daring to show up, he grudgingly added, "Browning did get two hits and only made three errors in eight chances which was pretty good in his condition." By July 1883, the Louisville club had hit players with a total of $140 in fines for violating the rules, including those against drinking—$130 of them to Browning alone. Yet the fines had little apparent effect on him. Benching might have worked, but the owners were reluctant to sit down their best player. "Browning and Leary have been drinking," O. P. Caylor reported in May. "The former was suspended, but Louisville wouldn't know how to play ball without Big Pete."

OLD JUDGE CIGARETTES Goodwin & Co., New York.

Pete Browning
(Library of Congress)

"So far as we Cincinnatians are concerned, Pete may get stone-blind drunk this week and remain so till Saturday night," Caylor wrote before the Eclipse visited Cincinnati in early July. "For Pete Browning sober is considerable of an ingredient of any ball game he interests himself in."

———

By mid-July, pennant visions danced in the heads of Kentucky baseball fans. Eclipse boosters found their dreams coming true when their boys whipped Cincinnati, 5–0, on July 10, in the opener of a big five-game series against the Reds. "The present champions met the coming champions yesterday afternoon, and were knocked out . . . in a way that opened their eyes," the *Courier-Journal* crowed. First baseman George "Juice" Latham helped by leaping to snare a line drive high over his head, then tagging the helpless runner off the base for an unassisted double play. "The boys played with more spirit and energy than they have displayed for a long time, and demonstrated beyond a doubt that they are by odds the better club of the two," said the *Courier-Journal*. And they did it without Browning, who did realize his greatest fear—getting hit by a pitch. In the previous series in roasting Louisville, Athletics pitcher Grin Bradley had smoked a ball that struck Pete in the leg, injuring it so badly that it forced him to miss a series of important games. Even when the Gladiator did return, his leg was so lame that he enlisted another player to stand at home plate and run to first for him when he hit the ball—a legal form of substitution in 1883, if the opposing club granted permission.

But Louisville's bliss was short-lived. The champion Reds reasserted their dominance over the next four cruel afternoons, winning all four games, by scores of 9–3, 11–2, 3–1, and 9–3. Immediately, the talk about "the coming champions" collapsed like a leaking balloon. "We have hoped beyond hope. There is no use hoping any longer," the *Louisville Commercial* keened. "We are not hogs. We know when we have had enough."

A scapegoat was quickly found in the person of shortstop and heavy drinker Jack Leary, who was having a terrible time getting on base. (He would bat a feeble .188.) The baseball writer for the *Commercial* nicknamed the weak-hitting infielder "Old Energy" and penned a sarcastic poem in his honor, dedicating it to "John Slugger Leary":

> *Old Energy sat in his easy chair,*
> *Smoking his pipe of clay;*
> *I'll do it, he said, I'll do it, be dad,*
> *I'll make a base hit this day.*

But even Louisville's hardest hitters accomplished little in the devastating series against Cincinnati. Shot after shot down the third-base line was smothered by Hick Carpenter, who may not have had a sprightly mind, but compensated for it with astonishing physical dexterity. "It isn't much use to hit in the neighborhood of third base . . . when Old Hickory is holding it down," one reporter noted. "Hickory doesn't think any more of stopping a base hit than Jack Leary does of striking out."

The Reds series left Louisville sportswriters so despondent that they refused to perk up even after the Eclipse went on to Columbus and won four straight. Even though the local club stood in third place, only three games behind, the *Commercial* reporter employed sledgehammer sarcasm to mock local baseball fanatics who still believed the Eclipse would capture the pennant. "The local club is immense," he wrote. "It is a consolidation of great ball players, and can just knock the spots out of any base-ball club in America, not excepting the Orioles, of Shepherdsville, nor the O'Leary Fairies, of Indianapolis."

That skepticism turned out to be well placed. The Eclipse lost five of their next eight games against the St. Louis Browns, then three of four to Columbus and four of five to the Reds in Cincinnati, to tumble nine and a half games out of first place by mid-August. "K-E-E-P C-O-O-L! Some of these days the Eclipse nine will snatch a victory from a first-class club," the *Courier-Journal* jabbed. In truth, the newspaper continued, Louisville fans had grown so disgusted that they would just as soon never see the team again. "If Gerhardt will lead his club out into the woods and lose them, he will confer a favor upon many base ball admirers in this city." Noting their penchant for dropping balls, the *Louisville Commercial* groused after a 9–0 loss to the Browns that the "Eclipse players couldn't have held a ten-dollar gold piece if somebody had placed it in the palm of their hand."

The *Commercial*'s correspondent even took out his frustrations on Cincinnati sportswriter O. P. Caylor, claiming that Caylor, whom he dubbed "the Ghoul" because of his pale, slender appearance, had badly skewed his coverage. "Physically, he is a ghost, with less blood in him than the meek and lowly turnip, which has been his principal diet for the last sixty-two years. Mentally, he is one of the nine goose eggs that the Cincinnatis earned in the first game at Louisville last week. As a whole he is that part of a horse's anatomy which is always nearest to the dashboard." For much of the rest of the summer, that same scathing Louisville columnist offered an amusing take on the local team by treating readers to conversations between two fictional ardent women fans,

Margaret Fresh of Market Street and her friend Isabella Smart. Written in the style of melodramatic Victorian-era romance novels, the sketches pitilessly lampooned the local club for daring to pretend it was offering Louisville high-quality baseball.

In one of his first items, the columnist reported that a "light of a great joy" had recently appeared in Margaret's eyes. "'Thank heaven,' she said devoutly, 'it has come at last,' and then she burst into a flood of happy tears. Leary had made a base hit."

Massive first baseman Juice Latham, who chomped on big wads of tobacco (hence his nickname) and wore a filthy uniform, was another favorite topic of the ladies' conversation. They contended he could pass for "a great hairy, shaggy Siberian mammoth." In one column, "the fair face of Margaret Fresh wore an expression of deep gravity" as she asked: "Isabella, have you heard the news?" When Isabella confessed she had not, Margaret broke it: Juice Latham had actually changed his shirt. "For a moment there was an oppressive silence and then a dull moan of agony, as the form of a fair girl fell heavily to the kitchen floor. Isabella had fainted: the awful information had paralyzed her."

The pair frequently discussed the club's pathetic acquisitions of broken-down veterans and outright drunkards. As Margaret stood at the window in the August heat, contemplating having to do the laundry the following morning, Isabella burst in with some momentous news: Louisville had just signed a new player:

> Margaret Fresh shrank convulsively back in the shadows. Her right hand wildly clutched at a round of the spectral clothes-horse, and her breath came in quick, short gasps. She trembled for a moment from head to foot, and then in one masterly effort overcame her terrible emotion. Directly she spoke. Her voice was hard, and cold, and steady.
>
> "Is the new player a drunkard?" she asked.
>
> "No, quite the contrary. I understand he is a prohibitionist," replied Isabella, lightly.
>
> "Has he a bad leg?" continued Margaret Fresh in the same cold voice.
>
> "No, his legs are straight and sound," answered Isabella as she looked up wonderingly into her companion's white, cold face.
>
> "Is his arm lame?" continued Margaret.

"Nay, he has not even a lame arm," answered the other.

"Surely he must have a sore thumb or a splintered finger," urged Margaret in an excited voice.

"No, sweet one, his hands are without a blemish."

Margaret Fresh stood firm and still for a moment like a Statue of Galatea, and then suddenly lowering her head until her ruby lips touched the pink and white ear of Isabella Smart, she said in a low, determined voice:

"Speak, Isabella, I command you; is the new player deaf and dumb?"

Isabella Smart hesitated for a moment and then slowly bowed her head [in] assent.

"Thank God," murmured Margaret. "He will not be entirely out of place in the procession."

By the time that column appeared, catcher Dan Sullivan was injured, Browning was limping, and the team was badly demoralized. "Move Up Joe" Gerhardt, the club's scrappy, tobacco-chewing player-manager, was taking it harder than anyone. (Gerhardt won his nickname by screaming to his base runners: "Move up! Move up! Take a step, take another, take a step! Move up! We'll all move up!") The son of a heroic Union general, the Prussian-born Joseph Gerhardt, young Joe had been "as proud as a boy with a pair of new copper-toed boots" when he landed the manager's job and became a stockholder in the Eclipse Club. Gerhardt knew he needed victories to boost his income. The defeats, and his inability to stop them, were grinding him down.

On the evening of July 25, when he was sitting in front of the St. James Hotel in muggy St. Louis, mulling over the next day's tough game against the Browns, Gerhardt suddenly felt a sharp pain in his left arm. He doubled up, vomited, and found he was unable to move the left side of his body. Stunned friends carried him to his room and summoned a doctor, who "pronounced the trouble a light paralytic stroke, caused by overexertion and undue excitement, and requiring absolute rest." Later that night, a reporter found Gerhardt lying in bed, his left side covered with blankets. He was in surprisingly good spirits. "I can use my leg now and the feeling has come back into my hand," Gerhardt informed the journalist. "My side is still numb, but I know from the way I am feeling that it will be better in a little while." In fact, Gerhardt seemed far less concerned about himself than his club's ailing pennant chances, expressing the concern that "my sickness will take the heart all out of the boys." Healthy, Louisville could have beaten anyone in the American Association, Gerhardt insisted. "We have had terrible bad luck, and that's what has brought on this stroke. I am a hard worker and a hard loser. I don't say much when I lose, but, oh, I feel it and it hurts me."

Gerhardt was an epileptic, and such paralytic attacks felled him periodically as time went on. His teammates, however, were convinced that Gerhardt's stroke owed everything to the viciousness of Browns pitcher Tony Mullane. Gerhardt had been suffering pains in his side ever since one of Mullane's savage fastballs had struck his chest on May 24, making the sound of a drum. "You can just bet your life that I believe that ball, and nothing else, is the cause of his being paralyzed tonight," fumed Louisville outfielder Leech Maskrey. When the men returned to Louisville the next night, they took their player-manager with them. "He was able to walk, but his left arm was useless and his left side was quite numb," the *St. Louis Globe-Democrat* said.

But, even now, the Eclipse players were professionals, and they were determined to go down fighting. The season's final days would demonstrate just how hard Joe Gerhardt's men could battle when all hope was lost.

————◄◊►————

AS THE CINCINNATI REDS SURGED AHEAD OF LOUISVILLE INTO third place, making their run at Philadelphia and St. Louis, O. P. Caylor overflowed with confidence. "If anyone thinks the Cincinnatis' chances for the flag are less than any of the other three, he is much mistaken," he wrote. "We cannot believe they are not the strongest team collectively in the Association." Starting to see luck go their way, the Reds turned back into the loose, swaggering team they had been in 1882. Suddenly, they were doing everything right. "Four fine double plays, remarkable running catches of difficult flies by Sommer, Jones, Corkhill, McPhee and Carpenter, and equally marvelous foul-bound catches by Reilly and Snyder, makes [sic] yesterday's game a jewel among games," Caylor wrote after a 3–1 victory over Columbus.

On July 21, the Reds managed to pull off the most celebrated scam of the season. It began when the ever-confused Hick Carpenter missed the team's train from St. Louis to Columbus and wired manager Pop Snyder that the earliest he could arrive was 4 P.M.—precisely the time the game was to begin. By then, unfortunately, Snyder would have to have his lineup in place; under 1883 rules, substitutions were not allowed after the game began, except in cases of extreme injury or illness. Determined to get his star third baseman into the game somehow, Snyder ordered backup pitcher Harry McCormick to grab a horse and carriage and head for the Columbus depot with Carpenter's uniform. Once he had Carpenter aboard, McCormick was to "drive like hell" back to the park while Hickory got dressed in the carriage en route. Snyder's next concern was delaying the start of the game until Carpenter had safely arrived. Here, Chick Fulmer, the Reds' handsome shortstop, came to the rescue. "I don't feel very well, and may be real bad at 4 o'clock," he assured Snyder. The infielder knew something about acting: he was known as "Uncle Tom" Fulmer in Philadelphia for his work off-season as a manager arranging popular stage performances of *Uncle Tom's Cabin*. Now, he intended to put his theatrical experience to good use.

When game time arrived, Fulmer was nowhere to be found. Launching a search party, the two teams found him in the clubhouse, curled up on a chest, complaining of terrible cramps. "Then he groaned in G flat . . . while everybody could see the cold sweat start out at every pore of his Parian brow. The Columbus boys at once thought of the Egyptian plague, and several faces blanched." While the players solicitously dosed Fulmer with ginger, hoping to get him into a condition to play, Columbus manager Horace Phillips went out on the field and apologized to the crowd for the delay, explaining to the grandstand "how desperately sick" the infielder was. Jimmy Williams, a club official and American Association secretary, was discussing how to deal with cholera when a carriage tore onto the grounds at full speed. Carpenter leaped out in uniform, and Snyder, seeing him, shouted, "Come on, boys." The remaining Reds—including Fulmer—calmly emerged from the clubhouse. Williams reportedly looked at Carpenter, then Fulmer, rubbed his finger up and down the side of his nose, and exclaimed, "Well, dog my buttons!"

"Fulmer in Cramps,"
by John Reilly, Cincinnati Commercial
Gazette, *July 31, 1883 (Library of Congress)*

The Reds relished their little trick. First baseman Long John Reilly, a talented illustrator, celebrated it in a cartoon published in the *Commercial Gazette*. It depicted Fulmer doubled over with his eyes shut in pain, his mouth wide open, and his tongue hanging out. Soon after that, Caylor was ordering more cartoons from Reilly. His funny, boldly drawn work began to appear on the front of scorecards sold at the games, though the twenty-four-year-old's greatest artistic contribution that summer was at the plate. He hit .311 and finished third in the Association in home runs and hits and second in triples, runs, slugging average, and total bases.

Between late July and mid-August, Cincinnati won thirteen of fifteen games to close within three of the league-leading Athletics and two of the Browns. In a league of drunks, actors, minstrel stars, cartoonists, tea merchants, dreamers, newspaper correspondents, bombastic grocers, epileptics, hot-tempered Irish managers, fainting catchers, fetishistic and hard-of-hearing sluggers, great shaggy mammoths, owners playing in their street clothes, inauspicious yellow dogs, and seriously confused left-handed third basemen, anything might happen as the great season approached its climax.

135

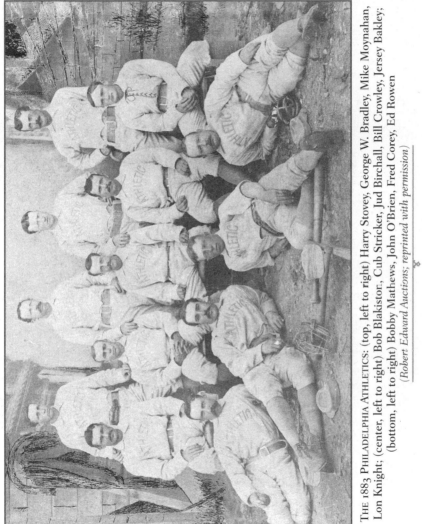

THE 1883 PHILADELPHIA ATHLETICS: (top, left to right) Harry Stovey, George W. Bradley, Mike Moynahan, Lon Knight; (center, left to right) Bob Blakistor, Cub Stricker, Jud Birchall, Bill Crowley, Jersey Bakley; (bottom, left to right) Bobby Mathews, John O'Brien, Fred Corey, Ed Rowen
(*Robert Edward Auctions; reprinted with permission*)

THE 1883 ST. LOUIS BROWNS, posing in front of their new "Bulletin Board" late in May. Stars include Charlie Comiskey (standing, left), Pat Deasley (standing, right), Bill Gleason (seated, far left), Jumbo McGinnis (seated next to Gleason), Tony Mullane (seated, fourth from left). On the ground are Hugh Nicol (far left) and Arlie Latham (third from left). The little man in the center, with the derby hat and incipient beer belly, appears to be club owner Chris Von der Ahe.
(Transcendental Graphics/theruckerarchive.com; reprinted with permission)

9

FIRST-CLASS DRUNKARDS

T WAS A PLEASANT SUNDAY EVENING, WITH A FRESH BREEZE cutting the July heat of St. Louis, and young lovers strolled along the streets, chatting and enjoying the night air. Along Grand Avenue, people were flowing into Sportsman's Park, where Von der Ahe was putting on a fireworks display, price of admission twenty-five cents for adults, ten cents for children. He had beautifully illuminated the park with Chinese lanterns that gave off a warm glow of red and gold, green and blue, "forming a picturesque scene in the clear, bright starry night." Von der Ahe was something of a fireworks fanatic, and in April 1882 he had sent away for "a very curious implement," a Japanese mortar used for daytime fireworks. It was a cannon-shaped device made of bamboo wrapped in steel wire, and as soon as it arrived from New York, he put it on display at Sportsman's Park. Now, on a Saturday night in 1883, he was playing again. With a startling flash, a rocket shot up in the air, erupting in piercing sparks and embers that sank to earth, followed by others. Unfortunately, the grand climax mistakenly went off with a stupendous explosion early in the show, and a display reading "Success to the St. Louis [club] of 1883" crackled to life. "It went off with a boom," said a reporter, "and showed up very brilliantly."

It was a fitting symbol, since the Browns themselves were showing up brilliantly. The club was in the thick of the pennant fight, winning game after game under the generalship of the little Irish chatterbox, Ted Sullivan. Not that there weren't challenges. Von der Ahe had impulsively benched one of the team's two starting pitchers at a time when he was sorely needed. The Athletics were getting hot again; they would win fifteen of the last twenty games of their big road trip. And the Browns were dealing with injuries. "Gleason is suffering with a lame leg," said one report. "[Second baseman George] Strief is also lame and sore, and Comiskey's sides and arms are all raw, the result of sliding while running the bases." As Comiskey recalled, he and his teammates varied the style of their sliding—head first, feet first, right or left—on the basis of which parts of their bodies were bruised by the bumpy, pebbly infields of the day. "It was much like broiling a steak," he explained. "If rare on one side, turn it over." Midway into the 1883 season, Comiskey was rare on all sides.

The Browns were also suffering from dismal offensive production by the outfield. Tom Loftus and Ned Cuthbert had both flopped, and Tom Dolan, a catcher thrown into the outfield, could hardly get the ball out of the infield. When Sullivan got wind that the National League's Detroit Wolverines were prepared to release Tom Mansell, he moved fast. The redheaded Mansell, twenty-eight, a brother of major leaguers Mike and John, all of Irish stock, was a solid professional hitter and outfielder, having won praise for capturing "horizon searchers" in his hands "like hickory nuts in a bag." But something had ruined his play this year. After showing up at spring training twenty pounds overweight, he had performed sluggishly and slumped to .221, earning the *Boston Globe*'s description of him as a "wretched fielder and a very moderate batter." Detroit manager Jack Chapman would have none of it, praising Mansell "in the highest terms as a batsman and fielder," and insisting he was forced to release him only to free up room in the payroll for new acquisitions.

Desperate to give his lineup some National League punch, Sullivan ignored the criticisms and any potential skeletons in Tom's closet, signed Mansell, and sent him on to St. Louis. There, on the scorching Tuesday afternoon of July 3, Von der Ahe discarded his suit jacket to watch in shirt-

Tom Mansell,
New York Clipper, *October* 27, *1883*
(Library of Congress)

sleeves as Billy Gleason hit line drives and fly balls to Tom, who captured each one and threw the ball "back like a shot" nearly the length of the field. "Nothing wrong with that man," Gleason called out. "He is all right." Sullivan planned to play him the following day, in the big Independence Day holiday doubleheader, with one game in the morning and the second in the afternoon. Unfortunately, at the scheduled starting time of 9:30 A.M. on July 4, Mansell was nowhere to be seen. He had climbed aboard a horsecar earlier that morning, thinking he had plenty of time, but failing to factor in how sluggish the St. Louis system was. Fifteen minutes after game time, he arrived at Sportsman's Park, and raced to dress in five minutes. The game, which had been held up for him, began at 9:50 A.M. Though he was late, Mansell proved worth the wait. He went 3-for-3 en route to a .402 American Association batting average.

Having picked up one strong outfielder in the West, Sullivan headed out East for another. He had his eye on Ed Glenn, a promising twenty-two-year-old left fielder for the outstanding Richmond Club, of Virginia, which would join the American Association in 1884. But Sullivan told Von der Ahe that he would also stop in Philadelphia to try to buy slugger Fred Lewis from the floundering Phillies, who were securely holding last place in the National League. "Yes, Ted, you can hit one bird with a double stone," Von der Ahe responded. It was one of the German owner's classic malapropisms, yet there was a kernel of wisdom in it, for when Sullivan missed out on Glenn with one stone, he hit Lewis with another, buying his contract for $800.

In nabbing Lewis, Sullivan was once again overlooking a player's skeletons. Lewis was an arrogant, dull-witted, barrel-chested center fielder whose heavy drinking plainly presented a discipline problem. But he could drive the ball long and hard, and the Browns badly needed that right now. Reds first baseman Long John Reilly described him as "a queer character": a batter who cared so little which pitchers he faced that he couldn't even "recall them by name," much less reflect on their best pitches and strategy. "They all looked alike to him," Reilly noted, "and he hit them all." Since the peddling of human beings in baseball through the sale of their contracts was still a novelty, the Lewis deal drew amused comment. It "shows the market for flesh and blood is as good as it was in the days of slavery," cracked the *National Police Gazette*. "St. Louis is engaging players by the bunch, like you buy radishes," Cincinnati sportswriter O. P. Caylor opined, warning that Von der Ahe was destroying team chemistry by introducing so many foreign elements. "Better let well enough alone."

For his part, Lewis was "much pleased" to leave the wretched Phillies behind for a team in the thick of a pennant race. "He is a man of fine physique, showed splendid fielding points and is a terrific batsman," a

Fred Lewis,
New York Clipper, *November 17, 1883*
(*Library of Congress*)

St. Louis reporter enthused after watching Lewis's first two-hour practice in a Browns uniform. "From all appearances he will be one of the heavy guns of the nine and will carry out all that is promised for him." Though Lewis was the heaviest man on the team, tipping the scales at 190 pounds, he could be surprisingly graceful. In his debut with St. Louis, Lewis made a lovely running catch in deep right-center field, then slammed three hits, including a triple. Like Mansell, he would feast off American Association pitching.

Sullivan's midseason acquisitions dramatically improved the Browns' pennant chances. With Mansell in left and Lewis in center, joining little Hugh Nicol (another National League alumnus) in right, St. Louis suddenly possessed the Association's elite outfield.

Yet, for all their talent, the Browns remained a collection of obstreperous and temperamental young men, up to and including their manager and owner. Soon after taking Jumbo McGinnis out of the starting rotation, Von der Ahe benched a player who was, if anything, even more critical to the Browns' hopes: the gritty, Irish-born Pat Deasley, the club's only first-quality catcher, who had reportedly failed to report on time for one practice and had plied himself with "spirituous liquors." Deasley had already been lost to the team for many games through a series of agonizing injuries, one of the reasons the Browns had trouble winning at the start of the season, so Sullivan could not have been very happy. Once again, Von der Ahe insisted that he had been compelled to step in to enforce discipline, leaving unsaid that his manager had failed to do the job. "I have determined . . . to draw the reins very tight and insist upon the men doing as the rules require them to," Von der Ahe declared through his mouthpiece, Reid. "I dislike being harsh, but I intend making the men work for the championship and carry out their part of the contract. They are all big salaried and should certainly live up to the requirements. If they do not I will inflict the penalties at any cost. It is too serious a state of affairs to permit any indulgence and it will not be tolerated."

VON DER AHE HAD GOOD REASON TO BE CONCERNED. A NUMBER of his players were notoriously hard drinkers, even by the standards of a business filled with them, and it was difficult to keep watch on their nocturnal activities. In theory, an 11 P.M. curfew hung over players' heads, and on the road most managers did bed checks. Ballplayers often spent their nights in the hotel, people-watching or talking baseball, puffing on cigars, or playing friendly games of billiards. Others might stroll the neighborhood or take in a show—a comedy, minstrel performance, or vaudeville extravaganza—at twenty-five cents to a dollar a ticket. But many athletes, addicted to adrenaline and adulation, would sneak out after curfew in search of more unsavory recreations. Like thousands of other men away from home and on their own in a big city, they found their way to the red-light districts and crowded bars, to houses of prostitution, to gambling parlors, or to low dives, where shapely young women undulated to the jangling notes of a piano going out of tune.

Some young men, plunged into that world, drank to excess, to the point that they showed up at the ballpark the next day with throbbing headaches or slurred speech. The *Chicago Tribune* maintained that a ballplayer, who was generally good for little else in life, could make a princely sum of $350 to $500 a month, "with his traveling expenses borne by the club, and himself carted about the country in palace-cars and fed at first-class hotels." The least he could do was "present himself on the field in fit condition to tender something near an equivalent for such extravagant compensation. . . . The 'black list' . . . should be relentlessly carried out" to enforce discipline. But it wasn't. Baseball, confronting the necessity of filling out the rosters of two major leagues with talent, often looked the other way. As the *Pittsburgh Dispatch* pointedly asked in an editorial, if every player who drinks is banished, "who will play base ball?"

The *Pittsburgh Commercial Gazette*, much like the *Chicago Tribune*, found it astonishing that any professional ballplayer would squander his extraordinary good luck by becoming a drunkard. After all, many men toiled six days a week, ten hours a day, doing brutal, dangerous physical labor for a pittance. The paper noted that:

> a ballplayer's path in summer time is on beds of flowery ease. He gets a big salary, travels all over the country, stops at good hotels, and has the best of everything. He is paid by the public to furnish one hour and a half of amusement each afternoon, and he certainly should be able to keep clear of whiskey during the season, especially as he had all winter

to get even. The great trouble with some men on the Allegheny club is that they look on base ball merely as a pretext to open their pores and enable them to sweat out the whiskey drank the night before. They regularly fill up and regularly sweat it out at the expense of the reputation of the management and the regret and sorrow of all lovers of ball playing hereabouts. Without whiskey the Alleghenys are the equal of any club in the association.

When Ormond Butler quit the perils of umpiring to take over the Alleghenys, reputed to be an assembly of drunkards, some wondered if he had made a wise decision. "He will soon find that the abuse which he received from the spectators was extremely pleasant in comparison with managing the smoky city team," said one observer. Sure enough, within two months, his men were scorning his orders. Meanwhile, the press was attacking him viciously, contending that he did not have "the spunk of a louse." Within days of Butler's taking over, three members of the Allegheny club—Jackie Hayes, George Creamer, and the Association's top hitter, Ed Swartwood—engaged in some "slugging and brutal kicking" in an early-morning fracas at Harff and Cramer's saloon in Cincinnati. Tom's brother, Mike Mansell, and Reds pitcher Harry McCormick were also involved, although, the *Cincinnati Enquirer* insisted, they "did not participate in the disgraceful affair except in their efforts to pull the ruffians off of their prostrate victim." Butler complained that the press got the story wrong. "I know the *Enquirer's* story was unjust," he said, "because the disturbance in front of the saloon occurred between 10 and 11 o'clock in the evening, and McCormick was not arrested for fighting, but for firing a Jackson cracker in the street. He had a revolver with him and it was thought he had discharged a shot from that." Apparently, the notion of a ballplayer carrying a concealed revolver in front of a saloon late at night did not especially trouble the manager.

Butler insisted that the persistent report that the Alleghenys were "'lushers,' in other words drink too much, is entirely undeserved, at least since I took charge. I find the members gentlemanly and willing to obey any orders which I give." In an interview four years later, though, Butler admitted that his players had bamboozled him. "I had a number of good drinkers on my team, but I was keeping a close watch on them," he said.

"They went to bed early every night, and I saw that they were sober, but when they came down in the morning they had red eyes and big heads, and a couple of times I smelt beer in the rooms." Certain that someone must be providing the men refreshment, Butler carefully monitored the staircase leading to their floor. Night after night, he could find no evidence. One night, he was smoking in his hotel's billiard room, trying to figure out how his players were "working" him. "Suddenly, I saw something white shoot past the window and go flying up into darkness." Curious to know what it was, Butler stuck his head out of the hotel window and looked up. "And what do you think I saw? . . . There was one of the gang pulling like blazes on a rope, the other end of which was fastened to a big water pitcher. . . . Those fly lushers had bribed a bell-boy to fill that jug about every half hour, and they kept it up until they were too weak to pull up the line." Butler did not last out the season. "Personally Butler is a gentleman, but his forte is not managing an unruly ball club," the *Dispatch* noted.

One of the most somber stories of the 1883 season was the fall of Ed Nolan, a pitcher of such incomparable brilliance that he had earned the nickname "the Only." In 1877, the Only Nolan was a national celebrity, one of the best pitchers anyone had ever seen, with blistering speed and a killer "downshoot," or sinking curve. He threw an astounding thirty-two shutouts for the independent Indianapolis Dark Blues, who toured the country and took on all comers.

Hoping to cash in on Nolan's following, the National League imported the entire Indianapolis team into its circuit in 1878. But early into that season, it became clear that Nolan had badly damaged his arm with overwork. He took to drinking heavily. On one day in August, Nolan refused to take the field, saying his brother had died back in Paterson, New Jersey, and he wanted to go home to mourn. When the club discovered that no brother was ill or dead, it expelled Nolan, and he wound up for a time on the National League's dreaded blacklist.

After a couple of comeback attempts, and his release from the blacklist, Nolan signed in 1883 with the American Association's Pittsburgh Alleghenys. Considering the Alleghenys' bibulous reputation, the team was just about the worst he could have joined. From the start, his spring was a disaster. His arm still hurt and a bad cold plagued him, and his temper was frayed by the time his club embarked on its first road trip in May. Returning to his New York hotel late after a night on the town, Nolan found manager Al Pratt waiting for him with a $10 fine. Flying into a rage, Nolan informed Pratt that he would give him a better cause to fine him. While the manager slept, Nolan drank all night, swilling one cocktail after another, running up a tab that he charged to his team. This time, Nolan received a $100 fine and a hasty trip back onto the blacklist. The "shameful jamboree" probably marked the end of Nolan's celebrated career, the *Pittsburgh Dispatch* noted with some sadness. "There was a time, a few years since, when the 'Only' was considered one of the finest pitchers in the land, but he has weakened wonderfully of late and is of little use to any team. . . . Nolan was a good fellow at heart, but too much of the ardent knocked him out."

At a meeting in June, the club directors considered reinstating him, in part because the Alleghenys had failed to land George Bradley as a replacement, and in part because every player on the club pleaded that the likeable pitcher be given one more chance. Even manager Pratt noted that Nolan had apologized profusely for his binge and had otherwise followed the rules. To prove he was serious this time about changing his ways, Nolan took a solemn oath of abstinence before his parish priest. Reluctantly, the directors gave him one last try. But in less than three weeks, he was back to drinking, and the Alleghenys wanted nothing more to do with him. "They have dumped 'the Only Nolan,' whose dissolute habits have at last reaped their reward," the *Cincinnati Enquirer* reported. Nolan had been "once more thrown on the cold charity of the world and free lunch rooms." He was never great again.

Von der Ahe did not want his stars to end up like that.

⸺◇⸺

ALTERNATING THREATS AND PUNISHMENTS WITH OPEN AFFECTION, the owner threw a big dinner on the Tuesday night of July 24 for his players and their families at Bodeman's Grove, near Gravois Road and Arsenal Street, a popular destination for German immigrant picnickers. The resort, with its handsome columned house, tall trees, sloping plush green lawns, and gleaming blue pond, offered a bucolic escape from the noisy, dusty city. The splashy dinner was the kind of bighearted gesture that made Von der Ahe, for all his foibles, well liked by his players. In a few days, the Browns would set off for their final road trip of the season, a crucial twenty-eight-game odyssey that would take them to every other American Association city, and Von der Ahe wanted to show them his appreciation and support.

Just as characteristically, he blew his top two days later, when the Browns lost their final game of the home stand, a 5–4 heartbreaker against the Louisville Eclipse. When Arlie Latham entered the clubhouse, a furious Von der Ahe was there to greet him.

"Latham, I've fined you five dollars."

The astonished Latham asked why.

"For running in from third base that time you got thrown out at the plate," the owner answered.

Latham, merely playing the Browns' standard game of highly aggressive running, had tried to score on a double steal, the kind of bold, risky attempt that had helped St. Louis win many times. Von der Ahe, surely, would have joined in the applause had the exploit succeeded.

"You have no right to fine me. I used my best judgment. I thought I could get there. I won't stand for it," Latham said, getting heated.

"If you talk that way to me I'll make it fifty dollars," the owner barked.

"The third baseman thought for a minute," reported the *St. Louis Post-Dispatch*, "and walked away." Sullivan apparently defended his player, for he and Von der Ahe did "some very loud talking." Then the owner launched into a postgame diatribe, singling out Deasley for more abuse. On that note, the men headed for the train station, and the grueling road trip began.

Safely away from their flammable owner, the Browns quickly won two games in Louisville from Joe Gerhardt's crippled club. Arlie Latham, wearing padded pants to give him some protection while sliding, sprinted so recklessly in catching a foul ball that he "went through the boards" of the Cincinnati grandstand "like a battering ram" and needed help dislodging his leg. Despite such effort, the Browns blew three straight ninth-inning leads in one stretch and lost five of six, including three of four to the roused and suddenly dangerous Cincinnati Reds. Along the way, manager Sullivan paid the price for his hands-off approach to the players' after-hours activities. He virtually lost control of his men. On the Saturday night of August 4, several hours after St. Louis's sole victory in the series at Cincinnati, the Browns' new slugger Tom Mansell returned to the lobby of the Grand Hotel and strode straight through the door of an elevator, failing to notice there was no car inside. He plunged several feet down an open shaft, gruesomely gashing his right knee. A doctor summoned to the scene dressed and bandaged the wound and told the Browns' new star hitter that he would not be able to play for ten days to two weeks. George McGinnis, who had accompanied the outfielder into the hotel, remembered that he didn't have his room key, and had gone back to the desk to pick it up. "On his return, he found poor Mansell down in the hole," Von der Ahe recounted. A few days later, Mansell returned to St. Louis, his knee heavily bandaged, and "was transported with considerable difficulty" from the depot to his apartment on Grand Avenue for weeks of recuperation. He was so seriously injured that when he tried to rejoin his teammates in New York City at the end of August, the club sent him back home for more rest.

Naturally, reporters were convinced that the Browns' new outfielder had been drunk when he fell down the shaft. The *Cincinnati Enquirer* reported that Mansell and McGinnis spent the evening "with several residents of the city who were inclined to be convivial, and by the time they had visited several Over the Rhine saloons and tossed off sundry and numerous bowls of Cincinnati's 'amber,' they were loaded to the gunwales." Von der Ahe, trying to control the damage to his club's reputation, insisted that he had launched his own investigation and found the report to be "an infamous misrepresentation." Mansell "was as straight as a man could be." But the *Enquirer* remained skeptical. "Tom, undoubtedly, is a good fellow, but the night he did the grand and lofty act down the elevator of the Grand Hotel he was either drunk, tired, or the red lights on Vine street had made him near-sighted." Upper Vine Street in Cincinnati's Over the Rhine neighborhood was notorious for its saloons, gambling dens, dance halls, and burlesque theaters.

While Von der Ahe was busy issuing denials, another scandal erupted. One week after the elevator debacle, Fred Lewis and Pat Deasley, teammates on the 1881 Boston Red Stockings now reunited on the Browns, created a late-night ruckus outside a Columbus billiard hall. According to the *Ohio State Journal*, Ted Sullivan had hunted the two men down when they missed curfew. Possibly tipsy, they reportedly chased their manager out of the joint, while some of their teammates "made things lively for [Sullivan] by frequent blows in the region of the head." Deasley and Lewis then fled the scene, disappearing into the gas-lit streets of muggy Columbus. Later that night, evidently roaring drunk, the two became so rowdy that police felt compelled to arrest them for disorderly conduct. Refusing to go peacefully, the ballplayers "had to be clubbed vigorously" by three Columbus officers "before they submitted."

The ugly incident served the Browns right, critics maintained. "Lewis was dropped by the Philadelphias for his lushing," O. P. Caylor noted. "St. Louis deserves to lose for taking up men who make beasts of themselves." The *Boston Globe* concurred, calling Lewis "a hard ticket" that the Phillies had sold off "on account of his bad habits." Deasley, meanwhile, was "far too ignorant to have any character at all, and has gone downhill very fast since leaving Boston." Both men were ordered to stand for trial. Instead, they skipped town with their team, forfeiting $15 in bail.

Ted Sullivan hotly denied newspaper reports that his men had assaulted him, saying he had simply found the two men playing billiards in a saloon adjoining their hotel and "told them it was time they were in bed." Then he had gone to bed himself. Later that night, he contended, Lewis and Deasley got into a loud argument with some Columbus players. The police, playing favorites, let the local ballplayers go and arrested the St. Louis men. Sullivan only learned that his stars had been jailed the following morning. By then, he found the two "so penitent and so regretful" that he decided their wretched night in jail was punishment enough. "He refrained from telegraphing to Mr. Von der Ahe about the matter and tried to hush it up to save the reputation of his nine, several of whom felt keenly the reflection upon their character as an organization." More likely, he feared that an enraged Von der Ahe would immediately suspend them if he heard of it, robbing his lineup of two key players.

Sullivan's denials earned him only ridicule from the *Cincinnati Enquirer*. "Throwing two or three beer glasses at a manager's head and running may be a new way of asking for a chew of tobacco or the time of day, but it is a way that most people would look upon as some kind of assault, Mr. Sullivan to the contrary." Deasley and Lewis, meanwhile, sent off a protest to the *St. Louis Post-Dispatch*, calling its account of the incident "contemptible and malicious." But the newspaper stood by its report. "It will be observed that Messrs. Deasley and Lewis do not take the trouble to say that the statements were untrue, and as neither man could come within a mile of spelling either 'contemptible' or 'malicious,' it is doubtful if they knew what they were trying to say in the telegram which was dictated for them." The paper pointed to one educated man as the true author, saying: "Manager Sullivan knows he will be blamed for the want of discipline and this telegram is an attempt to square himself." Club discipline was much worse than previously revealed, it argued. Deasley and Lewis had been arrested earlier in St. Louis, while fistfights between players had repeatedly broken out, with Tony Mullane battling Bill Gleason in one incident, and Tom Dolan tussling with Deasley in another.

Though Von der Ahe talked down the Mansell injury and the Deasley-Lewis fracas in the press, he was getting angrier by the day about the severe discipline lapses on his club, and he blamed Sullivan for failing to get the men in line. There was little to do about it, Von der Ahe concluded, except head east, join the men, and assert authority himself—whether Ted Sullivan liked it or not.

10

CAP ANSON'S NIGHTMARE

TIRED AND GRUBBY, CAP ANSON WAS IN NO MOOD FOR AN argument when the train bearing his Chicago White Stockings hissed into Union Station in Toledo, Ohio, on the steamy Friday morning of August 10, 1883. In the midst of a punishing road trip, Anson's men had just dropped two out of three to lowly Detroit. As they disembarked, a *Toledo Blade* reporter took note of their deeply sunburned faces, so dark that they could have been suspected of being "tainted with black blood."

This was supposed to be their off day, crammed between the Thursday finale in Detroit and a big Saturday contest in Buffalo, and they could have used the rest. But Albert Spalding, club president, had shoehorned in an exhibition game that Friday afternoon. Although Toledo had only about fifty thousand residents, it was a baseball hotbed, home of the Blue Stockings, one of the top clubs in the game's best minor circuit, the Northwestern League. A big crowd could be expected to hand over thousands of quarters to see the hometown boys take on the kings of the National League. That would boost Chicago's profits—and why not, since they were passing through Toledo anyway? No reason, except that the men were getting worn to a frazzle.

But it was not just the constant work, recent defeats, and ordeal of travel that had Anson in a foul mood. He had been hearing, with mounting disgust, about Toledo's rising twenty-five-year-old catcher, Moses Fleetwood Walker. A tall, graceful young man, Fleet Walker was a rarity in 1880s baseball in that he was a college-educated gentleman. The *St. Louis Globe-Democrat* reported that he caught "magnificently" and declared that his throwing was "never excelled" in that city. The *Sporting Life*, which had a national reach, observed that Walker was "looming up as a great man behind the bat." The *Pittsburgh Dispatch* reported that he was "said to be the whole team, and a dog under the wagon"—meaning well-equipped with talent.

Anson, however, wanted no part of this nationwide celebration of Walker. He didn't even want to set foot on the same field with him. For Walker was a light-skinned *black* man—and in Anson's opinion, no such individual had a place in a white man's world, pretending to be a white man's equal. Many of his Chicago players staunchly agreed. Before assenting to the exhibition game, Anson had sought assurances that Walker would not play, and the Toledo club had indicated that Fleet needed a rest and probably would be benched. Anson accepted the hint as a promise, counting on the Blue Stockings to keep their black man out of his path. He didn't like Walker's presence in white professional baseball one bit, and he had a low opinion of the Toledo club for permitting it.

Adrian Constantine Anson—named not after the Roman emperors, but, more prosaically, after two towns in Michigan where his father had once lived—had formed his rock-ribbed convictions of white supremacy early in life. It started with his dealings with the ragged remnants of a Pottawatomie Indian tribe that lived on the plains just beyond his hometown, the pioneer village of Marshalltown, Iowa. "I fancy they were not as fond of us boys as they might have been," Adrian recalled with amusement, "for we used to tease and bother them at every opportunity."

One night, as a teenager, he awoke with a start to see two Indians standing in his room, one at the head of the bed, the other at the foot, each wielding a tomahawk. "That they had come to kill me I was certain, and that they would succeed in doing so seemed to me equally sure,"

Anson recalled. He tried to scream, but could not, and watched in terrified silence as they vanished through the open doorway, disappearing into the darkness. In the morning's light, when he dared to leave his bed and alert

his father to the strange visit, the old man laughed and told the boy he had dreamt it all. But as long as he lived, Cap Anson fervently maintained that the visitants were real. "I saw these two Indians as they stood at the head and foot of my bed as plainly as I ever saw a base-ball, and I have had my eye on a ball a good many times since I first began to play the game," he said. But even if he had not imagined the encounter, the Indians' wordless warning never pierced his heart. For the rest of his life, he would demean and harass those whom he insisted on pigeonholing as his inferiors.

Cap Anson
(*Library of Congress*)

Blacks, in particular, stirred Anson's feelings of supremacy. In his 1900 ghost-written autobiography, the retired base-ball legend wrote unblushingly of Clarence Duval, batboy and mascot of the White Stockings, as a "little coon" and a "no account nigger." Such virulently racist comments appeared frequently in baseball books and articles of the time—as acceptable, if not entirely respectable, public language. Sportswriter Henry Clay Palmer wrote at length about "the little darkey" Duval in such books as his 1892 volume *Sights Around the World With the Base Ball Boys*. With sadistic relish, Palmer described in detail the various humiliations the players inflicted on the friendless boy, from pelting him with food to dressing him up like an organ grinder's monkey, then taking him out in public on a leash.

St. Louis Browns manager Ted Sullivan shared Anson's fondness for reducing blacks to crude comic stereotypes—much like the producers of the minstrel shows that had made Lew Simmons a star. In Sullivan's memoirs, a collection of the stories he loved to tell to get laughs, Ted wrote of local men who attended an autumn exhibition game in 1883 in Pensacola,

Florida. "In center field the cedar trees were packed with coons, so thick were they on the trees that they resembled a flock of blackbirds or crows." Serving up some of the dialect humor that was immensely popular in the nineteenth century, Sullivan quoted one "big coon" who was initially unimpressed when One Arm Daily stepped up to pitch against the home club: "Why dem St. Louis babies thinks so little of our white club, dat they are putting in one-armed men on dem." When the crowd saw Daily neatly pick up a ball as if he had two arms, another man supposedly turned and cried, "Which of you niggers said dat dat one-armed man couldn't play?" Later in the game, Daily drove a line drive into the trees that struck one of the spectators painfully in the back, to the amusement of his fellow African Americans. "O Lordy, if dat man had two hands I would have been killed," the victim cried, according to Sullivan.

As of that 1883 exhibition, a mere twenty years had passed since President Abraham Lincoln had issued his Emancipation Proclamation, theoretically freeing all slaves in states still at war with the Union, as a matter of military necessity. Yet even Lincoln longed to be rid of African Americans altogether, having concluded that whites and blacks could never get along. "You and we are different races," Lincoln told black leaders during a White House meeting in August 1862. "We have between us a broader difference than exists between almost any other two races." Most blacks refused, justly insisting they were Americans as much as anyone. As the war went on, some 200,000 African Americans, with Lincoln's strong encouragement, joined the fight to save the Union and win the freedom of their race. Their strength turned the tide of the war and added enormous impetus to the movement for equal rights. But many white northerners surely shared Lincoln's original hope that blacks would leave. "Who believes that Whites and Blacks can ever amalgamate in America? Or wishes it to happen?" asked Walt Whitman in a May 1858 editorial in the *Brooklyn Eagle*. "Nature has set an impassable seal against it. Besides, is not America for the Whites? And is it not better so?"

Many white baseball players certainly felt it was better so—and because of their fierce opposition to integration, which long predated the twentieth century, baseball's color line was not to be ended for good until 1947. Citing a desire to avoid divisive controversy, the National Association of Base Ball Players passed a December 1867 resolution "against the admission of any club which may be composed of one or more colored persons." Although they were denied that association's sanction or assistance, blacks went right on playing America's game, however. The number of black clubs exploded during these post–Civil War years. The *Washington Evening Star* of September 21, 1869, reported on a contest at the National Baseball Grounds between the Alerts, a newly formed black club, and the Olympics, an established white club. Far from inflaming political divisions, the game brought out a large crowd of peaceful, happy people. "Good feeling prevailed throughout, the game being equally enjoyed by the contestants and spectators," the *Star* said.

By the late 1860s, Octavius Catto, an infielder and captain of the superb all-black Pythians of Philadelphia, had emerged as perhaps the game's first black star. An extraordinary man, Catto was an educator and civil rights leader, fighting for the right of blacks to ride on Philadelphia's horsecars, a crusade that led to legislation banning segregation of the city's public transit. In the next decade, another black star rose to prominence, a brilliant young pitcher named John "Bud" Fowler. The son of a barber in Cooperstown, New York, Fowler became an amazingly skilled hurler. In April 1878, as a twenty-year-old star for a semipro team in Chelsea, Massachusetts, he stunned the baseball world by beating the National League champions, the Boston Red Stockings, 2–1. Soon the pitcher would become the first African American in professional organized baseball, landing a contract with the Lynn (later Worcester) Live Oaks of the International Association, baseball's second best league at the time. Another member of the league, the Maple Leaf Club, of Guelph, Ontario, signed him to play in 1881, but when he showed up, his putative teammates "refused to play with him on account of his being a colored man."

By 1883, attention was turning to a new young black star. Fleet Walker was the son of mulatto parents. His father was an ambitious and intelligent man, a barrel-maker turned physician turned minister of the Methodist Episcopal Church in the town of Oberlin, Ohio, a hotbed of abolitionism in the mid-nineteenth century with a proud tradition of supporting black students. Fleet managed to attend the preparatory school of Oberlin College in 1877, and to move up to the college itself a year later. There, he obtained an education far beyond any achieved by Adrian Anson and most other white ballplayers, studying Greek and mathematics and reading Livy, Horace, and Cicero. Along the way, he also learned to play piano, another mark of social distinction. His surviving transcript shows that his classroom attendance dropped off the longer he stayed— a trend that coincided with his growing obsession with an increasingly popular sport on campus called baseball. In 1882, he went to the University of Michigan to play ball.

Walker had his heart set on becoming a professional ballplayer at a time when the doors that had been briefly pried open by Reconstruction were slamming shut again on blacks all over America. Though his skin no doubt worked against him, Walker had something that made some baseball executives willing to overlook it: talent as a catcher, which teams sorely needed. Although the National League barred black players, by August 1881 Walker had won a professional job playing for the Cleveland Whites, a fine team sponsored by the White Sewing Machine Company boasting several future major-league players. The presence of a black man among the Whites stirred interest, but seemingly no animosity—until the club ventured south, to Louisville, where it quickly became apparent that Walker would not be treated as just another ballplayer. The first sign of trouble was at the St. Cloud Hotel, where the management barred him from eating breakfast with his teammates. This was no isolated incident: he frequently had to find his own accommodations, since blacks were increasingly being barred from "white" hotels, restaurants, and even some railroad passenger cars. As word spread that a black ballplayer had arrived in the city, local rednecks began mulling over their response to this innovation. That muggy afternoon, while the thermometer climbed to 89 degrees, more than two thousand people paid their way into Eclipse Park to see what would happen.

To the disappointment of many, the Louisville players adamantly refused to take the field with Walker. "The prejudice of the Eclipse was either too strong, or they feared Walker, who has earned the reputation of being the best amateur catcher in the Union," said the *Courier-Journal*. In any event, Walker was instructed to watch the game from the stands in his street clothes. The Whites' first baseman—not yet hardened in the difficult and dangerous art of catching—attempted to take his place. When his hands gave out after one inning, however, the sweating crowd, curious to see Walker's stuff, "at once set up a cry in good nature for 'the nigger.'" The Eclipse club's vice president, defying the wishes of his own players, went down on the field and personally asked Fleet to play.

The twenty-three-year-old catcher—who must have felt great trepidation, appearing in the South for the first time and facing white supremacists who emphatically did not want him there—was uncertain whether to risk playing. As he walked in front of the grandstand, the crowd began chanting, "Walker! Walker!" He hesitated, but finally threw off his coat and vest and stepped out to play in his shirtsleeves and pants. Furious that Walker was about to play, Eclipse second baseman Fred Pfeffer and pitcher John Reccius stalked off the field. The crowd hooted, and a new argument erupted.

When it appeared that the Louisville players would make good on their threat to walk out, the Cleveland manager again relented, agreeing to bench his star. He didn't want to lose his share of the gate receipts. But even the manager's abject surrender did not satisfy some in the crowd. They were still outraged by the mere presence of a black man. While Walker was putting his collar and jacket back on, a man named Charles Fuller rushed onto the field and grabbed Fleet in an attempt to forcibly eject him from the ballpark. In that explosive moment—Walker might have faced a lynch mob, had he defended himself—others raced out and broke Fuller's grip. Walker somehow kept his cool, straightened his clothing, walked back to his seat, and watched the game. "When it was seen that he was not to play, the crowd heartily and very properly hissed the Eclipse club and jeered their misplays for several innings," while cheering on the visiting club, according to the *Courier-Journal*—to no avail, since the Eclipse won, 6–3.

The city's newspapers hissed along with the critics. With dripping sarcasm, the *Louisville Commercial* headlined its game account "The Utter Respectability of the Eclipse Nine Will Not Permit a Mulatto Catcher." It called on the club, made up of ill-educated, hard-drinking men who were not in the least respectable, to rethink its shabby behavior and let Walker play the next day—and to "have a watchman to guard Mr. Fuller who offered such an indignity to Mr. Walker." Nevertheless, that night, Walker "shook the dust of Louisville from his feet . . . and went home."

Two years later, the Toledo Blue Stockings of the Northwestern League, a new minor league, snapped up the young star. "He is said to be·

a plucky catcher, a hard hitter and a daring and successful base-runner," the *New York Clipper* reported. Walker "is . . . said to be one of the most efficient [catchers] in all points of play . . . to be found in the country," the *Missouri Republican* added. Still, the notion of a black man playing with whites caused a ruckus at the Northwestern League's meeting on March 14, 1883. The Peoria Reds petitioned the circuit to outlaw blacks, but a majority of owners—after an emotional debate—refused, apparently concluding that Walker was such a good gate attraction that he was worth the risk of inflaming feelings. Even so, such integration could probably never have happened were it not for Walker's great personal strengths. In a profession dominated by crude and violent men, here was an educated, polite, and steady fellow who comported himself with dignity and pride. He worked hard and never showboated. Moreover, as the incident in Louisville had demonstrated, he possessed tremendous courage and self-restraint, qualities a black ballplayer would need for survival if he chose to compete with whites.

Moses Fleetwood Walker
(*Transcendental Graphics*/theruckerarchive.com;
reprinted with permission)

WHEREAS WALKER HAD BRAVELY CROSSED OVER THE COLOR LINE to play baseball in white leagues, a surprising number of skilled black ballplayers were earning money in 1883 by playing on all-black teams. The "Negro clubs"—including such teams as the Cleveland Blue Stockings, the Cincinnati Brown Stockings, the Louisville Mutuals, and the Geneva Clippers—were sharing in that year's baseball boom, tapping into African Americans' obvious passion for the game. A growing black middle class was eager to part with their quarters to watch fine athletes of their color play the game.

The St. Louis Black Stockings were one of the best. They had been formed by black saloonkeeper Henry Bridgewater to compete in an all-black professional league. "When the league failed to organize we were compelled to make engagements with teams composed of white players," Bridgewater explained in an interview. The Black Stockings received strong praise from local sportswriters, even if they got fewer column inches than white clubs. When the Black Sox opened against a local nine of white amateurs on April 24, the *Missouri Republican* predicted the game would "not only be a novelty but . . . also open somebody's eyes regarding the ball-tossing abilities of the colored element." As it turned out, the black ballplayers—splendid in their uniforms of blue hats, bright white shirts and knickers, and jet-black stockings—clobbered the white team 8–1. "Several of the colored players worked like trained professionals," the *Globe-Democrat* noted admiringly. Seated among the crowd at Compton Avenue Park that day were white stars from the St. Louis Browns—George McGinnis, Hugh Nicol, the Gleason brothers, and Charlie Comiskey—who were curious to see how well the black men played.

The Black Stockings embarked on a nationwide tour later that week, and the *Globe-Democrat* proudly predicted that the St. Louis team would "make mince-meat of the colored clubs throughout the country." The *National Police Gazette* took a mocking tone, branding the Black Stockings "the champion moke club of St. Louis" and reporting that they would be taking on other "coon clubs" in the Midwest. In September, the paper reported that the "coons are doing good work in St. Louis, as they have knocked out all of the coon clubs with which they have come in contact." The *Register* in Rockford, Illinois, reported the Black Stockings' defeat of the city's vaunted white club, the Rockford Reds, with the headline, "The Coons Carry Off the Cake." In covering these games, some white sportswriters acknowledged African Americans' talent, but felt compelled to spice up their copy with racist jokes. The *Missouri Republican*, reporting on the Black Stockings opener, noted that "Little Harris," the team's catcher, "got caught between the bases yesterday, but wriggled through like an eel, although five men were on the line after him. A good-sized buck who ornamented the pavilion, threw up his hands which darkened the field and exclaimed, as Harris got second: 'Look at de little scamp! Fo' de Lord, his yere's waggin yet.'" When the Black Stockings arrived in Cincinnati during a tour that included Indianapolis, Dayton, Cleveland, Akron, and other cities, sportswriter O. P. Caylor touted the upcoming game as a "rare opportunity to see how colored men play ball. They are said to be peculiar in their style on bases and in the field." Caylor joked lamely that the Black Stockings would be wearing "flesh-colored hose," and he predicted that black players would mostly request high pitches. "Then if they are hit it will be in the head and will not hurt."

Ignoring such jibes, black audiences turned out in large numbers. Even in a cold drizzle, some seven hundred people—about five hundred of them black—watched the visiting Black Stockings take on the all-white Cincinnati Shamrocks, a professional independent club competing for business against the superior Reds. Most of the crowd rooted for the black visitors rather than the white home team. Ren Deagle, who went on to pitch well for the major-league Reds that season, struck out thirteen Black Stockings batters and led the Shamrocks to a 4–0 victory. But Caylor had to admit he was impressed with the visitors. "The colored club were a well behaved lot of young fellows, and played a plucky game."

As the summer went on, black baseball proved tremendously popular. A June series between the Black Stockings and the black Louisville Mutuals drew crowds as big as those attending the American Association's Louisville Eclipse games. In Detroit, "business was practically suspended in the barber shops" when the St. Louis Black Stockings and Louisville Mutuals paid a visit to Recreation Park—barbershops then being common black-run businesses in America. A *Detroit Evening News* reporter joked that the Black Stockings played so well that there was a "strong suspicion" that their pitcher, William "Bud" Davis, was actually Jim McCormick, the great National League star, "blacked up," minstrel-style. The spectators enjoyed themselves thoroughly, mixing it up with the players. At one point, the Black Stockings' best hitter was "dancing around the home plate in a frenzy of expectation, while the pitcher fondled the ball and delivered it with provoking deliberation." Growing tired of the crowd's taunts, the batter supposedly "flung down his bat, glared ferociously at the stands and shouted: 'What's de matter wid who? What's de matter wid you?' But the crowd gently guyed and exhorted him 'not to get wild,' and there were no further interruptions."

When the Mutuals came to St. Louis in August, a fine crowd of 1,200 turned out—most of them, this time, "curious or enthusiastic Caucasians." Once again, the Black Stockings' best hitter amused the audience with his gyrations at the plate, which were apparently much more emphatic than those of white hitters of the time. Interestingly, a description of him in the *St. Louis Globe-Democrat* has a remarkably modern ring: "He was not quiet for a moment, but divided his attention between casting furtive glances at the pitcher and tapping the home plate with his bat. His motions were nervous, peculiar and indescribable. Bobbing up and down like a jerky jack-in-the-box, he lost no opportunity to drum the plate. First it was one rap, then one, two, then straighten up for an instant and repeat."

Other blacks played a less dignified role in 1883 baseball—as team mascots. These young boys, whom the players considered good luck charms, were kept on hand to collect bats, fetch foul balls, and run errands. They also served as handy targets for vindictive players. Early in the season, the Athletics hired a black batboy and mischievously named him "Joe Quest," after the famous white ballplayer. Joe the mascot quickly lost his job when the A's began losing, as the players, searching for a scapegoat, branded him a "Jonah." Similarly, when Metropolitans manager Jim Mutrie got the urge to hire a mascot, he "hunted up a little darkey . . . to guard his team's bat bags and bring them luck." According to the *Cincinnati Enquirer*, Mutrie's "little 'coon'" turned out to be a Jonah as well. "Jim started out last night to look for a bigger one, and it was rumored that he captured one," a joking reference to fugitive slave hunting.

Such was the ugly world in which Fleet Walker competed. Neither a mascot nor a boy, he had to endure teasing and abuse as a man. And, unlike professionals on all-black teams, he had to go it alone, without the strong support of fellow players who understood, or cared, what he was enduring in integrating baseball. To be sure, there were some white players capable of rising above racial prejudice who quickly came to respect Walker. At Columbus in 1883, the members of the city's American Association ball club invited Fleet to join them at their newly inaugurated downtown clubhouse, where they liked to hold impromptu concerts. Pitchers Frank Mountain and John Valentine were fine singers, and left fielder Harry Wheeler was said to be one of the best harmonica players in the country. Walker fit right in. "He is a great favorite with his fellow associates," the *Ohio State Journal* reported. "He favored the boys with some excellent piano solos at the club room last night. Give him a good reception, boys, he is a perfect gentleman."

The biggest baseball star in Chicago, though, had no desire to share songs, the ball field, or anything else with Walker. Cap Anson was too stern a man, too much invested in the old school, to condone racial integration. On August 10, Anson and his men—including second baseman Fred Pfeffer, who had put up such a stink about Walker two years earlier in Louisville—took the field at Toledo's Presque Isle Park, which was located near the mouth of the Maumee River on land that later became the Chesapeake & Ohio Railroad's coal-loading dock. Anson made a point of stressing to Blue Stockings manager Charles Hazen Morton that he and his men would be playing "with no damned nigger" that afternoon. Morton was roused to anger and ordered Walker to warm up; he would play right field. The "beefy bluffer," as the *Toledo Blade* called Anson, "was informed that he could play his team or go, just as he blank pleased."

When Walker came out, the managers bickered violently, and each side threatened to walk away. The *Blade* found Anson's conduct disgraceful, given that Walker was "a gentleman and a scholar, in the literal sense[,] . . . entirely lacking in the bummer instinct" and obviously "the superior intellectually of any player on the Chicago club." Anson, having already spoiled his off day with this obnoxious stop in Toledo, finally backed down; there was no sense throwing away the gate receipts at this point. But he was boiling mad, and he would never forgive the insult. "We'll play this here game, but we won't play never no more with the nigger in," he vowed. Even the *National Police Gazette* savored the captain's humiliation, cracking that "Anson weakened like a whipped cur and went on to play the game, with nothing more to say."

There is no record of Walker's reaction to the day's events. But the game proved to be a grueling one for the Chicago men. Toledo hammered pitcher Fred Goldsmith for sixteen hits and pushed the contest to extra innings—the last thing Anson and his men wanted or needed. In the tenth, the Blue Stockings actually seized the lead, but in the bottom of the inning Chicago scored twice to salvage an ugly 7–6 victory. A foul mood permeated the air. The insult of Walker's appearance would be branded on Anson's heart, and what would have otherwise been just another meaningless exhibition game became one of the most consequential games of baseball ever played.

Anson vowed that he would never again share a field with a black man. He was determined to devote his considerable influence, for the rest of his career, to making sure that no other white professional would, either. Regrettably, he succeeded. One year later, when the White Stockings arranged another exhibition with Toledo, Chicago took care to extract an ironclad pledge from Morton that Walker would not play. Although "the management of the Chicago Ball Club have no personal feeling about the matter," club secretary Jonathan Brown assured Morton, "the players do most decidedly object and to preserve harmony in the club it is necessary that I have your assurance in writing." This time, afraid of losing a big gate draw, Morton complied.

These were difficult years for African Americans. Reconstruction was coming to an end, southern Democrats were cracking down on black opportunity and rights, and, in 1883, the Supreme Court delivered a stunning setback to civil rights in a decision that stated that, though states could not deny blacks rights, under the Fourteenth Amendment, private businesses could. Yet even as the lines of segregation were hardening, Fleet Walker was preparing himself to step into a role that no black man had ever played—crossing major-league baseball's color line.

When the American Association expanded in 1884, adding the Toledo club to its ranks, Walker became the first recognized black major-leaguer—sixty-three years before Jackie Robinson took the field for the Brooklyn Dodgers. Midway into the 1884 season, another black player, Walker's brother Welday, briefly joined the Toledo team, filling in for five games in the outfield. Fleet's title as the first black major-leaguer has been challenged: William Edward White, a Brown University student who played one game for the National League's Providence Grays—on June 21, 1879—was the son of a white Georgia businessman and, evidently, a mulatto slave mother. But Fleet Walker was the first major-leaguer to be seen as a black player, recognized as such by everyone on and off the field. It seems only fitting that the American Association, the first major league to market baseball to immigrants and working people, making it more truly America's game, was also the first to welcome a black star into its ranks.

Still, during Walker's brief tenure at this level of competition, his considerable strength of character was severely tested. His 1884 battery mate, hard-throwing Tony Mullane, deliberately tormented Fleet that season. Walker was "the best catcher I ever worked with," he admitted years later, "but I disliked a Negro and whenever I had to pitch to him I used to pitch anything I wanted without looking at his signals." One day, Walker signaled for a curve, and Mullane dangerously crossed him up by firing a fastball. The catcher walked out to the pitcher's box. "Mr. Mullane," Walker said, "I'll catch you without signals, but I won't catch you if you are going to cross me when I give you a signal." And for the rest of that season he caught everything Mullane pitched "without knowing what was coming." Walker endured other slights from his teammates as well. In that season's team portrait, Fleet Walker was nowhere to be seen. Only white players appeared, as if Walker never existed.

Late in the season, prejudice against Walker grew markedly more sinister. In September, Toledo manager Morton received a letter from Richmond, Virginia, home of another American Association team. "We, the undersigned, do hereby warn you not to put up Walker, the Negro catcher, the days you play in Richmond, as we could mention the names of seventy-five determined men who have sworn to mob Walker if he comes on the ground in a suit. We hope you will listen to our words of warning so there will be no trouble, and if you do not, there certainly will be. We only write this to prevent much bloodshed, as you alone can prevent." By the time Toledo arrived in the capital of the late Confederacy, Walker had suffered a fractured rib and might not have played in any event. But, given that roving gangs had taken to terrorizing and lynching blacks in order to reassert white supremacy in the South, Morton took the threat seriously and made sure Walker sat the game out—as he would do again, after another letter from Richmond warned Morton not to start Walker when the Virginia club came to Toledo.

By the end of September, the Toledos decided the time had come to give Walker his release—ostensibly because of his injuries, but quite possibly because the management was tired of the controversy. His parting reviews were as warm as those that had greeted him at the start of 1883. "During his connection with the Toledo club, by his fine, gentlemanly deportment he made hosts of friends who will regret to learn that he is no longer a member of the club," said the *Sporting Life*. The *Toledo Blade* called him "a conscientious player" who was "very popular with Toledo audiences."

For the next five years, Walker played for a succession of minor-league teams: Cleveland of the Western Association; Waterbury of the Eastern League; and Newark and Syracuse of the International League. He did so well that he opened a saloon at the corner of High and Sheriff streets in Cleveland. In 1887, at Newark, Fleet Walker teamed up with George Stovey, a superb pitcher, to form the first all-black battery in organized baseball. During that season, some seven African Americans played in the International League, including Bud Fowler, demonstrating that black ballplayers were every bit the equal of whites. Yet white players began to grouse about having to mix with blacks. Many, no doubt, were worried that talented blacks would squeeze them out of their jobs. Some threatened to bolt to other leagues where they would not have to share the field with Negroes. On July 14, at their midsummer meeting in Buffalo, International League directors chose the way of least resistance. "Several representatives declared that many of the best players of the League were anxious to leave on account of the colored element, and the board finally directed Secretary White to approve no more contracts with colored men," said the *Newark Daily Journal*. Only those already playing could remain, ensuring that blacks would eventually be phased out.

Five days later, Cap Anson's shadow fell across black baseball again. Anson brought his White Stockings to Newark for an exhibition game and once again demanded that the blacks—Stovey and Walker—be removed. That same season, Anson blew up when he learned that Newark was about to sell Stovey to the New York Giants—which, had the deal gone through, would have meant Chicago would have to play against the black star. At the last minute, "a howl was heard from Chicago to New York," recalled Sol White, an early player who published a book in 1907 documenting the struggles of his fellow blacks. "This same Anson, with all the venom of a hate which would be worthy of a Tillman or a Vardaman [southern senators] of the present day, made strenuous and fruitful opposition to any proposition looking to the admittance of a colored man into the National League." New York backed off and refrained from hiring Stovey.

Anson's lobbying had lasting consequences. In 1888, the Ohio League's owners voted to bar black players, including nineteen-year-old Sol White, who had batted .370 for its Wheeling club. The decision drew a powerful and measured objection from another of the league's players, Fleet Walker's brother Welday. "The law is a disgrace to the present age," Welday wrote, "and reflects very much upon the intelligence of your last meeting, and casts derision at the laws of Ohio—the voice of the people—that says all men are equal." If it was against the rules for blacks to play ball, he argued, it should be against the rules for black people to buy tickets and patronize the local club. Otherwise, only a man's character and talent should count. But such logic could not convince the lords of baseball, and the color line was drawn. In 1888, the International League limited its teams to one black player each—two, in the case of Syracuse. After the 1888 season, black infielder Frank Grant left that minor league; in 1889, only Fleet Walker of the Syracuse Stars remained. When Walker retired at the end of that season, the curtain fell. More than fifty years would pass before another black was accepted into the International League.

Black players could not fully explain the vicious crusade that had been waged against them. They only knew that Cap Anson was their tireless enemy, working to keep them out of organized baseball. "Just why Adrian C. Anson, manager and captain of the Chicago National League Club, was so strongly opposed to colored players on white teams cannot be explained," wrote Sol White. But the afternoon of August 10, 1883, seemed to have fueled Anson's determination. He could not stand losing, and he never forgot being shown up that day by being forced to take the field against a black man.

Anson had his way when he was alive, and partly because of him it took baseball many more decades to integrate. Until his death, he was regarded as a paragon of virtue and a man who had greatly elevated baseball's reputation. Anson's virulent racism, his crusade against a culture of merit in baseball, either made no impression on many of his white contemporaries or won their quiet approval—since many shared his belief that blacks degraded the game.

But now history stands over the great player's memory like the two silent braves at the foot of his bed, sternly rebuking the meanness of a man who would seek to feed his own ego by bullying and intimidating others. In showing that he feared to meet African Americans on the ball field—where any questions about equality are quickly settled—Anson left an indelible stain on his own character.

11

FLINGING THE WATCH

I T WAS PROBABLY THE WORST DECISION THAT ATHLETICS CAPTAIN Lon Knight had made all season. For days now, his ace, Bobby Mathews, had just about heaved off his arm—pitching a three-hitter against the New York Metropolitans on Wednesday, July 26, 1883; giving up fifteen hits while losing to the same club on Thursday; beating the hard-drinking Pittsburgh Alleghenys on an eight-hitter on Saturday; and beating them on another eight-hitter on Monday. "Mathews as a pitcher seems to be all gone," O. P. Caylor, the Cincinnati sportswriter and Reds official, opined that week. "We feared Philadelphia would be too much for him." As dogged a competitor as Mathews was, he had absolutely nothing left on Tuesday, July 31, after throwing four complete games over a six-day stretch. But Knight started him anyway—not in the pitcher's box, but in right field, instead of giving him a much-needed rest. It proved a disastrous move.

The Philadelphia crowd had much to cheer that afternoon, as the home team beat the Alleghenys in a 16–12 slugfest. But in the second inning, when Mathews tore off to steal second base, he slammed a leg into the bag and collapsed in agony. He had twisted his ankle so badly that he could not even limp off the field. His teammates had to carry him. This was terrible news for the first-place club.

STOVEY, L. F., Athletics
OLD JUDGE
CIGARETTE FACTORY.
GOODWIN & CO., New York.

Harry Stovey
(*Library of Congress*)

For weeks to come, in the heat of the pennant fight, the Athletics would have to muddle through without their ace pitcher, the man who kept them from being an "ordinary" team. The injury might have been devastating, had it not been for the luck of the schedule: during Mathews's convalescence, the Athletics faced the very dregs of the American Association—Pittsburgh, Baltimore, and Columbus. Making the best of the situation, Knight replaced Bobby with a rotation of hurlers: Fred Corey, Grin Bradley, and a rookie from New Jersey named "Jersey" Bakley, who was rushed back from Harrisburg in the Inter-State Association, where he had been out on loan. Though none of them was as good as Bobby at flummoxing professional hitters, together they managed to get the Athletics through the immediate crisis.

Someone else also came to the rescue: the team's twenty-six-year-old first baseman. Tall, slender, speedy Harry Stovey—clocked that summer rounding all four bases in an impressive fourteen seconds—had been a fine player in the National League. Now he was blossoming into a superstar.

In early August, worshipful fans presented Stovey with a handsome badge depicting a baseball diamond, with ivory insets for bags. On the bar were the words "Home Runs, 1883," with the number to be filled in later. Harry would go on to club a record fourteen of them, while also leading the Association in doubles (31), runs scored (110), total bases (213), extra-base hits (51), and slugging percentage (.506). Stovey's energy, daring, and panache rallied his teammates as the pennant race neared its climax, and his daring, hard-driving style of play beautifully captured the spirit of the American Association.

"Gathering Them In,"
by John Reilly, Cincinnati
Commercial Gazette, *August 13, 1883*
(Library of Congress)

After three weeks trying to heal, Mathews finally attempted his return on August 21 in an important home game against the still dangerous Cincinnati Reds. That morning, he strode onto the field at Athletic Park and began to warm up. But when he attempted to let loose, possibly favoring his sore ankle, he badly strained his back. In agony, he found it impossible to pitch that day. The next day, Bobby gamely tried again, toughing it out this time, but lost to the Reds, 8–6. There was worse in store. In his next start, two days later, Mathews's still-painful ankle gave way in the fourth inning, and he hobbled off the field, injured again. "The Athletics are losing their grip," the *Boston Globe* observed, after Philadelphia dropped its third straight to Cincinnati.

On August 28, the recuperating Mathews stopped in Providence to visit with his old friend Joe Start, then turned up in the stockholders' box at Boston's South End Grounds, where he had pitched so splendidly the year before. The people there who knew him well could instantly tell that something was seriously wrong when they saw his exhausted face and pained movements. "He does not look as well as he did when a Red Stocking," the *Globe* reported. "His nine, the Athletics, is meeting with hard luck of late and it does not seem as if they could win a pennant." Without a healthy Mathews, or a pitcher to replace him—which, surely, would be a miracle at this point in the season—it was difficult to see how the Athletics could hold back Chris Von der Ahe's Browns, even with the red-hot Stovey.

THOUGH HIS PLAYERS WERE CAROUSING AT NIGHT, AND HIS BOSS was undermining his authority on an almost daily basis, Ted Sullivan steadied his men and kept the team unified, focused, and aggressive on the ball field. After his Browns suffered defeats in Louisville and Cincinnati, they won all four games in Columbus, three of four in Baltimore, and three of four in Pittsburgh. On the morning of August 27, the standings showed that the Browns had actually moved one half-game ahead of the Mathews-less Athletics:

	W	L	PCT.	GB
St. Louis	52	25	.675	—
Philadelphia	50	24	.676	½
Cincinnati	47	30	.610	5
New York	43	32	.573	8
Louisville	41	35	.539	10½
Pittsburgh	25	52	.324	27
Baltimore	23	53	.302	28½
Columbus	23	53	.302	28½

Next stop for the Browns was New York's Polo Grounds, a tough venue for any visitor. The New York Metropolitans were a strong club, and their right-handed ace pitcher, Timothy John Keefe of Cambridge, Massachusetts, was putting in one of the greatest seasons in major-league history. Grit ran in the family. Tim's Irish-born father, a carpenter named Patrick, had been trapped in the South during the Civil War and was given the choice of imprisonment or service in the Confederate Army. With two brothers fighting for the Union—both would die in 1862—he chose imprisonment, and spent three years making bullets in a prison factory. After being repatriated to Massachusetts, Patrick had high hopes for his son, and he felt miserably disappointed when Tim insisted on wasting his life on baseball. After starring for Troy in the National League—his microscopic 0.86 earned run average in 1880 is rated the lowest in major-league history—Keefe came to America's biggest, most vibrant city in 1883. Having mastered a killer change of pace to go with his fastball and curves, he would go on to win forty-one games this season and lead the Association in some impressive categories: hits and walks per inning (only 0.963); innings pitched (a stunning 619); strikeouts (359); and complete games (68). On July 4, he pitched both ends of a doubleheader against Columbus, winning the first on a one-hitter and the second on a two-hitter.

Tim Keefe
(Library of Congress)

Keefe helped make the Mets a very good team, one destined to win the pennant in 1884. Still, they were something of a redheaded stepchild to their owners, the Metropolitan Exhibition Company, led by a young tobacco merchant named John B. Day and Truthful Jim Mutrie. The company owned two teams, the American Association's Mets and the National League's New York Gothams, and Day and Mutrie made it a point to steer financial resources and their best players to the franchise in the older and superior league. The pair had started off in 1880 with a club they called the Metropolitans, an independent team run on a shoestring, much like the Athletics or Browns before their Association days. Mutrie's idea was to fill the Mets roster with players from the disintegrating Rochester Hop Bitters, a very good professional team named after, and designed to promote, a patent medicine of limited curative value but loaded with highly therapeutic alcohol. Unfortunately, he and Day lacked the $500 in train fare needed to get the men down to New York. Mutrie first tried to raise the cash from area sporting-goods dealers, but baseball's reputation was in such disrepair that he was unable to collect a dollar. Finally, an old friend, Jack Lynch of the Washington Nationals, and later of the Metropolitans, suggested that Mutrie talk to the prominent book publishers Charles Dillingham and Walter Appleton, as they were "lovers of baseball and liberally inclined." To Mutrie's delight, they agreed to join him and Day in backing the club.

Lynch, it turned out, was also instrumental in locating a home field. While the ballplayer was getting his shoes shined at Earl's Hotel at the corner of Manhattan's Canal and Central streets, a precocious newsboy asked why Lynch's club went all the way to Brooklyn to play its games. "Why don't you go to the Polo Grounds and give us New York boys a chance to see the games?" he asked. Up until that time, no major-league team had played ball regularly in Manhattan; even the National League's New York Mutuals of 1876 were a ferryboat ride away in Brooklyn. In the 1870s, the Polo Grounds, located at 110th Street between Fifth and Sixth avenues, were exactly what the name suggested—a grounds where polo matches took place. Mutrie was dismayed to discover that it contained stables for the polo ponies and "was in poor shape for baseball." Still, the level, grassy field was surrounded by a fence, which made it useful for baseball, and the polo clubs rarely used it anymore. Although the grounds had previously been considered a bit too far uptown to draw spectators, having been carved from undeveloped meadows north of the city, the site had already been engulfed by New York's relentless northward expansion. Now the city's new elevated railroad was but a brief walk away. Mutrie took the plunge, rented the space, and laid out a baseball diamond. Soon, Day and Mutrie were packing in customers and reaping tremendous profits.

In 1883, the first year New York was represented in two major leagues, the Gothams and the Metropolitans shared the park, sometimes at the same time. The owners did it by dividing the spacious field into two cramped halves, separating them with a portable eight-foot-high canvas fence. On occasion, a ball would sneak over or under it, interrupting the game on the other side. The divided field removed all doubt that the Metropolitans, once the darlings of New York, had been relegated to second-class status. The Gothams, who charged an admission of fifty cents and catered to wealthier League fans, had first dibs on the superior Fifth Avenue side of the grounds. Their side featured a new double-decked grandstand. The Metropolitan club, which charged twenty-five cents for admission and appealed to a lower class of customer, had to make do with a shabbier stand that had been moved from the old site to the Sixth Avenue side.

Operating a club in a city as big, brassy, and money-obsessed as New York could present its challenges. On the rainy Saturday of April 7, during the spring exhibition season, a pair of young men came to the Polo Grounds and asked to speak to an employee, supposedly about buying a horse. "The employee was busy at the time, and after answering their questions left them to saunter out alone," a later investigation revealed, as reported by the *New York Herald*. But, rather than leave the ballpark, the visitors craftily concealed themselves at the Mets' Sixth Avenue gate. When a crowd formed, expecting a game would go in spite of the rain, the men coolly opened the gate and charged each person queuing up a quarter to get in. "After making quite a little haul the men cleared out and left the gate standing open," the *Herald* said. By then, Day and Mutrie had decided to call off that afternoon's game on account of the weather, only to confront about five hundred people seated in the Metropolitan club's grandstand. They had paid their way in and "refused to be pacified" until they got their money back. The furious Day organized a manhunt. Gothams manager John Clapp and the Polo Grounds watchman tracked down one of the thieves in the barroom of a roadhouse on Harlem Lane. They hauled him back to the ballpark, where, in the presence of a police detective, a number of spectators identified him as one of the men who had taken their money. The culprit, Harry Sheldon, lived near the ballpark at the corner of Fourth Avenue and 109th Street. Life in the big city required constant vigilance against rip-off artists.

It was here, on the Sixth Avenue side of the Polo Grounds, that the St. Louis Browns came to play on August 27, followed soon thereafter by their owner. One can only imagine Ted Sullivan's dismay upon discovering that Von der Ahe was on his way, no doubt to micromanage, second-guess his decisions, and undermine his authority, even though the Browns had won ten of their last twelve games, all on the road. Five months earlier,

Von der Ahe had gathered the men in the clubhouse and declared that they were under Sullivan's sole management, and that Sullivan would hold them responsible for their conduct. Back then, he claimed to be interested in a strong-willed manager with "a mind of his own." By late August, he seemed to have forgotten all of that.

Upon arriving in the mighty metropolis—the city he had first set foot in seventeen years earlier as a young immigrant from Westphalia—Von der Ahe immediately checked out the mental state of his players, who had made ugly headlines during the long road trip with their embarrassing late-night escapades. According to the *Republican*, he found them in remarkably good spirits and perfect discipline. "Nothing could be more unfounded than the reports of dissensions in the ranks of the St. Louis club, and they are all absurd fabrications," the newspaper reported, faithfully passing along the owner's spin. "Mr. Von der Ahe found everything quiet and placid, the men in the best condition and spirits and in considerably better shape than any of their present or prospective antagonists. There is no quarreling and no slugging going on"—except against enemy pitchers. Then he settled into his seat at the Polo Grounds to watch the action. In the Monday opener, St. Louis clobbered the superb Tim Keefe and the Mets, 8–3, before four thousand fans, to retain a half-game lead over the Athletics.

Von der Ahe's professed satisfaction with Ted Sullivan's managing was short-lived, unfortunately. In the second game at the Polo Grounds, on Wednesday, August 29, Sullivan finally gave a break to the exhausted Tony Mullane. He had been filling in for George McGinnis, who had rested for an entire week because of an aching, dead arm. It became obvious that the hefty McGinnis was still having problems, though, when New York pounded him without mercy, jumping to a 3–0 lead in the first. Von der Ahe, watching from the grandstand with increasing frustration, called Sullivan over and ordered him to replace McGinnis with Mullane. The request was "so absurd," Ted recalled, "that even the players laughed." Flatly refusing, Sullivan tried to explain to his boss why the switch would only hurt. "It's no use now," he supposedly told Von der Ahe. "The Mets have a deciding lead." It was more prudent to risk the loss of that game than to bring in Mullane yet again, tiring him out before the next game, and risking an arm injury that would effectively end the Browns' pennant chances. The Mets coasted to victory, 7–1, dropping the Browns to second place, .005 behind the Athletics in winning percentage. Von der Ahe was furious. The *New York Clipper* tried to point out the obvious point that the owner seemed unwilling to accept: "If President Von der Ahe wishes to see the St. Louis champions he had better let his manager run the team, and not interfere with him, otherwise defeat will likely follow."

Already angry that he had been defied in the afternoon, Von der Ahe grew angrier still late that night, when he made an impromptu bed check at the Broadway Central Hotel, at Broadway and Third. He found several beds empty of their assigned players, who were apparently out enjoying the nightlife of America's biggest city. Von der Ahe had just finished telling the St. Louis press before he left that he intended to crack the whip, and here was Sullivan failing to enforce his will. All season he had grappled with what he saw as Sullivan's poor decisions, weak discipline, and outright insubordination. Way back in the first week of the season, Sullivan had refused to yank Captain Loftus from the lineup at Von der Ahe's orders, forcing the owner to release the man—and then Sullivan had insisted on choosing the new captain himself. This very day, he had spurned orders to replace McGinnis in the box. Von der Ahe had been forced to deal with constant complaints about Sullivan's decisions: from Jack Gleason, who felt he had been played out of position; from McGinnis, who thought he had been overworked by the second game of the season; and from Dave Reid, who had long deplored Sullivan's every move. Von der Ahe had been forced to step in time and again to fine and discipline the players: McGinnis, for getting too fat; Deasley, for imbibing "spirituous liquors"; Latham, for foolishly trying to steal home; Lewis, for drinking too much. The owner had been forced to make excuses when Tom Mansell fell down an elevator shaft, and when Deasley and Lewis got arrested in Columbus.

Talking himself into a rage, Von der Ahe confronted Sullivan sometime after midnight. Though the manager had led the team to a remarkable number of wins on the road, with a strong chance of capturing the pennant, Von der Ahe was convinced that Sullivan was hurting the club by failing to enforce discipline, and he warned him to shape up. Astonished by the accusation, Sullivan "retorted warmly and . . . they had a very bitter passage of words." When Sullivan pointed out that he had turned the Browns around and made them one of the best teams in baseball, Von der Ahe pooh-poohed the notion. Von der Ahe complained that he, the owner, "had had most of the management to do himself and had to take hold several times at great inconvenience to himself." No doubt, he considered this hasty trip to New York a prime example of that.

For Sullivan, that was the last straw. "Chris had been interfering with me for a week or so before the climax came, and finally I could stand it no more," Sullivan recalled. "I told him I had enough of his interference and that he could take his club and run it." Ted pulled out the beautiful gold pocket watch that Von der Ahe had given him that spring—the one inscribed with the owner's thanks for Sullivan's efforts—and flung it at him. "I should not have done so, but I was at the impulsive stage of my life where I could not bear his inconsistency—especially when I had the Browns at the top of the list." Sullivan demanded his release, and Von der Ahe, red-faced with fury, gladly granted it.

At the height of the pennant race, with a month to go, in the middle of a big series in the great metropolis of New York, the Browns were suddenly bereft of the manager who had turned the next-to-last-place team of 1882 into a baseball machine on the verge of a championship.

THE EMBITTERED SULLIVAN QUICKLY EXPOSED SOME OF THE Browns' dirty laundry. "I have brought this club up to its present standing, and it is hard, after putting it in a fair way to win the championship, to be treated thus badly," he told the *New York Times*. "Mr. Von der Ahe understands but little about base-ball, and if I had obeyed all of his orders during the season, the club would be nearer the foot than the head in the race."

Sullivan caught a train for a long and lonely trip to St. Louis, leaving his pennant-contending club and its owner behind. As Von der Ahe cooled off, he seemed to realize he had made a terrible mistake. He pleaded with Sullivan to return. But the manager stubbornly refused. "He says he was badly treated by President Von der Ahe, and that he would never go back again to the club," the *Philadelphia Item* reported. Von der Ahe announced that, from here on out, he himself would manage the team and enforce its rules, though he turned over the daily leadership of the club to Charlie Comiskey, Sullivan's longtime protégé and friend.

Back in St. Louis, the stunning shakeup got mixed reviews. "Mr. Von der Ahe thinks that he, with the assistance of Comiskey, can successfully manage the affairs of the club for the remainder of the season," the *Globe-Democrat* reported, adding, doubtfully, "Whether he can or not will be seen by the future success of the club." By contrast, Dave Reid of the *Missouri Republican* was ecstatic that the arrogant little popinjay from Dubuque was gone. His paper hailed the departure:

GOOD-BY, SULLIVAN!

<hr/>

**The Browns at Last Relieved of
Their Disturbing Element.**

<hr/>

**Charley Comiskey to Manage the Club
the Balance of the Season.**

<hr/>

**Joe Quest's Debut at Second Base
Entirely Satisfactory.**

The last two lines referred to Sullivan's final gift to the club: the acquisition of yet another seasoned National Leaguer for the concluding weeks of the Browns' pennant drive. The five-foot-six Quest, the former star second baseman of the Chicago White Stockings, had great speed and quick reflexes, at least when he was at the peak of his performance. But he had not been quite the same since seeking his release at the end of the 1882 season, fleeing an ugly scandal and, perhaps, a husband's wrath.

A handsome, witty fellow, Quest had long eyelashes, a carefully waxed handlebar mustache, and a meticulously tailored wardrobe. Though he was short and starting to lose his hair, he had a suave way about him, and he had earned a reputation as one of baseball's most successful womanizers. "Joe, though not exactly a dude, is and has always been a mad masher," the *Cincinnati Commercial Gazette* asserted. "It has been his business ever since he played ball to break the fragile female heart. In nearly every case Joe has loved not wisely, but too well. His 'small difficulties' in Chicago have been as frequent as the moons of summer." One sportswriter playfully described him as a champion racehorse—almost, one might say, a stud: "He has plenty of style, is richly coated (it cost $6.50), is strong in the loins, has a good mouth, and is an excellent breaker (of cheap female hearts). He is in good health and is jogged every morning." Rumor had it that Joe's morning jog in the summer of 1882 came courtesy of a Mrs. Waters, an attractive woman who shared his boardinghouse on State Street.

In November that year, Hiram Waters, the thirty-one-year-old husband of Quest's lady friend, put a gun to his own chest and pulled the trigger. Hoping to uncover a titillating scandal, local reporters hustled to the victim's boardinghouse that night and began asking questions. The building's gossips had much to say. Mrs. Waters had gone to Boston a month earlier, supposedly to meet up with her lover, who was identified only as a well-known man who shared the same Chicago boardinghouse. While she was gone, her husband heard stories about his wife's infidelity. After drinking heavily off and on for four weeks, he went to his room and tried to kill himself. Neither the *Inter-Ocean* nor the *Chicago Tribune* named Mrs. Waters's suspected lover.

The *Chicago Herald* was the first paper to break the silence, identifying the man who had boarded with Mrs. Waters as none other than Joe Quest. "It seems Mrs. Waters became completely infatuated with him. She would go to the Base Ball Park at nearly every game last Summer, and was out with him frequently." Other big-city newspapers, including the *Philadelphia Item*, picked up the story and spread it further. While the press probed his private agony, Hiram Waters clung to life with the aid of a doctor who kept him under the influence of opium most of the time. Although the physician couldn't extract the ball from Waters's chest, he believed his patient might yet survive. Four days after the shooting, a "weary and excited" Mrs. Waters arrived from Boston and rushed to her husband's side.

Ted Sullivan, with his usual indifference to a player's personal foibles, sought out Joe Quest to fill in at second base for the weak-fielding George Strief, who could be moved to the outfield. But Quest brought something more than talent to St. Louis at its crucial hour—namely, a brain stuffed full of the hardball tricks and strategies he had learned while playing for Cap Anson alongside Mike "King" Kelly. Debuting for St. Louis on the day Sullivan quit, Quest "played a brilliant game, his one error being off a difficult shooting ball owing to rough ground. His batting was thin, but his handling of the ball in his double plays was very rapid."

Thanks in part to Sullivan's wise decision to rest Mullane, the Browns beat the Mets in the next two games, then took the short train ride to Philadelphia for a four-game September showdown against their last serious pennant rival. The Athletics had won 55 games and lost 25. The Browns, at 55 and 26, trailed by half a game.

When Sullivan returned to St. Louis to gather his belongings before returning to Dubuque, a reporter was waiting to get his side of the blowup. Sullivan chose to respond with dignified discretion. "There were some warm words which ended in my throwing up the management. That is the whole story," he said. But he felt the sting, much as he tried to hide it. He had worked hard to build this superb club, train it, and make it the best-coached and most aggressive team in the American Association, only to be compelled to leave before he could harvest his pennant. The worst part was that he still cared about his Browns, in spite of all he had been through. "I'm with the boys yet," he told the reporter, "and I am just as anxious to see them get there as ever."

And then he climbed aboard a railroad car, sat down, and went home.

12

JUMPING JACK

NYBODY WHO FOLLOWED PROFESSIONAL BASEBALL KNEW HOW much Bobby Mathews meant to the Philadelphia Athletics. Though the pitcher weighed only "a little over 100 pounds"—140, actually— "his importance is equal to the figure of a ton avoirdupois," the *Missouri Republican* had observed in early July, using a highfalutin word for weight. "Taken out of the Athletic team, he leaves that force a very ordinary one, and one which would win but few games. If he lasts through the excessive work he is being put to, he will probably win the pennant for the Philadelphias. If he does not, then there are chances for a very hot race."

He had not, in fact, lasted through the excessive work, and the race had indeed turned very hot. By the start of September, his dead arm hurt. His ankle was so sore he could barely walk, much less push off of it to get power behind his pitches. He had wrenched his back, and pains shot up his body when he moved the wrong way. If Philadelphians had truly known how he felt, they would have been deeply depressed about the Athletics' pennant chances, despite the team's half-game lead heading into the climactic home series of the 1883 season.

Instead, fanatics were smiling and chattering as they poured into Athletic Park on September 3, 1883, for the first of three against the St. Louis Browns. Months of struggling between the teams representing two of America's most baseball-crazed cities—the classy, hard-driving A's and the coarse, hard-bitten Browns—had come down to a series of vital importance to both. The people of Philadelphia knew it, and they began crowding the park early, even though Mondays were traditionally light for turnout. As a crowd grew into a mob, the Athletics crew nervously opened the front gate. The surging mass of men, eager for good seats, snapped it right off its hinges in a frenzy to get inside. This was the biggest crowd since the mob scene on Memorial Day. Half an hour before game time, every seat was filled. Ushers pointed latecomers onto the field, where they stood ten deep along the foul lines and the outfield fences. Boys had propped themselves up on every part of the fence where they could gain a precarious foothold, "with doubtful chances of holding on until the game was done." So many people were drifting across the field that pregame practice had to be canceled. The game was then delayed for fifteen minutes as police strained to push the crowd behind the foul lines. The captains huddled over ground rules, just as they had on Memorial Day, deciding that any fair balls hit into the crowd would be doubles. Von der Ahe, suddenly deprived of his manager, took his seat. If he was worried about the loss of Ted Sullivan, he was not letting on.

Philadelphia second baseman Cub Stricker was ready to play, having shaken off a dental disaster on August 30, two days before, when a ball smashed him in the face during practice, dislodging some of his teeth. But now Mathews, who had gamely struggled to an 11–5 victory over the New York Metropolitans on Saturday, was simply too weak and in too much pain to work. George Bradley, another crusty veteran who was just about finished as a major-league pitcher, got the nod. He took a 5–3 lead into the sixth inning, when the Browns struck back, their trademark aggressive base running flustering the Athletics into bobbling the ball. "The great strength of the St. Louis Club is the dashing manner in which they run bases and the manner in which their runners are coached," the *Philadelphia Inquirer* conceded. "They are by no means heavy hitters, but they manage to make every hit count." Four Browns runners crossed the plate in the waning innings, driving the Athletics down to defeat, 7–5, right out of first place.

Von der Ahe was ecstatic. "The Banner in Sight," the *Missouri Republican* headlined its analysis. "St. Louis has at last gained the position to which her magnificent work of late has certainly entitled her—first place," the paper crowed. "Their victory shows a diamond in a cluster of brilliant emeralds, and shows their magnificent quality of ball playing at this supreme moment. . . . Our chances for the championship are now better than those of any club in the association. Cincinnati concedes the banner to St. Louis."

That wasn't the worst of the trouble for the Athletics. The team was out of pitching now. Manager Lew Simmons couldn't hand the ball back to his ace for game two on Tuesday, because Mathews was still incapacitated, pathetically sore, and hobbled from his Saturday start. With the pennant slipping away, and with Bradley and Mathews spent forces, Simmons had little choice: he would have to gamble, giving the ball to a college kid, a rookie who had become a national buffoon, the butt of bad jokes in baseball circles. For weeks, Simmons had searched frantically for a pitcher who might fill the breach during the final four weeks of the season. In early September, just as the Browns headed for town, the *Philadelphia Record* passed along some important intelligence to local fanatics. Simmons had found someone. An unlikely twenty-two-year-old would be given a try-out. "If he is effective he will be retained for the remainder of the season," the *Record* said. It was an act of desperation, but at this point, a desperate chance was better than none at all.

His name was Daniel Albion Jones Jr. His late father, also named Daniel Albion Jones, was a Connecticut dentist, revered in the community as a public speaker and philanthropist. The ballplayer's mother, Emeline Roberts Jones, had married the dentist at the age of eighteen. For some reason, she had quickly become "intensely interested" in her husband's line of work—to the elder Daniel's apparent shock and discomfort, since well-bred women simply weren't supposed to have anything to do with such work, other than to cower from it. After watching him toil—and nineteenth-century dentistry could be awfully grisly—she began experimenting with teeth that her husband had extracted from patients, secretly practicing at filling them until she had a two-quart jar's worth of her work to show him. Reluctantly, he took her into his practice in May 1855. Four years later, he made her his full partner—the first woman in America to establish herself in a regular dental practice. By then, this odd couple of dentists had a daughter, and young Dan followed. Hard times struck the family in June 1864 when the elder Daniel died, leaving Emeline to fend for herself with a three-year-old son and a six-year-old daughter. The widow carried on her work, traveling with a portable dentist's chair through eastern Connecticut and Rhode Island, while bravely providing for the children and giving them every advantage. In 1876, she began a lucrative practice in New Haven, and the son she doted on prepared for college at the Hopkins Grammar School before entering Yale with the class of 1883. By then, young Dan had mastered the art of throwing a baseball, and he quickly became the college's star pitcher, leading Yale to successive Ivy League titles—in effect, making his team national champion. He had also mastered the arts of singing and whistling, skills he put to good use with Yale's glee club. He joined the Delta Kappa Epsilon fraternity, whose members have included five U.S. presidents.

Yale baseball team, 1883; Daniel Jones is standing at center.
Al Hubbard is seated next to him with catcher's mask
(*Transcendental Graphics*/theruckerarchive.com; *reprinted with permission*)

Jones was pondering a career as a lawyer, but he needed money if he was to attend law school after his undergraduate studies. The obvious answer, given the great talent with which he had been blessed, was professional baseball. Even before his spring semester was over, pitching-starved professional clubs entered into a fierce bidding war for his services. The Athletics, Orioles, and Phillies offered him fabulous amounts, bigger money, even, than was made by some of the game's established stars. In the end, the National League's Detroit club—having dumped Tom Mansell's contract to help free up the money—outbid the others, reportedly paying the college kid a whopping $625 per month, at a time when a $400-a-month baseball salary was considered lavish. Jones made clear that making money for the summer was his top priority. "He can only play ball until Sept. 15, when he resumes his studies," the *Detroit Evening News* reported.

Thus, without a day's experience in the professional ranks, Dan Jones jumped straight to baseball's top league. There, he won six of eleven decisions, letting up ten hits for every nine innings he pitched—fair work for a rookie, though not much to cheer about, given the fevered anticipation he stirred and the enormous salary he commanded. The *National Police Gazette* considered the Jones hiring, all in all, little short of a disaster. "The Detroits slung out big money, took chances in a lottery, and got badly left," the paper observed. "Again and again they tried to make a pitcher out of this big soap-bubble, but they might just as well have tried training a pet poodle dog." Still, Jones's paycheck was not the thing that sparked the most talk. The thing that had people buzzing, if not laughing out loud, was the absurd way he threw.

The twenty-two-year-old hurled a fastball with a motion unlike any ever before used by a major-league pitcher: He leapt up into the air as he released the ball, flinging his arms and legs out in a manner that reminded reporters of a child's jumping jack. It was a ludicrous sight, a college boy's silly stunt that seemed completely out of place at baseball's top level. "Towards the close of the game, when performing his particular jumping act, he was the laughing stock of players and spectators," the *Buffalo Commercial Advertiser* reported. "Even some of the Detroiters mimicked his clownish actions, and Galvin at the bat laughed in his face." The sportswriter obviously found this young hotshot more than a bit annoying.

Though Jones was a "handsome fellow, and fresh as a daisy," he was clearly not as wonderful as he and his press clippings had led the public to believe, he observed. "If the blush of modesty ever mantled his cheek, it is not within our knowledge. He may be a 'great pitcher' in the estimation of some critics, but if so, then the standard by which he is judged good must be a low one."

By September, Detroit agreed. Far out of first place, it unceremoniously dumped the outlandish pitcher and his enormous salary. By then, the desperate manager of the ailing Athletics, Lew Simmons, was there to swoop in and grab him, regardless of the pitcher's obvious limitations. Simmons reportedly made the young man a handsome offer of $500 for one month's work (pending his try-out)—less than Detroit had given him, but still enough to make Jones one of the game's best-paid players on a per-month basis. Yes, people would laugh at the lad's freakish pitching motion, and they might well mock Simmons for spending so much money on such a bizarre player. But there were simply no strong professional pitchers to be had. If Jones, now bearing the nickname of "Jumping Jack," could somehow help the hobbled Athletics stay in the hunt during the final month of the season, Simmons would consider him a bargain.

PUFFING ON A FAT CIGAR, THE POT-BELLIED VON DER AHE WAS A conspicuous sight in his checkered three-piece suit and derby. He traded quips in a thick German accent, shook hands boisterously, and thwacked the backs of well-wishers, before settling, with a sigh of happiness, into his grandstand seat at Philadelphia's Athletic Park to watch his Browns do battle in the second match of this four-game series against the Athletics. He had reason to feel good. The Browns were in first place, on the brink of the pennant. Tom Mansell was back in left field, though the slugger's knee was still stiff after his plunge into the elevator shaft. And the owner surely felt that the big crowd that day was a testament to his wisdom in helping to found the American Association. The critics might scoff, but Americans loved the Beer and Whiskey League. Now it was time to enjoy. With a weakened Bobby Mathews, the Athletics did not look so indomitable anymore. No one could seriously think that a college kid would fill the breach, even one as heavily hyped as this Yale boy. Von der Ahe sat back to see what all the fuss was about.

Dan Jones strode to the pitcher's box in front of the biggest crowd that had ever watched him play. The fanatics seemed more subdued than they had been on Monday, perhaps sensing the implications of this game. This strange young man with a cocky demeanor, dark mustache, and sparkling eyes held the fate of the 1883 season in his hands that day. "There was perfect silence when he took his position," the *Philadelphia Times* reported. Bill Gleason, the brawny volunteer fireman, decidedly no college man, took his place in the batter's box and glared at the rookie. Jones nervously pitched three balls wide of the plate. He got the ball back and held it in his hands for a while, staring in at his catcher. Jones knew what he had to do. "Then he jumped two feet in the air, and while Gleason gazed at him in astonishment the ball traveled squarely over the center of the plate and one strike was called," the *Times* said. "'Jumping Jack' jumped again, and Gleason aimed at a ball two feet from the end of his bat. He jumped again on the next ball and Gleason was called out on strikes."

Von der Ahe and the Philadelphia crowd could barely believe it. It was ridiculous, ludicrous. Spectators looked at each other, laughed, and pointed in amazement as Jones made his celebrated leap three or four times per inning, usually when there were two strikes on the batter. "No one else can get it. It is taught exclusively at Yale," the *Philadelphia Press* informed its readers. "His antics in the pitcher's box, by jumping up and cracking his heels on every other ball pitched, was very amusing to the crowd." It was less so to the Browns hitters, who had trouble adapting. "You don't know whether Jones or the ball is coming for you," one player explained in frustration. Through five innings, Jumping Jack led 6–1. Then he poured it on, retiring the last twelve men in succession. In the eighth inning, with the Athletics leading 11–1, the deliriously happy crowd began taunting the Browns by whistling the "Dead March" in unison. When Jones struck out the last batter to end the game, recapturing first place for the Athletics, spectators flung their derby hats in the air and jumped onto the field. They quickly surrounded the pitcher, heaved him up, and bore him on their shoulders to the dressing room. The Yale boy was an instant Philadelphia sports hero—"the most popular man who ever played ball on the Athletic grounds," the *Philadelphia Press* declared the next day.

Von der Ahe, whose tantrums had just cost him a manager, was furious over the thrashing his team had received at the hands of this bizarre specimen. Immediately after the 11–1 debacle, Von der Ahe ordered the men to report to his hotel room. "The boys soon came up," the *New York Times* reported. "There was not a smile. They arranged themselves around the room—some on the bed, others on chairs, and still others lounged on the velvet carpet of the wealthy president's room. Von der Ahe gazed upon the crowd, and the crowd with their still unwashed faces glared back at him."

Finally, Von der Ahe spoke. "Vhy did you loose dot game today?"

There was dead silence. Then Arlie Latham, glancing at his teammates, offered an answer. "Why, you see, boss, we had devilish hard luck." Yes, nodded his fellow players, hard luck explained it.

"Von der Ahe gazed upon his nine. His nine glared back. He knew they had often won games for him. He also remembered how many fines he had paid and how many bad bonds he was on. He turned his eyes upon the stolid countenance of Lewis, and then a smile rippled across his Teutonic face as he said: 'Vell, boys, if it was hard luck dot settles it. You can't win a game ven you have hard luck. Dot's so. Dot vas all right.'" The players, relieved that he had no further destructive stunts in mind, all shook Von der Ahe's hand, then "fled down to the dining room, where they terrified the colored waiters with their orders for supper."

Athletics Captain Lon Knight faced a tough choice in game three: he could either go with one of his struggling pitchers, who were a good bet to lose, or gamble that Jumping Jack had enough pop left to pitch effectively for a second straight day. He went with Jumping Jack. Unfortunately, the tired Jones proved much less intimidating this time, "and his prance showed little of the pristine vigor that reduced the temperature for St. Louis the day before." Before a third straight sellout crowd, the Athletics jumped to the lead in the first inning, thanks to an error and wild throw by Joe Quest. The Browns struck back in the fourth, when Athletics shortstop Fred Corey fumbled a pop fly with two out, letting the fleet-footed Arlie Latham scoot across the plate with the tying run. A seesaw battle ensued. In the bottom of the ninth, the Browns—who had won the pregame coin flip and were batting last—came up, trailing 5–3. Hugh Nicol led off with a single, sneaking to second and third when

Jones's pitches got away from catcher Jack O'Brien, who was still getting accustomed to the new man. Then Quest looped the ball to short center field, sending second baseman Cub Stricker madly back-peddling. Stricker "tripped and fell as his fingers closed on the ball," and Nicol, tagging up, narrowed the score to 5–4.

There was now one man out in the ninth, with nobody on base. The Athletics were two outs away from a victory that would drop the Browns one and a half games behind. But "things began to look shaky once more," the *Philadelphia Record* noted. George McGinnis blasted a long drive to deep left field that sent the Athletics' Jud Birchall sprinting straight to the fence. At the last moment, Birchall turned his face into the blinding glare of the sinking afternoon sun and made the difficult catch for out number two. The Athletics appeared to be home safe when Tom Dolan skied a pop-up in front of home plate. But the new pitcher's inexperience cost the Athletics. "It was clearly Jones' ball, but he seemed loath to try for it, motioning for O'Brien to take it," the *Record* said. The exhausted catcher made a valiant effort and got his hand on the ball, but it bounced off, and Dolan stood safe on first base. George Strief followed with a single through the pitcher's box into center field, and suddenly the tying run was on second, the winning run on first.

Bill Gleason, a .287 hitter that season, then came to the plate. An extra-base hit would give his Browns the victory. Gleason hammered the ball, scorching a grounder down the third-base line. Grin Bradley reached out reflexively, gripped the spinning ball, and tagged third for the force out, ending a magnificent, emotionally draining game. Jumping Jack, frazzled and exhausted, had delivered two crucial victories for the Athletics.

On Thursday, after three successive sellouts, the biggest crowd of the week stormed Athletic Park. Lew Simmons, personally collecting tickets, "estimated that his hands passed over no less than 13,500 pasteboards [tickets] at the entrance to the grounds." With season tickets and other admissions, that made for about 15,000 spectators, and a stunning 50,000 for the series. Much again was at stake: when the day was done, St. Louis would either be a mere half-game behind, or two and a half back, a serious deficit with only three weeks left in the season. Pennant-crazed Philadelphians were at the park hours before game time, and they swarmed onto the field when the stands were full. Police strung a rope down the foul lines and in the outfield to keep the mob away from the players. Several hundred boys and men hoisted themselves over the fence at the unattended corner of Twenty-sixth and Master streets, dropping down into the grounds without paying the twenty-five-cent admission.

Jumping Jack needed a rest. Matthews, unnervingly, was still too hobbled to pitch, so the duty fell by default to Bradley. The Athletics built him a 3–1 lead, but St. Louis battled back to tie it. As the game entered the late innings, the tension became excruciating. When the Athletics' Fred Corey led off the seventh inning, promisingly, with a double, the Browns fought desperately to hold him to second. A pop fly sent second baseman Joe Quest on a sharp run into right field to grab the first out. Another ball soared to right field, but the Browns' Hugh Nicol caught and returned the ball "so perfectly that Corey dared not move from second." Then, with two out, Cub Stricker slapped a grounder past third base to score Corey with the go-ahead run. The Athletics led, 4–3.

St. Louis entered the bottom of the ninth needing a run to tie, two to win. Quest, the first man up, hit a sharp ball to third baseman Corey, who made a great stop and gunned him out at first base. The next Browns hitter, Pat Deasley, got things going with a single. He quickly moved to second base when a pitch scooted past catcher John O'Brien. Now the tying run was in scoring position. The Athletics should have been able to breathe easier after Tony Mullane hit a weak fly ball to left field, but Jud Birchall, a twenty-four-year-old Philadelphia native in the middle of an undistinguished three-year major-league career, "muffed" it "most ingloriously." Fortunately for the Athletics, Deasley held to second, fearing he would have been doubled off or thrown out. Now, with only one out, there were two runners on base. "With one accord," the *Record* said, "every heart in the audience came up into its owner's throat as it all at once became evident that a good long hit by Strief, who was next at bat, would surely bring in one run, which would tie the game, and possibly two, which would win it."

The crowd fell silent as ball one was called. Bradley's second pitch flew right over the plate, and Strief walloped it, just as Athletics fanatics had feared. As "the ball sailed out over right field," Deasley tore for third base with every intention of scoring the tying run. Right fielder Lon Knight, recognizing immediately that the line drive was screaming his way, "turned and ran with the ball a few steps, and then turning, sprang up and caught it with both hands as it was passing over his head."

Before the crowd had time even to register what was happening, Knight threw a bullet to first baseman Harry Stovey. Base runner Tony Mullane, who had halted between first and second to see whether Knight would catch the ball, barely managed to get back to first in time. But Stovey fired the ball to Cub Stricker, catching Deasley dead at second base, to complete the double play, ending the game in stunning fashion. "The shout raised was instantaneous and deafening," the *Record* reported. The mob instantly plowed through the ropes, and two to three thousand people swarmed over the field. Knight was surrounded, and "nearly smothered in enthusiasm," while other players were "badly jostled" as they fought their way to the dressing room amid an "excited throng waving hats and cheering lustily." The captain's extraordinary catch had saved the game, the series, and, quite possibly, the season. It was an amazing turn of events: the Athletics—thanks to Jumping Jack and their own perseverance—had beaten the Browns in three straight, taking a daunting two-and-a-half-game lead in the standings with fourteen left to play. "ST. LOUIS SURRENDERS," the *Philadelphia Press* declared in a lead headline, adding: "St. Louis has gone Westward in sackcloth and ashes." But Dave Reid of the *Missouri Republican* thought that there was little for Philadelphia to crow about: "Nothing but the sheerest hard luck kept St. Louis from winning three out of the four games, and the superiority of the Western team was patent to everyone who saw the games," he wrote.

———◦———

KNIGHT'S CELEBRATED CATCH MARKED THE END OF THE ATHLETICS' home season for 1883, at least according to the official schedule. But the resourceful Lew Simmons had managed to tack on two more home games by persuading the Columbus Buckeyes to move two contests from its park to Philadelphia. There, the gate take would be much bigger (and there, of course, the Athletics would have the home-field advantage). Cincinnati and St. Louis wasted no time filing formal protests with Association headquarters, bitterly complaining that the Chicago White Stockings had used the same ploy to steal the National League pennant from the Providence Grays in 1882 by shifting a crucial series from Buffalo to the Windy City.

Von der Ahe was naturally livid, and he threatened to overturn the championship at the Association's annual meeting in December, should the Athletics end up winning the pennant by a game or two. "Playing games away from the cities in which they are scheduled is not right, and takes away the interest in the game," he complained, with great justice—but to no avail.

Jumping Jack Jones, who got the assignment to pitch the first of the two games against the Columbus club, chose to take it easy. Hampered by muscle cramps, he had stopped performing his celebrated jump, and "the crowd began to call out to him requesting an exhibition." The Yale man obliged, striking out a Columbus batter with the help of his leap, "to the intense satisfaction of the spectators." He pitched the Athletics to an easy 5–2 victory. His record in four days with the Athletics was three wins, zero defeats.

Bradley worked the second Columbus game at Philadelphia. In the fourth inning, with the score still 0–0, he fired a ball that Columbus second baseman Pop Smith fouled straight back. It glanced off the mask of catcher Ed Rowen and struck umpire Mike Walsh flush in the face, dropping him to the ground "as if shot." For a second, Walsh, who had been foolishly umpiring without a mask, lay motionless, "as one dead," while a doctor who had dashed down from the stands tried to bring him back to consciousness with water and then liquor. Walsh "was soon seized with convulsions, and his unconscious struggles were piteous to see." Finally, the prostrate umpire had to be hauled off the field comatose to his room at the Bingham House hotel.

The two teams, bereft of an official umpire, agreed to play the rest of the game as an exhibition that would not count in the standings. Lon Knight, careful to spare Bradley's arm, moved second baseman Cub Stricker to the pitcher's box. From that point on, the *New York Clipper* reported, "the game was of the burlesque order." Stricker whipped up the crowd by imitating Jones's absurd jumping jacks. Columbus won, and the Athletics' regular season in Philadelphia was over. The makeup game would be played in Columbus, where it should have been played in the first place. Later that night, when Walsh came to, he found he had suffered a broken nose—the price for failing to wear a mask, a mistake fewer umpires would make as time went on. That night, in a state akin to shock, he caught a train with the Athletic and Columbus clubs for Columbus.

Though the Athletics held the lead, they now faced as severe a challenge as they had seen all season: winning the pennant while finishing up with thirteen straight games on the road. The Athletics would pass through Columbus, Cincinnati, St. Louis, and Louisville before returning home either as champions or failures. Jumping Jack, who had passed his audition in dramatic fashion, packed his bags and traveled with his new teammates for the first time. He was going to miss the first couple of weeks of his senior year at Yale.

Philadelphia buzzed with triumphant chatter about the Athletics and their quirky new hero. The *Item* sent off the first-place club with a couple of celebratory cartoons. One showed the balding Lew Simmons, standing in his three-piece suit, pulling on the string of a jumping jack toy. "This is what beat you, Von der Ahe," read the caption. A scrunched, gnomish figure, with a curly mustache and a monocle, labeled Von der Ahe, is seated below on the edge of his chair, shaking his fist. "Vas dot so?" the figure asks. "Vell, by tam, I gets me two shumping Jack pitchers when I get me mit Cent Louis!"

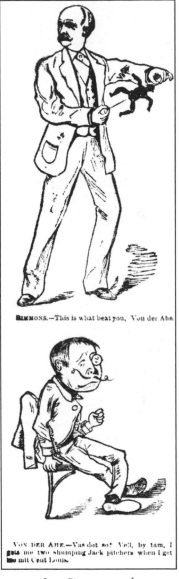

SIMMONS.—This is what beat you, Von der Ahe.

VON DER AHE.—Vas dot so? Vell, by tam, I gets me two shumping Jack pitchers when I get me mit Cent Louis.

Lew Simmons and Chris Von der Ahe, Philadelphia Item, September 9, 1883 (Library of Congress)

13

HURRICANE IN ST. LOUIS

CHARLIE MASON, LULLED BY THE RHYTHMIC CLICK OF THE wheels over the tracks, stared vacantly at the little towns and telegraph poles that leapt by his coach window. Leaving behind the cigar store and "Athletics headquarters" he had just opened at 139 North Eighth Street with some of the money that had poured into his pockets this year, the thirty-year-old co-owner of the Philadelphia Athletics was on something of a rescue mission, taking a fast train from Philly to Columbus so he could watch over the boys as they finished up there. Then he would accompany them to Cincinnati and, finally, to St. Louis, for the series that would, in all likelihood, decide the 1883 American Association pennant.

Winning this thing wouldn't be easy. Those Browns, even without the help of the manager who had brought them so far, would surely be terrors in their yard—unless Von der Ahe suspended more of their stars. Fortunate enough to spend their last fourteen games at home, they would be sleeping each night in the comfort of their own beds and waking refreshed, while Mason's Athletics would be on the move, eating bad food, racing to catch trains, breathing ash and getting singed by cinder through the open windows of the cars, grabbing rest in sleeper berths and strange hotel rooms, and playing every day before hostile fans.

Sportswriter Al Spink remembered these Athletics as "a happy-go-lucky crowd, both owners and players," who "did pretty much as they liked both on and off the field." It might have seemed that way to someone used to Von der Ahe's slightly more heavy-handed approach, but Mason applied discipline in his own way. A former professional player who was only slightly older than the boys, Mason forged a bond with them. He knew how to take care of problems, steady the young men's nerves, and enforce a curfew, keeping them away from their habitual diversions of hard liquor and painted ladies. As one reporter noted, Mason "watched their movements as steadily as an old hen would watch her brood of chickens" and instructed the men to postpone their nocturnal "sightseeing" until November. "By this system every player retired bright and early, and all arose feeling refreshed and in perfect health." With all the chips riding on these last several games, he didn't need any exhausted, distracted, or hungover men on his hands.

The team had enough problems. They were still in first place, having just beaten the Columbus Buckeyes 10–3 in their road opener on September 9. But Columbus was Columbus—one of the worst teams in the Association, an expansion franchise that depended on a mediocre pitcher from the local school for the deaf and mute, the crudely nicknamed "Dummy" Dundon, who had lost his hearing at the age of five after suffering typhoid fever. The teams that were next up, Cincinnati and St. Louis, were much tougher adversaries. And Philadelphia still had a serious problem with pitching. Bobby Mathews had become little more than a physical wreck, and George Bradley was just about played out as well. He had managed to beat Columbus, and would be a gritty competitor to the last, but his glory days as a top pitcher were long over. That left the new kid, "Jumping Jack" Jones, the Glee Club whistler and lady dentist's son. Not even a week after his brilliant debut, unfortunately, there were already signs that the twenty-two-year-old was not going to be as strong as Lew Simmons had hoped. American Association batters were quickly adjusting to his ridiculous leap. What's more, after a full season at Yale University, twelve games for Detroit, and now several for the Athletics, Jones seemed tired and edgy.

That was another reason Mason had made this emergency trip. Sitting next to him in the swaying railroad car was Jones's college catcher, Captain Allie Hubbard. Though Hubbard was not really a major-league-caliber player, Mason hoped the former classmate and buddy would steady the young pitcher, the way a friendly old horse in the stall might calm a skittish Kentucky thoroughbred. With Mason's connivance, the Massachusetts-born catcher was traveling under the pseudonym of Benjamin West, hoping his foray into the degrading world of pro baseball could be kept a secret from his parents. They did not savor the idea of their Yale-educated son spending his September with hardened drunks and womanizers. But reporters quickly saw through the ruse and identified poor Hubbard.

The pair arrived in Columbus in time for the Wednesday, September 12, game. "West" sat on the bench, getting a feel for the professional game and watching his college pal take the field without him. As expected, Jumping Jack "greatly amused the spectators by his peculiar movements." But the joke had worn thin for his teammates, who could plainly see that enemy batters were starting to whack Jones hard. Columbus jumped out to a 5–3 lead, and seemed to be coasting toward victory, until the irrepressible Harry Stovey blasted a home run to tie the game in the eighth inning, helping to push it to extra innings. In the top of the tenth, Stovey came through again, slapping a single and dashing all the way home on a triple by Lon Knight. Columbus threatened again in the tenth, and though Jones shut the Buckeyes down to win, 7–5, it was clear he was no longer dominant.

Behind Bradley, the Athletics swept the series with an 11–5 win the next day. Stovey was brilliant yet again, making a one-handed stab of a line shot that might have been good for a triple, saving at least two runs. But the Athletics knew their next Ohio foe would be much tougher. Although the Reds were out of the pennant race by now—seven games behind with nine to play—they had a splendid winning percentage of .618; a pitcher, in Will White, who was one of the best in the game; the most powerful offense in the Association; and a keen desire to play spoiler. Certainly, they were capable of quickly wiping out the three-game lead that the Athletics had smuggled through Columbus.

Jumping Jack got the nod for the opener at Cincinnati's Bank Street Grounds, and 2,200 people paid their way in to see the famous leaping twirler. For the first time, the Athletics teamed Jones with his college catcher, hoping Hubbard might coax a better performance out of him. "They are without doubt the strongest college battery ever turned out," O. P. Caylor enthused. But would the college battery be a strong professional one? Not in Cincinnati, where the Yale pitcher seemed more like a sideshow freak than a serious competitor. Each time he went to his "peculiar delivery," he won "cheers and laughter" from the Cincinnati crowd. "It was really amusing and was in exact imitation of a jumping jack," Caylor reported. "He jumps fully two feet from the ground, throws his heels up as he jumps, and delivers the ball as he alights." Reds first baseman John Reilly promptly sat down and sketched a hilarious caricature of Jones in motion, which was published a few days later in the paper.

But Jones's jumping utterly failed to deceive the strong Reds hitters. "Though the Cincinnati nine had never faced him before or saw him pitch," Caylor observed, "they sized him up from the first and thumped

"Jumping Jack" Jones,
by John Reilly, Cincinnati Commercial Gazette,
September 19, 1883 (Library of Congress)

him" for thirteen hits. The Athletics, by contrast, could manage only four scattered singles against the Reds' incomparable hurler. "Will White is not a jumping jack," Caylor remarked wryly, "but he manages to pitch a good, steady game standing still." Cincinnati ended up slaughtering Philadelphia, 11–0. It was a "Waterloo" for the Athletics, a shockingly inept performance for a first-place club this late in the season, and a warning sign that Philadelphia might not make it to the finish line in first place, with the Browns close behind them.

Having lost faith in Jones and fearful of overworking the weak Bradley, Mason saw little choice in the second Cincinnati game but to start the Athletics' crippled ace, Bobby Mathews. Taking advantage of a stiff September wind, the Reds proceeded to pound poor Bobby. This time, though, Will White was no better, finding that "his arm was as unruly as a colt" after his shutout performance three days earlier. The Athletics built a 10–4 lead before the weakening Mathews surrendered eight runs in the seventh inning. Philadelphia fought back to tie the game, 12–12, sending it into extra innings. In the bottom of the tenth, the ubiquitous Harry Stovey dug in at the plate. Earlier that afternoon, he had clubbed a double, and then his fourteenth home run—the most that had ever been hit in a single season of big-league baseball. (Ned Williamson beat Stovey's record one year later; and a man named Babe Ruth later beat Williamson's, with twenty-nine home runs in 1919.) This time, Stovey snuck an infield single past White, dashed to second on a wild pitch, and got to third on an out. When a pitch ticked off the hands of catcher Pop Snyder, Stovey daringly broke for home as the catcher frantically raced for the ball. Harry outsprinted Pop to the plate with the winning run.

The frightfully narrow 13–12 victory halted an Athletics collapse, but it also laid bare the woeful state of Philadelphia's pitching. Jones couldn't get the job done. Mathews was a ruin. Bradley would have to do the best he could in the third and rubber game of the series, on Wednesday, September 19. As usual, he found himself treated to Cincinnati spectators' frowns, boos, and catcalls—the price he paid for his fierce competitiveness, marked by his nasty habit of hitting batters. "Probably no man in the profession is so disliked here as he," Caylor noted. "It does not follow, however, that he deserves it, for in many ways George is a good sort of fellow. He plays for his side with all his soul every time, and never ceases to work to win, all of which should go to any ball-player's credit."

He earned the spectators' ill will that day, though, pounding two Cincinnati batters with pitches and trying his best to intimidate others. But he could not scare off the Reds, who feasted on his delivery for seventeen hits, including three triples and two home runs, to the joy of the assembled Bradley-bashers. "The grin which had adorned the face of 'George Washington' left him in the ninth, and was succeeded by a look most ghastly as the red-legged lads jumped onto him," the *Enquirer* reported. "Oh! how he suffered," Caylor exulted. "The crowd of sixteen hundred spectators greeted his terrific thumping with volume after volume of glorified yells and shouts." Though Bradley himself hit a home run, Cincinnati humbled Philadelphia, 12–3. It marked the third straight time an Athletics starter had surrendered eleven or more runs, and the second loss in three games against a good club. The pennant that had seemed to be Philadelphia's was rapidly unraveling. And now, in this pitiful condition, the Athletics had to climb aboard a train and make the 300-mile trip west to St. Louis, where they would face their most talented rivals.

———◆———

CHRIS VON DER AHE AND THE BROWNS CAUGHT THE 10 P.M. TRAIN out of Philadelphia on Thursday night, September 6. After a "long and tedious journey" on the Ohio & Mississippi Railroad, they chugged into St. Louis on Saturday at 6 P.M. Giving the owner no chance to rest, reporter Dave Reid knocked at Von der Ahe's door at the corner of St. Louis and Grand that evening. Once he was welcomed inside, he began peppering Der Boss President with questions. Despite the trip's disastrous ending, Von der Ahe seemed to be in high spirits, speaking of the "pleasure it afforded him, of meeting old Eastern friends, in both social and business life." He was terse about parting ways with Ted Sullivan, stating that he had fired the manager, thus denying Ted the dignity of his claim that he had quit. "At one of the games McGinnis started to pitch, and was hit hard. I told him to put in Mullane, who was playing in that game. He disregarded my orders and I released him."

But Von der Ahe was more effusive about boisterous Philadelphia crowds—telling Reid with amusement about their habit of whistling the

"Dead March" in the eighth inning, whichever team was trailing—then going into the details of the games. The 11–1 defeat at the hands of Jumping Jack Jones was "a fair and square routing," he said, but it was the only real beating the Browns had suffered that week. The following day, the Browns lost by one run only because of uncharacteristically poor base running. "Just when the boys ought to have kept a cool head, they became over anxious," Von der Ahe said. "We outplayed the Athletics at every point and the game should have been ours." He attributed the final 4–3 defeat to wretched fortune and bad umpiring by Charlie Daniels. "We again outplayed them everywhere but they managed to work in their bull-headed luck and capture a game, which in every respect was rightfully ours. Daniels gave us the worst of it on close decisions." So, in his view, the Browns had been anything but overmatched in Philadelphia, and remained in a great position to beat out the Athletics for the pennant. "I wouldn't give our position for theirs. We have no more Cincinnati and Eclipse games, and they play both of these clubs away from home," he said.

For all his reputed ignorance of the sport, there was something to his analysis. The Browns began their home stand against the cellar-dwelling Baltimore Orioles, whose most useful acquisition over the long season may have been new road uniforms. "The old and trampish-looking gray uniforms" that had been "a genuine eye sore" had been junked, said the *St. Louis Globe-Democrat*, and replaced by "white flannel suits, blue caps and penitentiary-striped stockings." Thirteen thousand spectators filled Sportsman's Park on Sunday, September 9, to welcome their beloved Browns home. Shortly after the Orioles appeared on the field, "a gong sounded and then the well-known forms of the six-week absentees were seen filing from the dressing-room," according to the *Missouri Republican*. "A loud shout went up, which grew in volume, and was maintained until the men reached the diamond and broke for their positions. It was evident that the public were of the opinion that the lads were still in a good position for the championship." During the Browns' absence, Grounds Superintendent Solari had gotten the field into lovely shape and spruced up the grandstand, painting the top scrollwork blue, the middle of the stands white, and the wainscoting a dark red. It made "the grounds look brighter and prettier than they ever did before," as the *St. Louis Globe-Democrat* put it. The one disappointment was Tom Mansell's gashed leg, which had finally "straightened out" but was still stiff, forcing him to sit out more games. But the boys looked good without him, hammering Baltimore, 10–2, behind a five-hitter by Tony Mullane. Joe Quest, the club's newest star, "was especially applauded for his quick pick-ups and throws and sharp stealing of bases."

Von der Ahe's men were even more impressive the next day. They won 15–4 and made no errors in the field, a noteworthy achievement in those days of bare hands, bumpy infields, and baseballs that became lopsided as the game went on. Right fielder Hugh Nicol, the favorite of the small boys in the bleachers, was at the peak of his game. In six trips to the plate, "he made five corking hits and as many runs. These latter were made by as daring and reckless base running as was ever witnessed," said the *Globe-Democrat*. Twice the diminutive player dove face-first into home plate, touching it with his hand just ahead of the ball. The next day the Browns made it three straight against Baltimore with a 6–2 victory, to remain two and a half games behind the Athletics.

One more win would have made for a four-game sweep, slicing a game off Philadelphia's lead. But Orioles rookie Bob Emslie stunned almost everyone by holding the Browns to only three hits in a 3–0 shutout, embarrassing the Browns' batters before a large Thursday afternoon crowd, adorned by pretty women in lavish hats who had turned out for Ladies' Day. "Why is it that the Browns can not play ball, even a little bit, on 'ladies' day'?" one letter writer to the *Globe-Democrat* asked in anguish. Back in Philadelphia, a crowd milling outside Mason's new cigar store bellowed with joy when the news came over the telegraph wire. "About 100 persons shouted in unison: 'That settles it!'" Not quite—but the Browns were now three games behind the Athletics with only nine left to play. "Nothing short of a miracle will save the pennant to the Mound City," Dave Reid lamented. "There is a chance, but a slender one."

Owner Chris Von der Ahe, to no one's surprise, was livid over the defeat, and he complained bitterly to Captain Charlie Comiskey, according to the *Philadelphia Item*.

"See here, Sharley, I brodest [protest] dot game," Von der Ahe fumed.

"On what ground?" Comiskey asked.

"Oh, vell, I brodest it. Dot umpire vas no goot. You go dell him, Sharley, dot I vas looking at him."

Sportswriters in those days often made up such discussions, poking fun at the German magnate. But Von der Ahe's actual response to the Thursday defeat was almost as outlandish as that apparently fictional one. On Friday night, after an off-day, Von der Ahe gathered his men for a meeting in his home. The session was mainly to discuss 1884 contracts, but he also informed them that he had been forced to perform "a very unpleasant duty"—that of expelling slugger Fred Lewis, the Browns' only .300 hitter (besides the hobbled Mansell), leaving the club bereft of the veteran's services during the season's last, desperate days. "Lewis was intoxicated yesterday and the night previous and behaved very badly," Von der Ahe explained. "For his erratic conduct and drunkenness he received the full penalty of the rules—expulsion." The owner was particularly miffed that a drunken Lewis, that very morning, had "called to me in a loud tone of voice and asked for his release, using some rude language in connection with the demand." Though the New York Metropolitans were willing to buy his contract for $500, the enraged Von der Ahe preferred to swallow the loss and teach Lewis a lesson by expelling him. It was hard to imagine the Browns winning the pennant now, without Lewis's big gun, but St. Louis sportswriters applauded the owner for sending a stern message to his good-for-nothing players. "Lewis was a fine fielder and a good batter, but the curse of drunkenness has brought him this disgrace and he has no one to blame but himself for his downfall," the *Globe-Democrat* declared.

On the heels of their defeat by the Orioles, and bereft of their best hitter, the Browns suffered a "terrific thrashing" by the New York Metropolitans, losing 12–6 on "military day" at the park in the opener of the crucial three-game set. Instead of picking up ground on the floundering Athletics, St. Louis stalled at three games out, with only eight left to play. "It was a game that St. Louis could not afford to lose," the *Globe-Democrat* keened. "The results realized were unlooked for and disastrous, leaving the St. Louis Club a most discouraging prospect for the championship, which can now only be attained by extraordinary playing and good luck."

Still, on the following afternoon, a Sunday, some twelve thousand fanatics showed up, demonstrating that they harbored hopes for the Browns yet. The Mets took an unnervingly quick lead in the first inning on an RBI single by center fielder Chief Roseman. He had earned his nickname for his blood-curdling war whoops, but he was no Indian; the Chief was a New Yorker through and through, with the accent and brashness to prove it. As Roseman danced off first base, Browns hurler George McGinnis spun around to watch him. "How's that for a balk, Chawley?" Roseman shouted at umpire Charlie Daniels, in a voice that could be heard in the stands. From then on, the crowd seemed part of the game. Roseman endured its jeers for a while, then burst for second base in an attempted steal. As Chief went into his slide, second baseman Joe Quest caught the throw and slapped on the tag. Umpire Daniels bellowed "out at second!" and beckoned Roseman to return to the bench. St. Louis fanatics "vented their delight in a thundering cheer."

Later in the game, Mets second baseman Sam Crane took first, while his teammate Dude Esterbrook, coaching the runners, hoarsely yelled at him to "Go on! Go on!"—perhaps to rattle pitcher George McGinnis as much as anything. When Crane did take off, Comiskey caught a foul ball and whipped it to McGinnis covering first for a double play, prompting the crowd to mockingly chant, "Go on! Go on!" It was not a great day for Crane on the base paths. The game's most striking play unfolded in the seventh inning, when he lashed a ball into center field, where Tony Mullane picked it up with his left hand. As Crane tore for second base, the ambidextrous Mullane realized he did not have time to shift the ball, so he "tried a left-handed throw," according to the *Globe-Democrat.* "The ball went straight to Quest, Crane was caught, and the crowd cheered loudly and at length." The cheering rarely let up all afternoon, and St. Louis won handily, 7–1.

One game remained against the Metropolitans and their magnificent pitcher Tim Keefe. Owner Von der Ahe, having expelled Fred Lewis for life four days earlier, now decided, after only two games without him, that Fred deserved another chance. Since Von der Ahe had not yet telegraphed notice of the player's expulsion to Association headquarters, Lewis was still technically a member of the Browns. The owner's rage had passed, and it had been replaced by an equally characteristic impulse of forgiveness. He reinstated his slugger.

Four thousand fans flowed in that Tuesday, September 18, "and from first to last all were kept on the tip-toe of expectations," as the *Missouri Republican* put it. In a tense, see-saw match, St. Louis held a 3–2 lead

going into the ninth inning. The first Mets batter that inning, Chief Roseman, cracked a ball deep to center field that "should have gone to the
bulletin board." It didn't, for one reason: Von der Ahe had rescinded the
expulsion of Fred Lewis. Running hard, Lewis flung his hand up and
grabbed the ball, making "one of the best catches of the year." The out
was critical, because the next batter, Dude Esterbrook, drove a ball all
the way to the left-field fence for a double, which doubtless would have
scored Roseman with the tying run. In sliding into second, the Dude
injured himself, forcing rookie Dave Orr to take his place. Orr quickly
captured third when Browns catcher Pat Deasley dropped a pitch.

The tying run now stood ninety feet away, with one man out. Mets
manager Jim Mutrie, desperate to get the runner home, ordered batter
Bill Holbert to try a kind of suicide squeeze. Orr was instructed to take
a big lead off of third, then break for home the moment Holbert tapped
the ball. Pitcher Tony Mullane, though, picked up on what was happening and threw hard fastballs. Holbert swung at one pitch, then a second.
When he missed a third, striking out, catcher Deasley fired the ball to
third baseman Arlie Latham, who tagged the rookie Orr and "scooted
away over the field towards the dressing room," the *Globe-Democrat*
noted. For a moment the crowd reacted with stunned silence. Then it
sank in: the Browns had pulled off a crisp game-ending double play.
"When the truth did dawn upon them there was a great shouting," and
for good reason—instead of being knocked out of the pennant race, St.
Louis had shaved a game off the Athletics' lead. And the upcoming contests of Friday, Saturday, and Sunday against the reeling, pitching-starved
Athletics—games the Browns could, and perhaps should, win—could
decide the pennant.

With two victories over the excellent Mets, the mood in St. Louis
changed perceptibly. "Something like a ray of hope" was "creeping through
the darkness and it has spread into something like a sunbeam," Dave Reid
wrote in the *Missouri Republican*. In their conversations in the saloons
and clubs of St. Louis, men noted that the momentum of the pennant
race had shifted. "The excitement last night was up to fever heat and
there was an increased feeling of confidence in the nine," wrote Reid.
With a sweep, the Browns would leap into first place. "This week will be
a great one in baseball history," he promised. Von der Ahe seemed nervous

but hopeful, observing, to the *Globe-Democrat*, "Thank God there is no ladies' day this week."

———◇———

ON THE MORNING OF SEPTEMBER 21, AS THE TIRED ATHLETICS ROSE at St. Louis's Laclede Hotel and prepared for that afternoon's battle, the American Association standings showed that the Browns still had a chance:

	W	L	PCT.	GB
Philadelphia	63	28	.692	—
St. Louis	61	31	.663	2½
Cincinnati	58	35	.624	6
New York	49	41	.544	13½
Louisville	47	43	.522	15½
Columbus	31	61	.337	32½
Pittsburgh	30	62	.326	33½
Baltimore	27	65	.293	36½

This final showdown between the clubs would be a "tug of war," the *Missouri Republican* promised, "and d—d be the club that cries 'Crushed! Enuf!'" It began with a magnificent Friday afternoon turnout of eleven thousand fans. Sitting in Von der Ahe's private box was Missouri Governor Thomas T. Crittenden, who had caught a special train the previous afternoon from the capital in Jefferson City. He joked that, "as an added inducement to the St. Louis nine," he planned to award patronage jobs as police commissioners in the capital to whichever two Browns players performed best in the series.

The governor, a fleshy, thin-nosed man with a thick mustache, was obviously in high spirits, still glowing from his recent victory over a reign of terror in the state. He had vanquished the notorious and vicious James Gang, former Confederate guerrillas and now train robbers who had generated headlines across America that painted Missouri as an outlaw place, dangerous for business or travel. By offering a $50,000 reward, Crittenden had coaxed two members of the gang, Robert and Charlie Ford, to visit Jesse James at his home in St. Joseph, Missouri, where Bob

Ford shot Jesse James through the back of his head. In time, a court convicted Robert Ford of cold-blooded murder, only to have the governor issue a pardon two hours after the verdict, then send Ford $10,000, his share of the reward. The governor's critics—and there were surely many at Sportsman's Park—believed that the chief executive had behaved like a wanton criminal himself. The *St. Louis Post-Dispatch* called Crittenden's hiring "of two scoundrels to cowardly assassinate" Jesse James, instead of according him due process by apprehending him and putting him on trial, "a shame and disgrace to the State of Missouri." As a Union veteran long steeped in Missouri's bitter and grisly internecine feuds, Crittenden didn't care. He had broken the back of the gang and rescued the state's reputation.

The afternoon was a glorious one, "the sky blue and clear, and the cool breeze well tempered by the warm September sun," the *Philadelphia Press* reported. Because the stands were full, latecomers went onto the lush grass to watch from the deep outfield, necessitating an agreement that balls hit into the crowd would be ground-rule doubles. The parking lot outside the ballpark was full, "and those along Grand Avenue were soon overflowing, so that the thoroughfare was lined on either side with carriages, buggies, drays, huckster and express wagons and every species of vehicle," said the *Missouri Republican*. At 3:13 P.M., the captains of the two teams strolled out for the coin flip by umpire Charlie Daniels. Charlie Comiskey won. He elected to take the field, sending the Athletics to the bat. The Athletics had to face Browns pitcher Tony Mullane, whose motion was "clearly illegal," in their view, his arm regularly rising above his shoulder, giving extra power to his sinking fastball. "An umpire ought to be able to see it," the *Philadelphia Item* groused. "Somehow or other they have, so far, with the exception of Kelly, closed their eyes to it." The atmosphere was tense and tingly, promising a tight, well-played game by these talented rivals.

It didn't work out that way. The Athletics jumped quickly to a 1–0 lead. Then, still in the first inning, it was time for one of the craziest plays anyone in the park had ever seen. With runners on first and second, Athletics catcher Jack O'Brien hit a sharp grounder to shortstop Bill Gleason, who shuffled the ball to Quest for the start of a double play. But Quest dropped it, and the Athletics' Lon Knight, rounding third, boldly dashed for home. Quest quickly picked up the ball and fired a strike to catcher Pat Deasley in plenty of time. Meanwhile, Mike Moynahan bolted for third while the throw was coming home. Deasley, seeing this out of the corner of his eye, hastily tagged out Knight and flung the ball to third. It tipped off the fingers of Browns third baseman Arlie Latham, and Moynahan tore for home. Gleason, backing up Latham, relayed the ball to Quest, who fired it to Deasley, who tagged out Moynahan—the *second* runner put out at home plate on the *same play*, with the *second assist* by Quest. The utterly bizarre top half of the first inning was over, and the Athletics had been held to a single run.

Mason had promised the press that Jumping Jack Jones would start, and the crowd was surprised when little Bobby Mathews took the pitcher's box instead. The stiff and aching veteran, who had surrendered twelve runs in his last start, had little to offer but savvy and guts, but at this point, that was enough. Though the Browns got on base inning after inning, Bobby held on as the Athletics built up a 6–0 lead by the fourth, threatening to put the game, and the pennant, beyond St. Louis's reach. Mathews's luck finally ran out in the fourth, as the Browns hammered him for three runs. Even worse, while racing for a foul ball, Harry Stovey slipped on the turf and sprained his ankle badly. In great pain, he staggered to his feet and, with the help of his teammates, limped off the field, and out of the game, dealing a potentially devastating blow to their hopes of taking the pennant. At the climactic moment of the long season, Philadelphia's best hitter and runner—the soul of the team, and the difference in many victories—was suddenly shelved. Mathews had to wonder: What else could go wrong?

Yet Philadelphia kept on scoring, with three more runs in the fifth. For the second time that afternoon, an overanxious Arlie Latham cut in front of shortstop Bill Gleason to field a grounder, only to boot it, "to his own disgust and the displeasure of the spectators, who roundly hissed the performance." The Browns responded with their own three-run inning, capped by a memorable bomb. The restored Fred Lewis took a mighty swat at a Mathews pitch and sent the ball soaring high over the right-field fence, to the cheers of the thrilled crowd, including Governor Crittenden and the assembled politicians. "The home-run made by Lewis was very greatly admired by his Excellency, and it is commonly believed that if Lewis were a citizen of St. Louis he could have a seat in the Police Board without seeking the position." The clout pulled St. Louis to within three runs of the Athletics. It was 9–6, and the Philadelphia men could see their lead melting away.

The Browns kept bearing down on Mathews, who was weary and in pain. In the seventh, pitching carefully this time around the explosive Lewis, Bobby surrendered a walk. Lewis stole second and scooted to third when a pitch got away from Mathews and flew past the catcher. Then Joe Quest, not normally a threat, blasted a weak pitch to left center for a triple, scoring Lewis, as the crowd cheered wildly. But was it really a triple? Mathews immediately protested that Quest should have been held to a ground-rule double. A long wrangle followed as the members of both clubs crowded the umpire, all trying to talk at once. Finally, Daniels ruled that the ground rule did not apply, since the ball had not disappeared into the crowd. It was an important point, because one of Mathews's next pitches got past the catcher, sending Quest scurrying home. The Athletics' lead was down to 9–8.

Mathews was plainly exhausted, and the Browns continued to torture him in the seventh. They had a runner on third with two out when Tony Mullane sent a routine fly ball to left field. In horror, Mathews saw the ball pop out of Jud Birchall's hands; the left fielder anxiously juggled it before finally securing possession, for the third out. The Browns were that close to tying the game. But three outs were three outs, and Mathews strode off the field.

The Athletics built the lead back up to 13–8 with four runs in the eighth, when it was the Browns' turn to suffer a serious loss: catcher Pat Deasley, diving bravely to stop a wild pitch, split the skin of his middle finger wide open and had to leave the game. (A week later, it had come out of splints, but was "still a pretty bad looking object.") With a five-run lead, the Athletics might have ended the game with ease, had they had a fresh reliever to install in the pitcher's box. But they did not, and Bobby Mathews kept on struggling, long after it was obvious he had nothing more to give. The Browns scored three runs, narrowing the edge to 13–11. Browns pitcher Tony Mullane got through the ninth without surrendering another run, giving St. Louis a chance, though it was down to its last three outs.

The delirious crowd sensed that Mathews was ripe to be beaten. "Excitement was at its highest pitch. The crowd was howling and hooting," the *New York Clipper* reported. At that moment of fury and passion, as if on cue, darkness descended on the ballpark and the wind whipped up, "creating a panicky feeling among some of the spectators," the *Globe-Democrat* said. A sudden and furious breeze scooped up dust from the surrounding streets and swirled it, tornado-like, across the field. "A regular hurricane had possession of the park, and clouds of dust at times hid the players from sight," the *Clipper* recounted.

In the roaring wind, the Athletics players, desperate to escape with a victory before Mathews completely fell apart, surrounded umpire Charlie Daniels and shouted at him to call the game, for the safety of everyone. Daniels seemed inclined to do so, heading back to the bench "as if to get his coat and leave the grounds," when Chris Von der Ahe jumped up from the Browns' bench and ordered the umpire to get back to work. Charlie Mason, leaping from the Athletics' bench, also rushed over to the umpire, "and a regular controversy took place, the managers gesticulating, the players and the crowd yelling with all their might: 'Go on!' 'Play ball!'" according to the *Clipper*. Mason declared that he would let his men continue in a choking dust storm only under formal protest. Von der Ahe shouted back that he did not care, as long as the Athletics played.

And so the game went on in the strange Midwestern wind and darkness.

George Strief was up next. After the exhausted Mathews snuck two strikes past him, Strief blasted the ball to deep right field. Lon Knight dashed for the wind-whipped sphere, but a squall threw dust in his eyes while flinging the ball right into his face. He dropped it, letting Strief take second. Mullane next hit a high fly into the swirling wind, but Mike Moynahan froze to the ball and made the difficult catch. Bill Gleason followed with a tremendous lunge, driving the ball to deep center field. It looked good for a game-tying home run, and the crowd roared. But a powerful gust "blew the ball far back enough to allow Bradley to score a magnificent catch," the *Clipper* said—though he was "so far out and the dust was so great that Daniels at first was not able to tell whether a catch or a muff had been made." In fact, the Browns were certain it *was* a muff. Gleason initially refused to leave first base (Strief held second), insisting that

Bradley had dropped the ball. But Daniels ordered him back to the Browns' bench, ruling that the catch had been made.

Charlie Comiskey was now the last hope for St. Louis. He sent a sharp grounder down the line that Jack O'Brien, substituting for Harry Stovey, grabbed. O'Brien hopped on first base for out number three "with the air of a person of wonderful achievements," as the *Globe-Democrat* put it. Mathews and his Athletics, their sweat-soaked faces and uniforms powdered with red Missouri dust, had salvaged an exhausting 13–11 victory in a freak storm. "The Goddess of Good Fortune" had "smiled upon the boys from Philadelphia," reported the *Philadelphia Press*. St. Louis now trailed by three and a half games, with only five left to play.

A lesser team would have given up. Yet the Browns, who believed it was their destiny to win the Association pennant, refused to surrender. On Saturday, September 22, an even larger crowd came to see the hometown team seek its revenge against Jumping Jack Jones for his two victories over St. Louis in Philadelphia. Having been hammered in recent starts, Jones was beginning to wonder if his famous leap was even worth trying anymore. All it seemed to accomplish was to tip off batters that a fastball was probably coming. And so he retired it. "Everybody expected to see a mirth-provoking delivery, but saw only a very plain one," the *Globe-Democrat* noted with disappointment. But plainness proved to be no advantage. After Jones let up six runs in the first three innings, St. Louis walked away with a 9–6 victory, evening the series at one victory apiece. "The Athletics missed Mathews, whose generalship had done so much towards winning the game on the previous day," the *Clipper* contended. "Stovey played, but was not able to do himself justice, and in covering the circuit he rather limped than ran." The miserable Stovey, up at the plate with two outs in the ninth, watched three strikes pass him without even bothering to swing. While "a jubilant crowd filled the field," he sullenly limped away to a waiting horse-drawn bus that would take the beaten and battered Athletics back to the Laclede Hotel. Charlie Mason and co-owner Billy Sharsig, finding more than Jones's exhaustion and Stovey's injury to blame, sent a bitter telegram home to the *Philadelphia Item*: "We were completely robbed out of the game to-day by the umpire." After the first game, Von der Ahe had filed a formal complaint about the same man, Charles Daniels. By Saturday night, Daniels was ready to resign and had to be talked out of it.

What would the Athletics do now? Jones had lost again and was looking weaker than ever. The *Item* ran a cartoon of Athletics co-owner Lew Simmons, with clenched teeth and an agonized expression, holding the frayed end of a piece of string. "Great Caesar, the string of that 'Jumping Jack' broken again!" he says. "I'll get an iron chain next time." With one more victory, the Browns would be back in the race. There was nothing to do but pray, and play on.

————◇————

PERHAPS THE BIGGEST BASEBALL CROWD ST. LOUIS HAD EVER seen, "a moving, surging dark mass," the *Globe-Democrat* said, appeared at Sportsman's Park on the following afternoon for the season's final game between the pennant rivals. At 1 P.M., two hours before the game was to begin, "the enthusiasts began arriving, great crowds pouring out of street cars, carriages, omnibuses and express wagons, rigged up for the occasion." Virtually anything with wheels was being used to transport mobs of baseball fanatics. "Fashionable circles were also represented," the *Philadelphia Press* noted, with hundreds of expensive carriages "intermingling with the commoner vehicles" along the streets surrounding Sportsman's Park. "It reminds me of Derby day; upon my soul it does," said an Englishman who watched the crowd arrive. As late as 4 P.M., when the game was an hour old and already into the sixth inning, "the great human stream kept steadily pouring in." When fans were told the game was well under way, they didn't care. "They were not to be disappointed of at least a glimpse of the big game of the season, and they willingly paid the admission price, taking their chance of securing standing room, for seats were held at a premium, every available one having long since been taken and clung to as tenaciously as though glued to the occupant," reported the *Globe-Democrat*.

Along the outfield fences, "thousands were huddled and squeezed in all sorts of positions—some sitting, some lying at full length, while others in the rear stood on tip toe, straining every nerve to catch a glimpse of some applauded play." Among the forty police officers on the grounds were five mounted on horses. They were working feverishly to force back fanatics who would have otherwise swamped the outfielders. Even so, players were obliged to leap into the crowd for long fly balls that day. Those seated in the grandstand, surrounded by standing spectators, found the situation little better, many claiming they saw nothing of the game except when the ball was knocked high in the air. A number of fans clambered up on the roofs of the press box and upper deck, "which groaned beneath the unwonted pressure and threatened a calamity at any moment," the *Philadelphia Press* noted with alarm. Earlier that season, many people remembered, the upper deck had swayed and almost collapsed, prompting Von der Ahe to have it reinforced. Now, as people climbed on the roof, "many were the anxious glances cast by the ladies and their nervous escorts at the scaffolding and supports of the structure on which they sat." (It was a reasonable fear. The following spring, when the Cincinnati Reds opened their new ballpark, a portion of the stands did collapse, injuring dozens of people.) The scene outside the park was much the same. "On the tops of the roofs, hanging on the edging and cornices, seated on chimneys of adjacent houses, on the porches, fences, in fact every where from which a view could possibly be obtained could be seen a tired but interested looker-on, who, although unable to use his hands in applause of some good play, satisfied himself with a hoarse, dusty Comanche yell." The cheering and clapping of the massive crowd "sounded like the rumblings of an approaching thunder-storm."

All told, some 16,800 paid their way in, not counting those with season tickets. Von der Ahe had never seen anything like it. The coins collected and flung into a strongbox weighed so much that the strongest member of the Browns could not lift them; the dollar bills filled a large clothes-basket. When all three box offices at the park were overwhelmed, Von der Ahe put bundles of tickets in the hands of park attendants and sent them out into the streets to hawk them as fast as they could. "That it was a red-letter day in the base ball history of St. Louis is acknowledged, and that it will for a long time be spoken of as 'the big day' can not be doubted," the *Globe-Democrat* said. "The gathering was beyond a doubt the largest ever seen at a professional game of ball, played on any enclosed ground in America," Dave Reid added. That was not strictly true, but no one could doubt anymore whether baseball would survive; the game that had almost died several years earlier was booming as never before under the mercurial leadership of Chris Von der Ahe.

Harry Stovey, showing extraordinary grit, was back in the lineup, seemingly a mixed blessing for the Athletics. He was so lame he could barely hobble, and the Browns had denied him permission to use a pinch runner. Many Browns fans were delighted to see Grin Bradley, considered an easy man to beat, take the pitcher's box for the Athletics. Though Bobby Mathews had been pounded for twenty-three runs in his last two starts, he had also cagily won both games, showing that penchant for victory that made him the Athletics' most dangerous pitcher. It was up to Bradley, who had surrendered twelve runs and seventeen hits in his previous start, to somehow find a way to win, too. He decided his best approach was to establish his dominance early, in the usual manner. He hit leadoff batter Bill Gleason on the left arm, "causing him to drop his bat and walk around for awhile." That sort of pain would give these batters something to think about. Bradley won that initial battle, coaxing Gleason to ground out, and his Browns teammates quietly followed him.

The Athletics, on the other hand, were determined to make some noise, even though they were facing the redoubtable Tony Mullane, who would post thirty-five victories, with a league-leading .700 winning percentage and (applying a modern statistic unknown to him) a sparkling 2.19 earned run average, second best in the Association. Jud Birchall, leading off, "caused the small boys to cheer" when he lunged at a Mullane pitch for strike one. But he silenced them with a single down the line in right, which Comiskey protested was foul. Harry Stovey followed with a blast into the crowd for a ground-rule double, and Birchall scored on a sharp grounder to third. When Mullane uncorked a wild pitch, Stovey followed him home, limping in pain all the way. The Athletics led, 2–0, widened to 5–0 in the fifth, with the help of a run-scoring single by the unstoppable Harry Stovey, who scored himself. And Stovey still wasn't through. In the seventh, he hit his second ground-rule double of the day, then came around on two wild pitches to give his team a 6–0 lead, expanded to 7–0 the next inning. The Browns were in deep trouble, and Bradley was somehow finding a way to retire them, one man after another. The Athletics took a 9–1 lead into the ninth inning.

By that time, many angry, heartbroken Browns fans, especially hundreds who had stood all afternoon on the field, were pushing against those in front of them, and surging into the playing field, eager to get out and go home. Anxious to keep the diamond clear until the ball game was over, mounted police rode around the enclosure, swinging their batons and ordering the crowd to get off the field. The Athletics refused to play the ninth until the fans were pushed back.

After the crowd got shoved back, and slugger Fred Lewis walked to the plate, applause rippled through the park, then grew louder, in remembrance of Lewis's titanic shot two days earlier. "Fred smiled and looked as if he really was going to do something," the *Globe-Democrat* said. His appearance proved to be "exasperatingly deceptive," though, because Bradley coaxed him to ground out weakly to second base. Hugh Nicol—who, with a flare-up of malaria, was woozy and exhausted, and getting by only through "pure pluck"—followed with a grounder straight back to the pitcher, for out number two. The crowd got ready to break onto the field and head for the nearest exits.

But the scrappy Joe Quest refused to go down quietly. He plunked a pitch to center field, then raced to second on a passed ball. Bradley stared in at Arlie Latham, hoping to end the game then and there, before his arm got any weaker. But Latham smashed a sharp grounder down the third-base line that instantly looked good for extra bases. To everyone's surprise, Athletics third baseman Fred Corey made a "magnificent" diving stop. "Then, standing erect and taking good aim, he threw dead on the line to Stovey." It was over.

Instantly, hundreds of pent-up fans made a rush to cross the diamond to exit the park. Quest himself, who was headed for third, watched Corey make the play, then dejectedly trotted to the bench to collect his jacket before someone in the crowd walked off with it. Yet things were not as they seemed. Looking over his shoulder, he was stunned to see that Stovey had, in fact, dropped the ball at first. The Browns were still alive. Veering toward home, Quest tapped the plate with his toe, claiming the game was now 9–2. Athletics players raced in from the field, protesting angrily that Quest had never touched third and should be declared out. But umpire Charlie Daniels, who had been watching the play's conclusion at first while nervously eyeing the mob flowing over the field, had not seen Quest's detour to the bench as he rounded the bases. The run counted.

For the next several minutes, Daniels and the police worked fiercely to push the crowd back, clearing enough of a space so that the game could go on. Bradley would have to go out and throw again. George Strief promptly hit one of his pitches sharply on the ground, but it went straight to second baseman Cub Stricker, who scooped up the ball and "relentlessly forwarded" it to Stovey. This time, the star first baseman grasped it firmly—and with that catch, the series was over.

In one hour and forty minutes, the hated Bradley had pitched a three-hit masterpiece, winning perhaps the biggest game of the season. "HE WRECKED US," the *Missouri Republican* headlined the next day, adding, "Bradley Constituted Himself an Infernal Machine." The Browns, who had posted a .671 winning percentage under Ted Sullivan, had gone only 9–7, with a .562 winning percentage under his successor, Charlie Comiskey. And that had made all the difference.

The Athletics rushed to their waiting carriages, and "as they were driven out of the gates, they were heartily cheered and hailed as the future champions," the *Philadelphia Press* reported. Even if St. Louis were to sweep the Alleghenys in their final three-game series, the club could achieve a tie for first place only if the Athletics lost *all four* of their games against the Louisville Eclipse. "The knowing ones," said the *Press*, "laugh at the very idea" that St. Louis might yet pull it off. Philadelphians began working frantically on plans for a stupendous welcome-home parade to celebrate the pennant victory.

But was it really over, even now? The Browns, after all, were fully capable of beating the next-to-last-place Alleghenys three straight times. And the Athletics, far from home, were wretchedly weak and on the edge of collapse—facing a talented Louisville club that would love to play the role of spoiler. "The Athletics leave here in quite a crippled condition," the *Press* had to admit in its final report from St. Louis. "Stovey is away under the weather. Mathews' arm has given out and hangs limp and lifeless, from his shoulder. Jones is also complaining of lameness and [backup catcher Ed] Rowen has had his finger split."

No, it wasn't over yet. As the *Globe-Democrat* would remark with amazement a few days later, when few were laughing anymore at the idea of the Browns stealing the pennant away from the Athletics, "base ball is mighty unsartin, so that anything may be looked for."

14

LIMPING HOME

L EW SIMMONS HOPED HIS ATHLETICS WOULD CLINCH THE
pennant on the afternoon of Wednesday, September 26, 1883, in
Louisville, with an easy win over the Eclipse club in the opener of
a four-game set. But here he was, a nervous wreck. As another Louisville
player crossed home plate in the ninth inning, the smiling men surrounding him in the wooden grandstand at Eclipse Park broke out in applause
for the umpteenth time that afternoon, some waving their derby hats.
Simmons chewed on the stump of his cigar and flung it under his seat
with disgust. This didn't look good. It didn't look good at all. The Athletics
were blowing it, blowing it.

Simmons's smooth-tempered colleague Charlie Mason, having nursed
the Athletics for three-quarters of the road trip, had gone back home to
help prepare for the grand celebration in Philadelphia. The baseball-
crazed city was already planning a massive party, with a nighttime parade
and spectacular dinner. Simmons and co-owner Billy Sharsig would hold
down the fort here, in unseasonably cold and windy Kentucky. Simmons
had already negotiated with the Eclipse managers to move up Sunday's

game from the afternoon to the morning. He had had to fork over $300 to Louisville management to change the time, an enormous sum, given that American Association clubs only guaranteed visitors $65 per game. Both clubs knew that the gate take would be lousy on a Sunday morning in church-going Kentucky. But an early escape was essential if the Athletics were to get back in time for the big celebration.

Yes, the club was putting the cart before the horse. But to capture the flag, all the Athletics had to do was win just one of these four games in Louisville. Either that, or the Browns would have to lose just one of *their* three against the Alleghenys. That seemed easy enough: just one in seven games had to go Philadelphia's way. But, on that Wednesday, neither the A's nor the Browns showed much of an inclination to cooperate. As a minstrel star, Simmons was accustomed to performing under pressure, and he loved the spotlight. But, somehow, this week, his brassy confidence had started melting down. He was too much in love with baseball and his Athletics to be dispassionate about the outcome in Louisville. The thought that his beloved boys might fritter away the pennant, after coming so far, twisted his stomach in knots.

George Washington Bradley was in the pitcher's box for the opener. That made some sense, Simmons thought: three days earlier, he had turned in the club's most impressive pitching performance in weeks, beating the Browns, 9–2, in the rivals' season finale. Two days of rest were plenty by 1880s standards, and the club might as well use the best pitcher available to finish the job. As the afternoon had progressed, though, it had become depressingly apparent that sending Bradley out again so quickly might not have been such a swell idea. Grin had expended so much of his strength in that Browns game that he seemed to have little left for this one. He had trouble putting the ball over the plate—an obvious sign of fatigue—inflicting three passed balls and two wild pitches on his catcher, Jack O'Brien. Forced to throw weak pitches directly over the plate for strikes, he got hammered for fourteen hits.

For much of the afternoon, though, strangely, that had seemed good enough. The Athletics had fought back from a 4–0 deficit to take a 5–4 lead, while Simmons "chewed up four cigar stumps" in hellish anxiety. But just when Louisville appeared to be "very near going to pieces," and the pennant seemed in Philadelphia's grasp, Eclipse pitcher Sam Weaver found the strength to hold the Athletics back, letting his teammates get to work with the bat. Two runs in the sixth inning gave the Eclipse the lead; another in the ninth iced it, 7–5. Simmons looked nervously at the scoreboard. There was no relief from St. Louis. The Browns had been stockpiling runs all afternoon against the inept Pittsburgh Alleghenys. When the slaughter was over, the Browns had amassed thirty hits, forty-six total bases, and a 20–3 victory. Fred Lewis alone had three singles, a double, and a triple. Obviously, the Browns had no intention of rolling over so that the Athletics might win the pennant.

In Philadelphia, crowds of men and women, eager to celebrate the pennant win, swarmed outside the Athletics' club headquarters and the large windows of the city's newspapers, where the inning-by-inning scores, fresh off the telegraph wire, were posted for all to see. In front of the *Philadelphia Press* building, the busy intersection of Chestnut Street and Seventh was blocked by fanatics "who debated between innings the prospect of the favorites, and stopped long enough to shout or sigh as the score took a Philadelphia or Louisville turn." Although it was obvious that Louisville was playing a strong game, "an abiding faith in the good luck of the Athletic kept the crowd standing inning after inning." At last, the final results were posted: defeat. "Then the excited feeling broke forth in a groan which made the air mournful for blocks around."

There was good reason to groan. Slugger Harry Stovey was still limping around on the ankle he had sprained in St. Louis, robbed of the speed that had made him the Association's most fearsome offensive threat. He was no longer able to steal bases, stretch triples into home runs, or make dazzling plays on the field. And who would pitch? The Athletics had already—perhaps foolishly—used up Bradley, with only a defeat to show for it and three games to go. Jumping Jack Jones, after letting up twenty runs in his last two games, now admitted his arm was "lame." Bobby Mathews, who had let up twenty-three, didn't have to admit anything—it was obvious to everyone that he could barely move his arm. That night, "the Athletics' friends in Philadelphia burned the wires with importunities to get into the game and win the pennant," Simmons recalled. "We all were just as anxious, too." But it was too late to bring on new players. "Just now . . . Simmons is on the ragged edge," the *Cincinnati Enquirer* laughed.

On Thursday, Simmons, in loud suit and derby hat, strode into the park with head held high, clutching his cane. This would be the day. It had to be. He did not want to consider the gut-churning alternative. And, as luck would have it, he did not have to wait long for something to cheer. In the first inning, Louisville ace Guy Hecker, a twenty-eight-game winner that year, proved "very wild and hard to hold," according to the *Louisville Courier-Journal*, giving a workout to catcher Dan Sullivan. The Athletics, able to wait for the pitch they wanted, hit him hard. Jud Birchall opened with a sharp drive to right field that Chicken Wolf—who got his nickname for touching no meat but chicken, which he ate four times a day—had to chase down and catch. Harry Stovey followed with his requisite single. "Playing on one leg," Stovey hobbled to second on a passed ball and limped home on Mike Moynahan's hit to right field. The Athletics led, 1–0.

Louisville fans had come to the park hoping to see Jumping Jack Jones perform his famous leap. And, indeed, he seemed a reasonable choice to pitch game two. Louisville fans were surprised, then, to see a little man with a big mustache make his way, slightly limping, to the pitcher's box. Bobby Mathews, the Athletics' highest paid star, the player most responsible for Philadelphia's sterling season, had been given responsibility for producing the one victory the Athletics needed. Probably, he had demanded it.

Simmons's air of satisfaction proved short-lived. In the bottom of the first, Louisville slugger Pete Browning repeated Harry Stovey's round by slashing a single, reaching second on a passed ball, and scoring on a single. The Athletics battled back to take a 2–1 lead, but Mathews, who had been relying almost entirely on his oversized heart, ran out of strength in the fourth, and the Eclipse ripped into him for three runs to move ahead 4–2. The club added another the following inning. The Athletics cut the lead in the seventh, when Mathews himself drove a runner in from second with a single, but the Eclipse built it right back up in the eighth, to 6–3. "The crowd yelled repeatedly until a number were hoarse," the *Louisville Courier-Journal* reported. Mathews, wracked with pain, had turned in a heroic performance, arguably his best in many games. But it just wasn't good enough.

Trapped among the cheering revelers, Lew Simmons slumped angrily in his seat, sinking into the sort of gloom that always descended on him when his Athletics lost. He chewed on his cigar and flashed dirty looks at those who tried to talk to him. "Lew Simmons's manners usually intimidate one who is not acquainted with him," the *National Police Gazette* observed. "He has a 'git off my lip, I can't spit' style about him that breaks a stranger all up, and makes him believe he is going to get a black eye or a bloody nose if he crosses the path of Mr. Simmons." Some critics had accused the co-owner of being greedy, but others knew better. "Mr. Simmons . . . has his whole heart in the Athletics club," the *Philadelphia Item* contended, "and would rather come out of the season without a cent's profit than have his club worsted in the championship race. He is an enthusiast, and not the cold, calculating miser that some of the young men in the press picture him." Now, in Louisville, the enthusiast looked on, hoping against hope his team might rally for victory in the ninth.

Instead, the Athletics went down without a peep, losing 6–3. Philadelphia was reduced to only two more chances to win the pennant. Simmons, who cherished a gold-headed cane that had been given to him years before in recognition for his wonderful playing for the Athletics, suddenly snapped. "Lew Simmons brought his cane down on the benches with a whack, breaking it in two, and walked sadly off the grounds," the *Courier-Journal* reported. If the Eclipse could win one more game, the writer added, "it will take a log chain to hold Lew Simmons."

There was no help from St. Louis, of course. That afternoon, the Browns had an easy time of it. Tony Mullane carried a no-hitter into the ninth inning, and though the Pittsburgh boys scratched out two hits at the very end, "The Apollo of the Box" tamped down the threat to win, 6–2. If the Athletics were to win the pennant, they would have to find a way to do it on their own. The Alleghenys weren't going to help.

On the streets of Philadelphia, frustration was boiling into panic and rage. Co-owners Simmons and Billy Sharsig, who were supposed to be managing things in Louisville, "came in for their full share of condemnation, and the last two defeats were laid on their shoulders," the *Philadelphia Inquirer* said. Charlie Mason, following telegraphed accounts of the games, was alarmed and perplexed. He had left orders to pitch Jumping Jack Jones and Grin Bradley, in that order, in the first two games in Louisville: "These orders were disobeyed, but why Mr. Mason did not know. He regarded it as a very poor piece of head work to pitch Mathews . . . as he was suffering from a lame arm." Men feverishly making preparations to honor the Athletics sent frantic telegrams to Louisville urging Captain Lon Knight to start Jumping Jack on Friday, while Philadelphians obsessed over Thursday's loss. "The excitement all over the city was intense," the *Philadelphia Inquirer* noted. "Crowds surrounded the bulletin boards and newspaper offices, and the Athletics' defeat was the sole topic of conversation." Back in Louisville, Simmons feared the worst. "Our cup of sorrow overflowed," he recalled years later. "The boys were almost wild with grief, and they were keyed to the highest tension all the time."

Simmons's anxiety was only making the men press harder. The players, already feeling badly, recommended that the distressed owner stay out of their sight during the next game. "The boys would not even let me around where I could be seen. My face was the picture of distraction and they were blue enough," he later said. After a horrible, sleepless night, Simmons felt so desperate that he tracked down Louisville player-manager Joe Gerhardt before the third game and made a highly unseemly proposal. The Eclipse general did not feel the sort of animosity toward Philadelphia that he did toward St. Louis—the Browns' vicious Tony Mullane, after all, had almost killed him with a pitch—and Simmons thought Gerhardt might be willing to show the Athletics some mercy, just once, so Philadelphia could win the pennant. "Give us a show," Simmons suggested, using slang for throwing a game. Gerhardt, as a fierce competitor, flatly refused. Though the Eclipse had no chance to win the pennant, the men "wanted to beat the team that did have a chance." They weren't even playing for money at this point; they were playing for pride. Certain that further argument was futile, Simmons glumly found a place to hide at the park, out of sight of his men.

The Athletics were plainly in trouble. If the team's money pitcher, Bobby Mathews, could not deliver the one victory needed, who could? "*DANGER AHEAD*," the *Philadelphia Press* warned. A tie for first place—an ignominious finish, given that the Athletics had the pennant all but locked away with their brave work in St. Louis—was no longer a far-fetched idea. The Browns needed only to win their final game while the Athletics lost their last two. Bradley and Mathews had both failed; the only pitcher left was Jumping Jack, whose recent performances hardly instilled confidence. Without a healthy Mathews, the Athletics were just another club, and not a particularly good one. "It has been said all along that it is by the grace of the Supreme Being that they are in the position they now hold," the *Louisville Commercial* sneered, "and we begin to think so too."

Only five hundred spectators bought tickets to the third game on Friday, September 28—better than the paid turnout of twenty-two against the Orioles a week earlier, but less than one-thirtieth the size of the biggest turnout in St. Louis just days before. For their loyalty to a team long out of the hunt, those hundreds got a special treat that day: the last chance to see the Athletics' bizarre Jumping Jack. Jones's aching arm had been rested for five days, his self-confidence was back, and he was hungry for victory. He informed his mates that "if Louisville won that game they would have to walk over his dead body, for he would either do or die." The tense Athletics players swallowed hard and got ready to play.

Jones brought back his bizarre leap, providing "much amusement" to the crowd—although catcher Jack O'Brien, forced to dive for his wild throws, no doubt found the spectacle less enjoyable. Still, Jumping Jack seemed more effective than of late, and the days off seemed to have returned some zip to his fastball. When he hurled such pitches in tandem with his distracting jumps, Louisville batters were caught on their heels. Athletics batters, meanwhile, were hitting the tired Guy Hecker hard, though Louisville's terrific fielding contained the damage. For three innings, the clubs were locked in a scoreless tie. In the fourth, Athletics third baseman Fred Corey lifted the spirits of his teammates by leaping for a hot liner with one hand, the force of which caused him to roll over and over. And in the bottom of the inning, Philadelphia batters finally got to Hecker. Mike Moynahan slapped a single to left, stole second, and scored on a wild pitch. Jack O'Brien walked, went to third on a single by Fred Corey, then scored on a grounder to second base. Simmons, trying to remain in hiding, may have had to stifle his habitual cry of "Pretty work!" The Athletics' 2–0 lead was short-lived, as Leech Maskrey drove home two runners to tie the game in the top of the fifth. A rally in the sixth, however, earned the Athletics a 5–2 lead. At long last, the American Association pennant seemed in reach.

Then Jumping Jack went to pieces. In the seventh inning, he walked Juice Latham and Tom McLaughlin—no easy task when seven balls were required, under 1883 rules, to put a man on first. Leech Maskrey and Chicken Wolf next jumped on his pitches for hits. By the time the night-marish inning was over, Louisville had sent four men across the plate and taken a 6–5 lead. Now the crowd was roaring. The Athletics were failing again! In Philadelphia, fans in the streets were "worked up to a fever heat," their nerves tortured by the "dread uncertainty" of the outcome. In St. Louis, supporters of the Browns, their team idle until Sunday, took hope.

Still, the Athletics kept fighting. In the top of the eighth, with two strikes on the batter, a foul tip ricocheted off the A's gritty catcher, Jack O'Brien, knocking him down as the ball shot up in the air. "While lying flat on his back he just managed to reach the ball with his left hand and held it. For this remarkable play he was greeted with loud and prolonged cheers, and it was fully five minutes before the game could go on," the *New York Clipper* reported. Fortune smiled again on Philadelphia in the bottom half of the inning, as an error by third baseman Jack Gleason let the Athletics tie the game, 6–6. Jumping Jack Jones was bearing down now, and the ninth came and went with neither team scoring. It was a new ball game. Extra innings would decide the Athletics' fate.

In Philadelphia, the mob on the streets expanded all afternoon, until some 1,500 to 2,000 people crammed into the intersection of Seventh and Chestnut streets. "It was impossible for [horse]cars or other vehicles to get through, to say nothing of foot passengers," said the *Philadelphia Press*. The crowd waited for the outcome in anxious silence. At Eclipse Park, Simmons looked on queasily. In the top of the tenth, Jumping Jack did his job, retiring the Eclipse without a run. Now Harry Stovey pulled a bat from the box at the end of the bench and limped to the plate. Though his sprained ankle had turned him into a sad parody of himself on the base paths, Stovey remained a serious threat as a slugger. Hecker, either wary of Stovey or incapable of controlling his pitches at this point, kept the ball away from the plate, finally walking the batter. When the exhausted Hecker followed with a wild pitch, Stovey hobbled down to second base— not quite scoring position, this time, given the runner's lame ankle.

Captain Lon Knight stepped to the plate. Throughout the pennant stretch he had repeatedly made clutch plays that kept the Athletics alive. Now, he ripped a single to left field.

Stovey barely made it to third.

It was up to Mike Moynahan. He had enjoyed a fine day, going 2-for-4 at the plate and making nine assists at shortstop, with only one error. Hecker held the ball, stared at the plate, took a run, and fired. Moynahan swung and connected. At the crack of the bat, left fielder Pete Browning and center fielder Leech Maskrey dashed for the ball as it shot between them. Harry Stovey, who led the American Association with 109 runs scored, stumbled home, wincing, with number 110. Cub Stricker's midsummer night's dream had come true, in a sense, after all: Harry was the one man who had caught the train, and made it home.

At 6:30 P.M. in Philadelphia, a newspaper employee posted a new and final score in the window: Athletics 7, Eclipse 6.

Instantly, a shout arose in the city that "rent the heavens," with "round following round of cheers." In Louisville, Simmons emerged from hiding "with joy in my heart, and I told the boys to go and celebrate any way they liked at my expense, and they did." Somebody produced some bottles. Before the Athletics left the ballpark, Simmons laughed, "most of them were unable to walk straight, and they celebrated all that night." Simmons sprinted to the telegraph office and sent a dispatch back home. At Seventh and Chestnut, someone grabbed it from the telegraph operator and shouted Simmons's message to the throng, featuring a mocking pun: "Well, the boys got there! Send greetings to St. *Lose!* The pennant's coming home." The crowd erupted. "Men threw their hats into the air and shouted themselves hoarse," the *Inquirer* reported, while "the ladies waved their handkerchiefs, and in some cases even joined in the shouting." The news of the victory spread rapidly, "and in a short time the streets for squares were filled with enthusiastic men and boys, shouting the result of the contest to newcomers, who at once joined in and spread the excitement."

Athletics headquarters was overrun by a delighted mob. There was hardly room for the club's backers to squeeze in and put the final touches on plans for the grand reception. On the building across the street, a beautiful silken banner was unfurled, bearing letters in shining gold: "CHAMPION ATHLETIC." Throughout the gas-lit evening, said the *Philadelphia Press*, "men could be seen stopping each other on the street and exclaiming, 'Have you seen the score?' 'Seven to six.' 'Jones has won again!' and so on." The press joined in the excitement. "Well! Now it is settled. The

Athletic is the champion!" the *Philadelphia Record* beamed. "Bradley and Mathews were no good in Louisville; but Jones' jump did it."

After their years of neglecting a sport they thought was crooked, Philadelphians suddenly cared more passionately about baseball than anything. And Chris Von der Ahe, who had let his manager go in a moment of anger, had to settle for second place.

15

A GREAT BOOM
FOR BASE BALL

T HE *PHILADELPHIA EVENING BULLETIN* ARGUED THAT THE 1883
season had surely proved that baseball was the national pastime:
"It is a quick, nervous, dashing, brilliant kind of sport, in keeping
with our American characteristics." Moreover, the huge crowds and the
honest, hard work of the players had made clear that baseball's long decline
was over, and the stain of corruption scrubbed clean. A decade earlier, the
Philadelphia Item recalled, "the name of Athletic became a by-word for all
that was dishonest and corrupt. Players were known to stand in with the
gamblers, and pools were sold within a few feet of the ground, and in the
very room in which the players dressed." The gamblers had "killed and
buried the game in this city." Now baseball had risen from that grave. For
all the celebrating, the Athletics' final victory was not exactly impressive.
After Simmons had begged Louisville to lose, without success, the pennant
had in essence come down to one game, in extra innings, and one limping
runner crossing the plate. But no matter. The Athletics clutched the prize

they had come west to find. In Philadelphia, a dazzled reporter walked along Chestnut Street with an old-time baseball addict who, like thousands of others, had just rediscovered his love for the game.

"Have you the fever, too?" the older man asked the journalist. "I must admit that I have a touch of it myself. Not since 1874, when the gamblers broke up the games in the East, have I felt any interest in it, but now every one talks base ball." The man began reminiscing about baseball in Philadelphia from 1868 on, a reverie the journalist dutifully scribbled down; it filled up more than a full column of small type the next day.

Then the two went their separate ways, the reporter to file his story, the other to a business engagement. "Bye-bye," the fanatic waved as he turned away. "I will see you in the parade."

Pennant in hand, the Athletics cared nothing about the final game of the regular season, on Sunday morning, September 30. Harry Stovey sat out, resting his throbbing ankle. But his teammates on the field were almost as bad off—tired, sore, homesick, and, surely, hung over. The new champions played "with a certain degree of carelessness that was disagreeable to the spectators, and they made several very bad errors," the *Louisville Courier-Journal* complained. Eclipse batters cracked it open in the eighth inning, scoring nine runs off George Washington Bradley to bring down the Athletics, 10–5. When it was over, the Athletics admitted they had "played to finish the game quickly and get away." Later that afternoon, the Browns completed their sweep of the Alleghenys, ending the season just one game behind Philadelphia. Had Von der Ahe left Ted Sullivan alone to do his job, would St. Louis have breached that narrow gap?

After a quick lunch in Louisville, the bruised and exhausted champions headed for home. When they pulled into the station at Cincinnati that evening, the Athletics received the first of many warm receptions. The New York Metropolitans and their manager, Jim Mutrie, were waiting on the platform to offer their congratulations and to board the victory train. In gratitude for the damage New York had dealt the Athletics' most dangerous rivals—especially the Cincinnati Reds, whom they defeated ten times in fourteen games—the Athletics had invited the Mets to join them as their guests in Philadelphia. Two Reds players with strong Philadelphia connections also made it to the platform—Chick Fulmer, a police constable in the city, and Long John Reilly, both former members of the then-

"See, the Conquering Heroes Come," depicting the injured and
exhausted Athletics at the end of the 1883 season
(Transcendental Graphics/theruckerarchive.com; *reprinted with permission)*

independent Phillies—and they "made up in warmth what the Cincinnati
delegation lacked in numbers, and satisfied the Athletics that old Philadelphia players were rejoicing at their good luck," wrote a reporter for the
Philadelphia Press who was now traveling with the champions.

After an overnight journey, the train stopped in Pittsburgh, where the
two ball clubs paused for breakfast with umpires John Kelly and Charlie
Daniels, who would accompany the Athletics to their victory celebration. A
number of the men woke up that morning in sorry shape. Jumping Jack
Jones was suffering a painfully sore neck, and Harry Stovey tried to ignore
the pounding of his sprained ankle. Athletics outfielder Bob Blakiston, meanwhile, was "still somewhat discomposed" after having jumped up into his
berth the night before "in the approved slide-for-second style," only to bring
the whole bed crashing down on Lew Simmons in the lower bunk. Both
men, however, came through the accident in good enough shape to engage
in some baseball talk, which lasted from the moment they left smoke-
shrouded Pittsburgh until the train approached the suburbs of Philadelphia.

As the train steamed toward Philadelphia, squealing to station stops in
between, the players discovered ever-larger and wilder crowds waiting to

greet them. In Altoona, where the men stopped at the splendid Logan House, famous for its 104-foot-long dining hall, fanatics hailed one man as the hero of the hour: the Yale leaper, Jumping Jack Jones. "He was good natured enough to smile on the crowd as he passed back and forth from the Logan House dining-room," the *Philadelphia Press* reported. In Huntingdon, Harrisburg, and Lancaster, bigger and more enthusiastic crowds greeted the team. "'Jumping Jack' seemed to be the man whom everyone wanted to see."

When the train pulled into Harrisburg late Monday afternoon, several Philadelphia men who had spent the last two weeks feverishly planning the Athletics' celebration were waiting on a mobbed platform. The welcoming committee held back the crowd long enough for the Athletics, famished by the ride, to wedge their way through to dinner. As the ballplayers sat down to eat, fanatics rushed into the dining room, threatening to overturn the tables. The crowd was forced from the room and the doors closed. Outside, the *Press* noted, people took up "positions round the windows and commented on the appearance and appetites of the players," as if they were zoo animals at feeding time.

Back in Philadelphia, fanatics who were determined to welcome the team home threatened to overrun Broad Street Station, many of them eluding the railroad's efforts at crowd control. A main stairway to the station platform had been boarded up, and the railroad had dispatched an army of brakemen and conductors to peruse every person passing through a checkpoint. Their white caps and full uniforms showed that they were entitled to be there, and not just trying to get close to the Athletics. When people discovered they only needed to produce a railroad ticket to get onto the platform, "a rush was made for the windows, and the clerks found themselves with more work in hand than they could conveniently manage," the *Press* reported. "People bought pasteboards privileging them for a railroad journey which they knew they would never take." One man, barred entry, shook his fist at the conductor and stormed off to buy a ticket. "With a proud smile," he "threw down a quarter at the adjoining ticket window," and, "with a triumphant air," presented it to the same conductor. "Your train won't be ready for an hour," the official said with a malicious grin. "Take a seat in the vestibule."

By the time the Athletics arrived, at 7:30 P.M., about one hundred fanatics were crowding the platform. Many times more stood behind an iron gate, and by "climbing on each other's shoulders and screwing themselves into all sorts of awkward attitudes," managed to catch a glimpse of councilman and mayoral candidate William B. Smith leaping from the train, "his face and silk hat alike shining." The badges on the dignitaries told the waiting fans that this was the right train—the Athletics had, indeed, arrived! "It was time to cheer, and cheer they did. A lusty yell was sent up and re-echoed back from the depot's roof. Hats, handkerchiefs and umbrellas rose in wild confusion to do homage to the returned players."

The Athletics players quickly formed behind a waiting band. As it marched out, it struck up "The Star Spangled Banner," while policemen fought to clear a path for the procession. Cheers and shouts erupted as the

Athletics' victory parade,
Harper's Weekly, October 13, 1883 (Library of Congress)

dazzled players, in danger of being crushed at any moment, strode down the magnificent main staircase. It was a madhouse. "Half a dozen young ladies who had come to present the Athletics some choice bouquets of flowers were rudely pushed aside by the surging mob," said the *Philadelphia Press*, "and before they could recover themselves or regain their positions, those whom thousands of Philadelphians had come to welcome were swept down into the carriages," which would form the focal point of a massive parade.

Standing before them was the Evening Call Band, sponsored by a local newspaper, its fifty members dressed in scarlet helmets with gold mountings, dark blue coats trimmed with dark braiding across the breast, and light blue trousers with scarlet stripes. As the Athletics players climbed up into their carriages, the band struck up "Hail to the Chief." Two of George Bradley's sons, who had been waiting at the depot, sat proudly alongside their famous dad, just as the children of Roman generals did in the triumphs of old. The barouches rolled away from the station and around Penn Square at a brisk trot, while a crowd that had waited for more than an hour for a glimpse of their heroes "set up a deafening chorus of cheers and yells." A mighty parade—more than a mile in length, 7,708 men strong—was forming. At Broad Street, "the advance fife and drum corps began tooting and beating away at a lively rate, the marshals shouted to the dense crowd to fall back, and the triumphal march was begun amid the firing of rockets and Roman candles and the waving of thousands upon thousands of hats and handkerchiefs."

Tens, if not hundreds, of thousands of people lined the streets to watch the nighttime spectacle, the biggest crowd, some thought, since a tremendous parade eighteen years earlier had been held to honor the returning heroes of the Civil War. "If the crowds were great that gathered in 1865 to see the veterans of many a hard fought field marshaled for the last time by Meade, Hancock, Humphreys, Geary, Hartranft, Averill and dozens of others whose names had been cut with their swords upon their country's records, the crowds upon the streets last night appeared no smaller," an editorial in the *Philadelphia Press* contended. "The bands played; hundreds of flags fluttered in the breeze; the cheers could not have been heartier; the enthusiasm could not have been more real."

Jim Mutrie, riding with his Metropolitans, found the scene "simply amazing." "No such demonstration has ever been seen in this country. It was a great boom for base ball," Mutrie said. Fanatics along the route took up positions on housetops and fences: "They swarmed on door steps and clung desperately to the very signs suspended from the awning girders. They climbed the telegraph poles by the dozen and filled every door and window along the line of march." Police, waving batons, fought to force a path for the parade through the mobs occupying the street. The crowd, thankfully, was in no mood to fight back. "While the dense mass of human beings swayed back and forth the utmost good feeling prevailed. Every person seemed happy," reported the *Philadelphia Record*.

When the barouches passed the Hotel Lafayette, Roman candles shot off, "and almost simultaneously Broad Street was lighted up for squares down its imposing length by a succession of different colored fires"— gold, blue, green, and violet lights—"dazzling in their intensity" and "gorgeous in the extreme." Businesses, too, contributed to the beauty of the scene. The front of the Chestnut Street department store of the innovative John Wanamaker was "a glittering combination of lanterns, colored lights and waving flags." Suspended over the street was the banner "Welcome champions," with a display of flaming gas dots spelling out: "Well done." The *Philadelphia Press* had hung the flags of many nations from the upper windows of its building, "while above the doorway was an elaborate display of bunting drooped and festooned around the motto: 'Welcome home, the Champion Athletics.'" The Athletics' club headquarters, "handsomely illuminated with torches, colored fires and Chinese lanterns," offered the most fetching visions of all: "A group of the lady friends of the club were gathered in the lower front apartment, and as the barouches passed the door they threw flowers and kisses at champions, who responded gallantly to the delicate and delightful compliments." Along the route, countless admirers of Dan Jones waved jumping jack toys. At Eighth and Buttonwood, the Iona club "created considerable amusement" by hanging a big jumping jack from the roof and keeping it in continual motion.

The parade itself featured a vast array of marching bands, soldiers, ballplayers, and men carrying illuminated "transparencies" with slogans on them. Carriages and wagons glowed with lights and colored fire. Crowds saw, in succession, baton-wielding policemen, bands, marching boys, and carriages bearing the Athletics, the New York Metropolitans,

Our Jumping Jack (detail),
Harper's Weekly, *October 13, 1883* (*Library of Congress*)

the Philadelphia Phillies, and the amateur August Flower and Anthracite clubs. Umpires Kelly and Daniels were part of the parade, as were Billy Barnie and his fellow Baltimore owners. Behind them were local amateur teams, including one all-black club, social organizations, and scores of Philadelphians who simply wanted to march.

Marchers carried jumping jacks of all shapes, and a life-sized dummy of Browns owner Chris Von der Ahe on a stretcher. One transparency read, "Der ish von thing mine poys did lack, und dot ish dis, von Shumping Shack!" It was signed, "Von der Ahe." Another read, "'Twas Bradley's smile and Knight's clear eye / Which made der Bresident moan and sigh." And there was this: "Matthew's [*sic*] brains, O'Brien's style, Jones' jump and Bradley's smile, did it." Others were pithier: "Rah for Yale"; "Stovey sixteen home runs"; "Jumping Jack"; "A Cold Day for St. Louis"; "A Cold Knight for St. Louis." One sign parodied a classified ad: "For Sale, the Complete Outfit of a Base Ball Club, Address St. Louis." Street hawkers, meanwhile, did a brisk business selling portraits of the Athletics players.

The parade took a full hour and ten minutes to pass the reviewing stand. As the *Philadelphia Record* described the scene:

> Dignified-looking citizens, arrayed in broadcloth and stovepipe hats, drove by in open carriages and respectfully touched their hats; bands of masqueraders in the guise of Indians, Dutchmen, clowns, acrobats, Chinamen and dudes, capered along, performing a series of astonishing dances as they went past. . . . There were bands of music, fife and drum corps, dozens of base ball clubs composed of men, and scores of base ball clubs composed of boys, some in carriages and some on foot; social clubs, yacht clubs and various other sorts of clubs; squads of mounted men in citizen's clothes; humorous characters bestriding donkeys and mules; temperance cadets, companies of pioneers, advertising wagons and a general conglomeration of miscellaneous attractions too numerous to mention.

Along with hundreds of horses, one mule had the privilege of marching—an "antique gray" that, in the off-season, had pulled the milk wagon of Athletics second baseman Cub Stricker. In the carriages up ahead, Stricker "was one continuous smile." Joyful noises filled the streets: "The uproar was tremendous with the blare of brass bands, the shrill piping of the fifes, the rattling of the drums and the howls of delight emitted by the numberless small boys, who, as usual on such occasions, were here, there and everywhere." One band of revelers, passing Mayor Samuel G. King's reviewing stand, let loose "terrific blasts upon a score or more of tin horns, an instrument that has long since received his severest official condemnation."

Fans looked on with adoration and envy. "There was many a man and boy last night who would rather have been one of the returning champions than a great general or successful politician," the *Press* noted. Jones and Hubbard, mere college boys,

> have made their names more widely known than are those of two-thirds of the country's professors, authors, statesmen or lawyers. Perhaps it may have occurred to these two as they rode through the thronged streets, while boys and men hung to their carriages and shouted themselves

hoarse, that the honors, if real, were fleeting; that perhaps no such scene would ever arise from such a cause again; that if it should others would be the heroes of the hour, while their own triumphs would be as deeds writ in water, and that any reputation, to be enduring, must be based not upon contests which have no substantial results, but on those which promote the welfare of man's fellows.

Out in the crowd, pickpockets had a fine night. At district police stations, people complained of lost watches and other valuables. A man fell from a tree at the corner of Broad and Market streets and broke a wrist. A forty-five-year-old woman suffered a crushed foot when a horse lurched out of control at Broad and Lombard streets. As the parade approached on Sixth Street, dozens of people rushed forward, pushing out the supports of a large scaffold, and bringing it down "with a large crash." Remarkably, it struck no one. At the corner of Broad and Chestnut streets, a pregnant black woman was watching the parade when a young white man named Charles Emerson shoved her. "She requested him not to push so roughly, whereupon he braced himself against an iron railing and kicked the woman in the face, seriously injuring her," the *Press* reported. (The *Inquirer* claimed that he "accidentally" kicked her in the abdomen.) In any case, two police detectives swooped down and arrested the man. At Broad and Bainbridge streets, five-year-old Emma Moore was watching the passing parade when a large wagon knocked her down and ran over her, killing her instantly. Such were the vagaries of nineteenth-century life.

The Athletics were blithely unaware of all this, savoring their hour of glory. Near the Central Station, Mayor King stood on a platform, hat in hand, flamboyantly bowing to the passing champions. "They rose in their carriage and saluted him heartily," the *Press* reported. As the night grew late, the Athletics' carriages suddenly departed from the parade, bolted down a side street for Seventh Street, and delivered them to Mercantile Hall for the grand banquet, scheduled to start at 11 P.M. As the players entered the hall, where tables had been laid for 160 diners, a band struck up "Home Again." On the main table was a centerpiece of two floral baseball bats standing crosswise over a ball of red and white flowers, a gift from Bill Sharsig's wife. Even the eight-course banquet's bill of fare was designed with baseball in mind:

Oysters on the Shell.
"Take them on the Fly"

. . .

Spring Chicken. Asparagus.
"Out on a Foul."

. . .

Devilled Crabs. Escalloped Oysters.
"Doubled Up."

. . .

Chicken Croquettes. Chicken Salad.
"A Juggled Foul."

. . .

Fried Oysters. Lobster Salad.
"Hot Liners."

. . .

RELISHES.
Celery. Olives. Pickles.
"The former we get twice a month."

. . .

Dessert. Fruits. Mixed Cakes. Ice Cream. Water Ices.
"Freeze to your Base."

. . .

Coffee. Tea.
"Home Run."

The keynote speaker, Colonel Thomas Fitzgerald, an orator, publisher, philanthropist, and founder of the first Athletics club, seemed to share his audience's awe over the extraordinary scenes they had just witnessed. "Nothing in the history of ancient Greece or Rome will compare with the reception given to the champions tonight. It is certain that 750,000 men, women and children witnessed the procession," the colonel declared. "This triumph is wonderful when we consider that every man here [in America] is a sovereign and every woman a queen." Lew Simmons beamed. The anxiety of Louisville was over, and baseball had obviously reestablished itself in the hearts of Americans, never to fade again as dangerously as it had before the American Association came along.

Then it was time for awards. Each player received a gold badge bearing his name and the inscription, "Athletic Base Ball Champions of 1884" (denoting their reign until the end of the next season). "Not the least pleasant feature of the occasion," the *Press* observed, was co-owner Charlie Mason's formal presentation of a gold watch and chain to Harry Stovey, whose extraordinary grace and drive had sustained the club during its crucial final six weeks. Although the organizers had banned "liquors of any kind" that night, nobody seemed to mind too much, as the crowd enjoyed its feast to the strains of delightful music played by McCann's Great Western Band. At 1:30 A.M., when the party finally broke up, everyone went out into the gas-lit night "delighted with everything." Certainly, the club was delighted with its profit margin for the season: a whopping $78,320, based on a detailed balance sheet published in the *Press*. Lew Simmons, who earlier in the year had purchased a fruit farm near Vineland, New Jersey, now bought himself "a cozy family homestead, a fine house handsomely fitted up."

One great challenge for the Athletics remained: proving themselves against the National League champions, the Boston Red Stockings, in what was supposed to be baseball's first World Series.

CHRIS VON DER AHE CELEBRATED HIS BROWNS' WILDLY PROFITABLE season in typically spectacular fashion, by funding a massive entry in St. Louis's annual Trade Parade on October 5. Drawn by six large horses that were "led by colored grooms who were in full uniform," the *Missouri Republican* said, his float was a stunning showpiece depicting Sportsman's Park in miniature. It included "a substantial representation of the grand stand and scorer stand with a large crowd of spectators inside." Standing on a scaled-down diamond at their own positions were the real Browns.

They were "readily recognized by the crowd who sent up cheer after cheer as the familiar faces passed by." At some point, they turned over their places to boys dressed in miniature Browns and Athletics uniforms, who actually played with a ball, "a wire screen having been provided on either side of the float to keep the ball from escaping," the *Globe-Democrat* reported. As the float passed the corner of Fifth and Market streets, a bat rolled off onto the street. Before anyone could grab it, Arlie Latham "nimbly jumped down in the mud," the *Republican* said, "and rescued it again. His action was much cheered."

As disappointing as the Browns' finish was, Von der Ahe was never one to stew for long. After all, he had much to be proud of. The season had been a phenomenal financial success. While the *Globe-Democrat* estimated a profit of $50,000, Von der Ahe bragged he had cleared $70,000. And he had gathered many of the pieces for a great team for years to come. The immigrant grocer, in short, had worked wonders in this foreign land with the game Americans called their national pastime. In time, many St. Louis fans would come to forget him and what he did, but they would never stop loving, with a remarkable passion that burns on to this day, the game he had helped to save.

And before the season was over, Chris was already making big plans for 1884.

EPILOGUE:
WHEN THEY SLIDE HOME

HE PHILADELPHIA ATHLETICS, FINDING THEY WERE TOO severely injured to compete effectively in October, canceled what would have been baseball's first World Series against the Boston Red Stockings. Even so, the baseball annuals published the following spring celebrated the magnificence of the 1883 season. It was "the most glorious and satisfactory ever known in the history of the game," *Wright & Ditson's Base Ball Guide* mused. "Never was the glorious uncertainty of the game so well displayed! Never was the rivalry between cities more intense and the excitement more infectious! Never was the result of games both in the home and other cities more closely watched for! The press was as wild as the public, and almost more space was devoted to the exploits of the favorite team in a day than had hitherto been given in a week." The season's attendance figures were unprecedented. The Philadelphia Athletics alone drew some 300,000 people. "The class of patron was of the highest character, well showing that the public had regained their confidence in the game"—the violence aimed at umpire Ormond Butler by Philadelphia goons notwithstanding.

The future of baseball, foreboding only a few years earlier, now looked dazzlingly brilliant. "The month of May will see more professional clubs taking the field than was ever known since the game began to be played, more than thirty years ago," noted *Reach's Official American Association Base Ball Guide*. On opening day 1884, there were three major leagues competing for baseball lovers' patronage—the new Union Association, destined to last only a year, had been founded by entrepreneurs who had been frozen out of the National League and the American Association. In addition, there were at least eighty professional baseball clubs hailing from more than seventy cities, and they employed more than one thousand players whose aggregate salaries would top an unimaginable $1 million.

Professional baseball never again teetered on the brink quite as it had in the late 1870s and early 1880s. The stability won in 1883 dramatically and permanently strengthened the game. People trusted it again, and Americans resumed weaving baseball inextricably into the nation's culture. There were some stumbles, of course. An economic depression temporarily blunted interest in the game during the following decade, and the Beer and Whiskey League was fatally wounded in 1890, when the Players League, a third major league, founded by rebellious players in 1890, and lasting only one season, deprived the Association of many of its players and much of its prestige. As a result, in 1892, the Association's strongest franchises merged with the National League. Four Association franchises survive to this day: the Dodgers (who would leave Brooklyn for Los Angeles), the Cincinnati Reds, the Pittsburgh Pirates (having dropped the Alleghenys nickname), and the St. Louis Cardinals (who shed the Browns moniker).

Even though the American Association had come to an end, its unique approach, delightfully combining beer and Sunday baseball, came to be adopted by the leagues that took its place. By 1918, Cleveland, Detroit, and Washington had Sunday baseball. The following year, New York permitted it. In 1929, Boston allowed Sunday ball; in 1932, Baltimore. Finally, Philadelphia—the toughest nut to crack—surrendered in 1934, thanks to the hard lobbying of Connie Mack, owner of the Philadelphia Athletics.

--------⟨◇⟩--------

THE AMERICAN ASSOCIATION'S ATHLETICS NEVER RECAPTURED THE glory of 1883. Amid reports of heavy drinking, the club staggered to seventh place in 1884, and it never again rose above third place in the Association's final standings.

In 1901, the Philadelphia franchise of the new American League adopted the Athletics nickname and had better luck with it—for a time— winning six pennants in thirteen years under manager and part-owner Connie Mack, who had been a major-league catcher in the 1880s. In 1955, the Athletics moved to Kansas City. They relocated to Oakland in 1968, where they remain.

Harry Stovey, who in 1883 became the first major-league player to hit more than ten home runs in a single season, later became the first to hit one hundred in a career. Two times he held baseball's career record for home runs, yielding the crown to Roger Connor, who was finally bested by Babe Ruth. For decades, Stovey was considered among the greatest base stealers of all time. He owns another distinction suitable for trivia contests: in a way, he is why the Pittsburgh franchise uses the name Pirates to this day. The press began using that name for the team after Pittsburgh tried to make off with Stovey and second baseman Lou Bierbauer in an 1891 raid on the Athletics. Stovey retired after the 1893 season, returned to New Bedford, resumed use of the name he was born with, Harry D. Stow, and landed a job on the city's police force. While patrolling his beat along the city's grimy waterfront one day in 1901, Stow spotted a seven-year-old boy who had fallen in between two piers and was struggling in the water. He dove in to save his life. Soon he was promoted to sergeant for bravery, and later he became a captain. He died in 1937 at the age of eighty—to the last a loyal fan of the Philadelphia Athletics.

Bobby Mathews, the tough little pitcher who led the Athletics to their only American Association pennant, won thirty games in 1884 and another thirty in 1885. Then he lost his edge. At the time of his retirement in 1887, he had won more games than any other pitcher in major-league history— 298, counting his National Association years. That is still the most wins ever recorded by any pitcher who has been left out of the Baseball Hall of Fame. Yet for all his magnificent achievements, he left baseball a poor man. After struggling in odd jobs—he worked at Joe Start's road house near Providence for a time—he began to show signs of mental illness, the result of paresis from syphilis, the same illness that finished off his one-time Providence Grays teammate Old Hoss Radbourn in 1897. Eventually, the great pitcher wound up in a mental hospital, where he died in April 1898 at the age of forty-six.

Jumping Jack Jones, the improbable savior of the 1883 Athletics, never played another game in the major leagues. Within months, he was performing around the country as second tenor with the Yale College Glee Club. The group was bound from St. Louis to Louisville in early 1884 when their train derailed, killing and maiming some aboard. "Jones, who was uninjured, received much praise for the efforts he made in behalf of two of his unfortunate colleagues," the New York Clipper reported. The lucky survivor went on to graduate from Yale Medical School. He studied dentistry at Harvard, then went into practice with his mother. In 1884, he briefly played ball for the Meriden club in Connecticut, where he pitched to a rising catcher named Connie Mack, later owner of the Athletics. "A friendship began that never ended," the New York Times recounted. "The Athletics have always been Dr. Jones's patron team. He sat on their bench with Connie Mack whenever he visited in Philadelphia, or any city where they were playing, and he and Mack visited each other repeatedly. Mack valued highly his judgment on the pitchers the Athletics developed." The man known as Jumping Jack died at the Masonic Home in Wallingford, Connecticut, in 1936 at the age of seventy-five, two days before the death of Athletics co-owner Charlie Mason.

The other members of that championship club quickly went their separate ways. Jud Birchall died of heart disease in 1887 at the age of thirty-two, one measure of the hard lives and bad diets of men at the time. Catcher Ed Rowen died at thirty-four after suffering hemorrhaging of the lungs. Mike Moynahan was dead before the turn of the century at age forty-six. Catcher John O'Brien became a Philadelphia teamster and, by 1910, was suffering terrible pain from Bright's disease, a kidney ailment. Destitute and all but forgotten, he relied on the charity of the Elks Club to make his final days comfortable. A huge fan of Mack's Athletics, O'Brien devoured every word about them in the newspapers his caretakers brought him on his deathbed. "Frequently he expressed the wish that he could go to the city hall and talk over old times with Lon Knight," the Washington Herald reported. "When one pauses to consider the pathetic end of the former star, almost alone and forgotten by the masses who lionized him less than thirty years ago, what a lesson his death should be. . . . Baseball goes on, but the men who made the game are forgotten in the desire to do homage to the new kings of the diamond."

Pitcher George Washington Bradley jumped to the Union Association in 1884, was blacklisted, and came back to the Athletics in 1886 for a dismal thirteen games as a short stop. He found employment as a night watchman and then as a Philadelphia policeman, dying of liver cancer in 1931. Second baseman Cub Stricker opened a cigar store near Recreation Park, home of the Phillies, then returned to delivering milk by his familiar horse and cart. He died in Philadelphia at age seventy-eight. Captain Lon Knight took a desk job at City Hall, helping to run the Highway Maintenance Department. After a gas line in his house broke in 1932, he died of gas poisoning. Fred Corey suffered a hunting injury in 1886, receiving a load of shot in the left eye that ended his baseball career. In his later years, he worked a lathe in Providence. He died in a hotel room there in 1912, asphyxiated while reading in bed. Bob Blakiston returned to California, where he made sails at the Mare Island Navy Yard and worked as a janitor, then died of tuberculosis in 1918.

Lew Simmons, who fell out with his fellow owners, sold his share in the team, lost all $100,000, and had to hit the road again as a traveling minstrel player. He kept all his earthly wealth—mostly the proceeds from the previous night's show—in his pocket. "But I am just as happy and perhaps a little healthier than when I stayed awake night[s] to count my money," he insisted. In 1904, a Philadelphia magazine writer described the elder minstrel star's appearance at the Pen and Pencil Club: "In response to loud calls he mounted the little club stage with banjo in hand, and in a moment he had many there traveling backward to the best years of their lives. Old faces became flushed with youth." A quintet of college banjoists on hand looked on in wide-eyed amazement as the old man worked his magic with the strings. "Old! That's a misnomer. Men like Lew Simmons never get old. Never in his palmist days did he make the banjo talk in sweeter tones." Still, he never forgot baseball, and he loved to regale his listeners with tales of his glory as an owner of the pennant-winning Athletics. "It was in those days—the heyday of baseball—that the sport, if less refined, was more picturesque," he said in 1902. In 1911, while still touring in vaudeville, the seventy-three-year-old Simmons stepped off a curb on a busy street in Reading, Pennsylvania, dodged an oncoming ice wagon that was in the wrong lane, and was struck down and killed by a beer truck.

--------◇--------

AFTER WINNING THE LEAGUE'S FIRST PENNANT IN 1882, THE Cincinnati Reds never captured another American Association championship. In fact, most of the team very nearly didn't survive another year—they almost perished en masse during an October 1883 postseason stop for an exhibition game. After changing into their uniforms in their third-floor rooms at the Beckel House in Dayton, Ohio, they headed to the elevator. Instead of going down in groups, the team's biggest stars—Will White, Long John Reilly, Bid McPhee, Chick Fulmer, Joe Sommer, Charley Jones, Pop Corkhill—all playfully packed themselves into an elevator with a reporter. The perennially late Hick Carpenter refused to join them at first, worried that the "thing might break" under the weight. One of the players laughed, saying, "Crowd in, Hick, you might as well die now as any other time." Carpenter obeyed. Before the boy operating the elevator could even close the door, something snapped, and "the car shot down like a meteor" before the horrified eyes of teammate Phil Powers, who was standing in the hall. Carpenter instinctively grabbed for the elevator cable, but quickly "let go after the flesh on [his] forefinger had been gashed to the bone." When the car hit the cellar floor, "the shock was terrific. Every particle of glass in the elevator was broken out."

Rushing down the stairs, "expecting to find the mangled remains of some of his companions," Powers heard nervous laughter emerging from the shaft. To his intense relief, nobody had been seriously injured, though the boy operator got bruises and cuts on his face and various players complained of back and ankle aches. "A whiter-faced set of men were never seen than the Champions as they crawled out of the hole under the cellar," noted O. P. Caylor in the *Cincinnati Commercial Gazette*. Then they went to the ballpark and drubbed the Dayton club, 15–0. "The elevator must have fallen on the Dayton nine," Caylor joked. "White says it was the greatest 'down-shoot' he ever got off."

Having survived that horror, White took the manager's reins in 1884, but quit with a 43–25 record, saying he lacked the drive and temperament to do the job effectively. He pitched another full season, then retired in

1886 with a lifetime record of 229 wins and 166 defeats. Incredibly, he completed all but seven of the 401 major-league games he started. No one in baseball history ever pitched more innings in a single season than White's 680 in 1879, though Old Hoss Radbourn came close, with 678 ⅔ in 1884. The first major leaguer to wear glasses, White founded the Buffalo Optical Company in 1893. In 1911, at the age of fifty-six, he was teaching a niece to swim near his summer home at Lake Muskoka in Ontario when he suffered a heart seizure and drowned.

O. P. Caylor, the controversial baseball editor of the *Cincinnati Commercial Gazette*, part-owner of the Reds, and cofounder of both the American Association and organized baseball, threw aside any last vestige of journalistic objectivity in 1885 and took over as manager of his team. The

scrawny, pale sportswriter didn't do half badly, leading the Reds to second place. After a less successful season in 1886, he moved on to the big city, New York, as manager of the famous Metropolitans, a team on its last legs, stripped of its best players. When the Mets folded, he founded the short-lived *Daily Baseball Gazette* before landing a job at the *New York Herald*. There, Caylor began to suffer a scaring pain in his throat, while his body grew progressively weaker. Frantic to provide for his wife and child, Caylor kept pounding out stories even after he became desperately ill and lost his voice. He died in 1897 at the age of forty-seven. "Mr. Caylor was never rugged," said the *Herald*, "but his blows for the welfare of the national game were those of a giant."

Long John Reilly and Hugh Nicol
(Library of Congress)

Long John Reilly, the Reds' towering first baseman who moonlighted for Caylor by drawing baseball cartoons, eventually became a commercial artist. A voracious reader and keen student of human nature, Reilly "found the characters of Dickens on every field and Thackeray's folk on the highways and byways leading thereto," the *Cincinnati Enquirer* noted. "Had he cared to devote his pen to biography instead of the sketching pad, the ballplayer-artist might have been his own Boswell and the enthusiastic fans of the grand stand would have been the charmed devotee of the library fireside." He died at age seventy-eight at his home on Stanley Avenue in Cincinnati.

Chick Fulmer, the man who inspired one of Reilly's funniest cartoons by faking stomach cramps to help Hick Carpenter get into a game, suffered an unpleasant end to the 1883 season. The handsome shortstop, who had been delighting crowds in postseason exhibition games with his dead-on impressions of Jumping Jack's delivery and George Bradley's grin, took a foul off his bat right in the face. "His nose was broken by the blow, and he retired to the dressing-room, bleeding profusely from the injured member," the *Cincinnati Enquirer* reported. While setting his nose, a doctor had the sad task of informing Fulmer that it would never be "symmetrically beautiful" again. Fulmer insisted he "doesn't mind it as he is married." He called it quits for the season and, with bandaged nose, rejoined his wife and two young children back home in Philadelphia. He played one more season and retired.

In August 1939, a bony, eighty-eight-year-old Fulmer showed up at a Phillies-Reds game at Shibe Park. He was carrying a cane, but looked dapper in a dark suit with a diamond-patterned tie and old-fashioned high collar. Hailed as the "oldest professional baseball player alive," he spoke of the Reds' pennant-winning season of 1882. Reds manager Bill McKechnie, in uniform, draped his arm protectively around the old man with deep-set eyes and a beak-shaped nose. "We'll do it again," he promised Fulmer. The Reds did, capturing the pennant that year, and again in 1940. Fulmer saw his Reds triumph in 1939, then died the following February.

————◇————

ED "THE ONLY" NOLAN, THE HARD DRINKER BANISHED FROM THE Pittsburgh Alleghenys in 1883, worked in only sixteen more big-league games. Retiring from baseball in 1887, he joined the police force in his hometown of Paterson, New Jersey, the baseball hotbed that had also produced King Kelly and Jim McCormick. Officer Nolan died there in 1913 at the age of fifty-five. Even his obituary referred to his drinking: "He was one of those old time heroes who had friends in every city, and a personal following everywhere. A 'personal following' meant a coterie of good fellows in every city on the circuit, which welcomed the hero on his arrival and never let go of him until he left. There were champagne suppers without limit and small drinks without end."

New York celebrated its first pennant in 1884. It wasn't won by the city's "gilt-edged" National League team, but by its second-class American Association team, the Metropolitans, who had been shifted from the bad side of the Polo Grounds to an even shabbier field on the site of a former city dump. It wasn't until 1888, after the Mets had been folded —their best players shifted over to the League—that the club now known as the New York Giants finally took home the National League pennant. For John B. Day, the owner of the Giants, success was short-lived. He lost his fortune—and his club—in the war against the Players League. Day died impoverished after a lengthy illness in 1925. "Truthful Jim" Mutrie, who lost everything with him, died a poor man in 1938 at the age of eighty-six. Others would enjoy the riches they always knew New York baseball would yield.

American Association umpire Charley Daniels never forgot his most memorable brush with Von der Ahe's impulsive temper: the owner's decision in 1883 to hire a special train, at the enormous cost of $300, to rush him to a game in St. Louis rather than let the Association's most respected umpire preside. Daniels served as an umpire until 1889 and then disappeared from the public eye. In his old age, this gentle man shared a farm home near Colchester, Connecticut, with his brother, both of them unmarried and miserably poor. After his brother's death, the house burned down, and Daniels was forced to ask friends for shelter. In March 1932, at age eighty-three, he slipped and fell while trying to walk to town, slashing his head badly; a passing truck driver found him in a ditch. Daniels died the next day at Norwich Hospital. A sportswriter took it upon himself to raise money so that the famous umpire could get a decent burial.

Daniels's old colleague, "Honest John" Kelly, remained a top major-league umpire until 1888, stubbornly fraternizing, and even playing poker, with ballplayers. He also refereed some of the biggest boxing matches of the nineteenth century. After his retirement, he made a living off of the darker side of professional sports: he became a bookie and better, operating heavily at the racetracks, before opening his own gambling house in New York City. "I got into the gambling game because it was the most exciting one I could find," Kelly explained. He prided himself on running a house where gamblers were not cheated, and he refused to pay the New York police protection money. "They kept me busy buying new front doors because I wouldn't work to fill their pockets," he said. According to the *New York Times*, the honest gambler came to be blessed with "a host of friends, in and out of the fraternity, and was respected as a man by many citizens who thought only evil of professional gamblers as a class." Kelly died in 1926 of complications resulting from pneumonia. He was seventy years old, but he looked at least twenty years younger. "He had such a powerful physique, carried himself so erect and dressed so well that the years seemed to sit lightly on him," the *Times* noted.

Moses Fleetwood Walker left professional baseball after the 1890 season. He became an entrepreneur, literary man, and inventor, investing in the Union Hotel in Steubenville, Ohio; buying a movie theater in nearby Cadiz; publishing a weekly newspaper; and applying for patents, including for motion-picture equipment and an artillery shell. Embittered by life in America, he published a book in 1908 entitled *Our Home Colony: A Treatise on the Past, Present, and Future of the Negro Race in America*, which advocated black migration to Africa, the policy Abraham Lincoln had once espoused. "The Negro race will be a menace and the source of discontent as long as it remains in large numbers in the United States," Walker wrote. "The time is growing very near when the whites of the United States must either settle this problem by deportation, or else be willing to accept a reign of terror such as the world has never seen in a civilized country." But he proved just as wrong as Cap Anson. After a great struggle, America followed the path of integration, not racial division, in seeking to honor the founding idea that all men are created equal. Walker died in his home state of Ohio on May 11, 1924, about two years after Anson's death. Before either of these ancient adversaries was gone, however, a child had been born in Cairo, Georgia, who would change everything. His name was Jackie Robinson.

--------⟨○⟩--------

THE TEAM THAT TED SULLIVAN SO PAINSTAKINGLY BUILT, THE 1883 St. Louis Browns, shed their much-maligned scarlet stockings in 1884 and returned to classic brown. Under the guidance of Sullivan's protégé

Charlie Comiskey, they soon became an American Association power-
house, winning four straight pennants between 1885 and 1888, including
one world championship and another disputed one, soaring so high that
they were celebrated on cigar boxes as a symbol of excellence—all in the
face of Von der Ahe's constant interference. Although the Boston Red
Stockings (1872–1875), New York Giants (1921–1924), and New York Yankees (multiple times) tied that record of four straight pennants, only one
franchise has ever bested it: the mighty Yankees of 1949–1953 and 1960–
1964. "This team was the wonder of the baseball world for many a day,"
Alfred H. Spink wrote of the Browns. "The players were not stalwart looking but rather slight and slim waisted and when they met heavy nines like
Chicago and Detroit they suffered on the field in comparison." Nonetheless, the Browns "played wonderful and speedy ball and . . . they knew
how to win games," compiling the best overall winning percentage of any
club in American Association history.

Ted Sullivan would never get to manage his beloved Browns again.
In 1884, he won some measure of revenge by helping piece together the
St. Louis Maroons of the Union Association before clashing, once again,
with his club's headstrong owner and moving over to manage that league's
Kansas City franchise. Thanks to Sullivan, Lucas's Maroons—not Von
der Ahe's Browns—became the first team in St. Louis to win a pennant.
Sullivan went on to manage several other clubs in several other leagues,
big and small, including the National League's Washington club in 1888.
Connie Mack, a member of that team, remembered how Sullivan coaxed
first-rate service out of waiters at various stops during the team's trips.
When the waiter started serving, Ted dropped a silver dollar on the table.
The waiter, eyeing a bigger tip than he had ever received, delivered first-
rate service and big portions. At the end of the meal, Sullivan coolly
picked up the dollar and strolled out. "That silver dollar many times and
in many cities made the difference between a good meal and a bad one,"
Mack laughed.

After helping found a number of circuits, including the American
League, Sullivan became one of major-league baseball's first full-time
scouts. In 1903, he published a memoir that revealed what became of the
famous timepiece he had hurled at Von der Ahe's head before angrily quit-
ting the Browns in the midst of their pennant race. "[Von der Ahe] put

the watch in his pocket and . . . two months afterward, at Sportsman's Park, placed it back in my hand and told me not to be so high strung." Along with the watch, the remarkably generous Von der Ahe insisted that Sullivan take his pay for the remainder of the 1883 season. "But I would rather have won the pennant and enjoyed its glory," the manager recalled ruefully. In a 1910 recap of his career, *Baseball Magazine* noted: "Though a great hustler in after years, the rebuilding and remodeling of the Browns and the handling of them in 1883 surpassed anything Ted ever did in baseball." The unreconstructed racist, scout, and storyteller died in 1929 in Washington, D.C., at the age of seventy-seven.

Jimmy Williams, the secretary of the American Association, took over as Browns manager in 1884. But Williams encountered the same disciplinary problems that Sullivan had and similarly failed to last out a season. In 1885, Von der Ahe finally gave the job to Comiskey, who led the club to four straight championships. Inheriting some of his father's political skills, Comiskey smoothed over Von der Ahe's tantrums in a manner that the touchy Ted Sullivan could not. "The reason may be found in the fact that Comiskey never paid the slightest attention to the frequent outbursts of the boss but, penetrating the rough exterior, early discovered a heart as big as that of an ox," Comiskey's biographer wrote. Comiskey was also honest with Von der Ahe, explaining to him carefully what was going on, "and the mercurial magnate boasted to his friends that Charlie never worried him with any tricks, which to the sorely harassed executive meant a lot." Though he hit only .264 over his career, his contemporaries considered him a major star—mainly because of his fierce dedication to winning, a trait one contemporary called the "quality of gameness." He delivered hits in clutch situations, he played a heady first base, and he fine-tuned existing strategies, such as positioning fielders for specific batters. Eventually, he turned his back on his boss, Von der Ahe, defecting to the Players League. Years later, he would become an owner himself, creating the Chicago White Sox and helping to found the American League. He brought with him Von der Ahe's lesson of twenty-five-cent baseball and kept one-fourth of his massive park available for two-bit admissions. "It doesn't bring in quite as much money at the gate as the more expensive seats but it gives a greater number a chance to see my team and that is the big thing with me," Comiskey said.

Over the thirty-one years that Comiskey owned the White Sox, his team would win four pennants and two world championships. But Comiskey's club was indelibly stained in 1919 when several of his best players sold the World Series. It was baseball's darkest hour since the Louisville scandal of 1877. Such revisionists as director John Sayles in the 1988 movie *Eight Men Out* have pinned much of the blame on Comiskey, rather than the cheaters themselves, portraying him as a greedy capitalist who took advantage of the innocence of his players, virtually driving them into the arms of gamblers. It is indeed true that the owner was notoriously tight with his budget—one of his stars left to earn more money in semipro ball—but he was also deeply committed to his city, to baseball, and to the vitality of his club. In 1910, he built the first Comiskey Park and opened it to the public free of charge for special events, including amateur games, picnics, and church festivals. Many who knew him personally did not see him as a coldhearted capitalist. "In all the years I have known Comiskey, I have always found him the pink of kindness with always a respect and consideration for the rights and feelings of others," veteran sportswriter Alfred H. Spink wrote in 1909. When Comiskey died in 1931, he was one of the most revered figures in American sports, and few held him responsible for the 1919 scandal. Eight years later, he was enshrined in baseball's Hall of Fame.

August Solari, the Browns' groundskeeper, won a place in baseball history for inventing the use of tarpaulins to protect the infield from rain. Eventually, he quit to run a beer garden on the outskirts of St. Louis at the corner of Olive Street and Taylor Avenue. He advertised it in 1887 as "about the coolest and best place to pull up at while out on the road." Customers could "find him and a choice selection of wines, liquors and cigars on hand at all hours as well as the most tempting lunch to be found on the road."

The narcissistic Tony Mullane tried to jump to the St. Louis Maroons in the new Union Association in 1884, but got cold feet when he was threatened with blacklisting. Von der Ahe might have taken him back but, worried about a lawsuit by the Maroons if Tony played in St. Louis, thought it best to loan the Apollo of the Box to the American Association's weak Toledo team. There, he compiled a marvelous 36–26 record— remarkable, given that the rest of the staff was a feeble 10–32 and that, as a racist, Tony crossed up his black catcher. Rather than come back to St. Louis, as promised, in 1885 after the Union Association folded, Mullane signed with the Cincinnati Reds. Von der Ahe used his clout to have him banned from baseball for a year as a punishment. That was significant, since Mullane fell only 16 wins short of the 300-win plateau that would almost surely have earned him a spot in the Baseball Hall of Fame. After his ball-playing days, Mullane moved to Chicago, where he ran a saloon for a time before settling into a long career as a police officer. Operated on in 1911 for the third time for a brain abscess, he reportedly nearly perished. But he didn't: he retired from the force in 1920 and lived on until 1944. As a reporter had noted way back in 1883, "Tony does not 'kill' as easily as some people."

Little Arlie Latham, the sparkplug of the great Browns teams of the 1880s, went on to score one hundred or more runs in eight straight seasons. Thanks to his constant jokes and chatter, the infielder became such a prominent figure in the newspapers that Lew Simmons gave him a starring role in his 1888 production of the Broadway play *Fashions*. Arlie greeted audiences with the cry:

> I'm a daisy on the diamond!
> I'm a dandy on the stage!
> I'd ornament a horse-car,
> Or look pretty in a cage!

After his major-league career wound down in 1896, Latham moved down to the minor leagues for three seasons, happy just to keep playing the game he loved. He returned to the big show in 1909 as the first full-time coach in major-league history, helping the farsighted John McGraw run the New York Giants. During his three seasons with the club, Latham danced jigs and amused himself with other acrobatics. Giants outfielder Fred Snodgrass rated him "probably the worst third-base coach who ever lived." But Latham did teach McGraw's men how to steal bases. Under his tutelage they went from 181 per season to 347, the most ever in the twentieth century. In 1909, when Latham was fifty years old, he was still so spry that McGraw threw him into four games at second base for the Giants. Latham became, on August 18, the oldest man in major-league history to steal a base.

After leaving the Giants, Latham crossed the Atlantic, found a job at a hotel checking hats, and took on the unpaid role of international ambassador for American baseball. He even claimed to teach the game to the future monarch, the Prince of Wales. ("King George had only a fair arm," Latham confided later.) When he returned to the States, he parlayed his baseball connections into a job as press-box attendant at Yankee Stadium, where he marveled over the play of Joe DiMaggio and Phil Rizzuto. Arlie died in 1952 at age ninety-two. He was the last surviving player from the 1883 season.

The fellow whom Latham most enjoyed teasing, Chris Von der Ahe, suffered a crueler fate. During the mid-1880s, he reached a pinnacle of sorts. Through baseball, the immigrant owner had made a fortune that reportedly totaled $300,000. Rolling in loot and proud of his achievements, Von der Ahe commissioned a heroic, larger-than-life statue of himself— shoulders thrown back, chest pushed out, one foot thrust boldly forward— that he placed in front of Sportsman's Park and later used to top his

The Von der Ahe statue
(*Edward Achorn*)

cemetery monument. But the once frugal grocer surrounded himself with "a numerous army of flatterers and hangers-on" and "handled $1000 bills as if they were peanuts to feed to monkeys." After the American Association collapsed and he joined the National League, Von der Ahe found his fortune melting away at an alarming rate. His downfall was hastened by his fellow owners, who stole away his best players. The generous and goodhearted but disastrously hotheaded Von der Ahe was quickly picked clean by his associates. Reporters claimed that he deposited his watch with the hotel clerk before his last National League meeting for fear his fellow magnates would pinch it.

Desperate to boost attendance at Sportsman's Park, Von der Ahe added a racetrack and amusement park, advertising the place as "The Coney Island of the West," a farsighted attempt to make a ballpark an entertainment destination, a strategy adopted by baseball magnates today. But nothing worked. A costly fire at the ballpark set him back. He went through two bitter divorces. His son turned his back on him, and his creditors wrested away his ball club, selling it at a forced auction. At one point, he was arrested—kidnapped, in truth—and thrown in a Pittsburgh jail for welching on debts. After it all, he managed only to scrape together enough money to buy a saloon on the outskirts of St. Louis, virtually ending up as he began. Paying their respects to the ruined owner, the new owners, Edward C. Becker and Frank DeHaas Robison, sent their very first complimentary book of season tickets to Von der Ahe. He was too proud to accept it.

In April 1899, his former team—shedding the old nickname of Browns, and soon to be known as the Cardinals—staged a grand parade before the first Sunday game of the season. As the procession neared Third Street, someone saw Von der Ahe emerging from the doorway of a vacant building to listen to the brass band. "He looked about and saw the eyes of the crowd about centered on him," *Sporting Life* reported. "His face flushed a deep crimson. For a moment he hesitated, thinking to brave it out[,] but the struggle was too much for him and he retreated to the rear of the building." Brokenhearted, feeling tired and old, he could not repeat his earlier success with a saloon. In 1908, his former club played a charity game to raise money for him. Von der Ahe might have starved had it not been for regular gifts of money from his old manager, the supposedly stingy, heartless Charlie Comiskey, who paid him a visit in February 1913. "It certainly makes me feel good to think you came here just to spend three hours with your old boss," Von der Ahe told him. When Comiskey asked Von der Ahe how he was "fixed" for the future, he replied, "I've got a lot and a nice monument already built for me in Bellefontaine cemetery," and began to weep. Ailing for months, Von der Ahe suffered nephritis, a kidney disease, and cirrhosis of the liver from a lifetime of heavy drinking. He died on June 7, 1913, at the age of sixty-one.

St. Louis had not forgotten him. On the day of Von der Ahe's funeral, hundreds of baseball fans gathered outside his home at the corner of St. Louis and Grand avenues, crowding the street for blocks and standing with their heads bared. Flowers and testimonials filled the house. The Reverend Frederick H. Craft chose a baseball motif for his funeral sermon. "First base is enlightenment; second base is repentance; third base, faith, and the home plate the heavenly goal!" he declared. "Don't fail to touch second base, for it leads you onward to third. All of us finally reach the home plate, though some may be called out when they slide Home." For all he did to save and revitalize baseball, to popularize Sunday ball and beer, to lend color and dazzle to the game, and to found and lead one of the great franchises in baseball, Chris Von der Ahe deserves a plaque at the Baseball Hall of Fame. But his flamboyant personality, and the stories that he himself cultivated, left later generations with the impression that he was nothing but a buffoon, unworthy of such recognition.

The statue that had once stood outside his park, and which Von der Ahe had moved to top his burial monument, can still be seen in its pseudo-regal glory at Bellefontaine Cemetery. His pallbearers included five members of his 1883 Browns: Charlie Comiskey, Bill Gleason, Jack Gleason, George McGinnis, and, poignantly, Ted Sullivan, the man who had resigned that '83 team in a huff, throwing his watch at the fuming Mr. Von der Ahe.

He may have driven them all half-crazy, but in the end, they all loved and admired the German immigrant who had changed baseball forever.

ACKNOWLEDGMENTS

THIS BOOK WAS STRENGTHENED IMMEASURABLY BY GENEROUS men and women who love the history of this great game. Jeffrey Kittell, curator of the richly detailed website This Game of Games (http://thisgameofgames.blogspot.com/), was extraordinarily helpful, reading the manuscript through, making dozens of wise suggestions, and answering incessant questions. Jeff and Steve Pona of the St. Louis Baseball Historical Society drove me around their beautiful city, helped me visit the key sites related to Chris Von der Ahe and the Browns, and shared with me, a lifelong Red Sox fan, the magic of a hard-fought Cardinals game at Busch Stadium. John Thorn, the official historian for Major League Baseball, was unfailingly gracious and helpful. Eric Miklich, the man behind the illuminating website www.19cbaseball.com, read through the manuscript and made many helpful corrections and suggestions. He and his fellow early-baseball enthusiasts at the Vintage Base Ball Association also enriched my understanding of how baseball of this era "plays." Peter Mancuso, chairman of the Nineteenth Century Committee of the Society for American Baseball Research (SABR), jumped to my aid whenever asked, as did the participants in SABR's nineteenth-century listserv.

David Nemec, author of scores of baseball books, including *The Beer & Whiskey League*, was helpful both personally and through his work. Mark Fimoff put his brilliant analytical skills to work in helping to identify long-forgotten faces in old photos. Thomas Wright graciously provided help tracking down genealogical material. The great nineteenth-century baseball scholar Frederick Ivor-Campbell, though sadly no longer with us, was a continuing inspiration, and his widow, Alma Ivor-Campbell, intrepidly dug through his papers searching for information for me. Candy Adriance read through the manuscript, made countless helpful suggestions, and assisted me in obtaining documents. Historian Maury Klein, who read through an early version of this book, kindly shared his thoughts and knowledge of the craft with me. Robert Lifson and his colleagues at Robert Edward Auctions generously tracked down and shared wonderful vintage images.

David Miller and Lisa Adams at the Garamond Agency believed from the start in this tale of beer, Sunday baseball, and some of the most delightful characters in the game's history; I fondly recall David laughing over lunch about the Philadelphia crowd's initial reaction to Jumping Jack Jones. Stanley M. Aronson, MD, dean emeritus of medicine at Brown University, answered my many questions about nineteenth-century medical diagnoses. Howard Sutton, publisher, president, and CEO of the *Providence Journal*, was always supportive. Mike Tamburro, president of the Pawtucket Red Sox and an illustrious member of the International League Hall of Fame, was greatly encouraging, as was the late owner Ben Mondor, also a Hall of Famer, who opened the PawSox clubhouse on his eighty-fourth birthday to host an unforgettable launch party for my previous book. J. Thomas Hetrick, author of *Chris Von der Ahe and the St. Louis Browns*, kindly shared some of his expertise on the topic. Lauri Burke of the Barrington (Rhode Island) Public Library graciously tracked down books and documents for me through interlibrary loan. The Sterling Memorial Library at Yale University provided me with useful information about Jumping Jack Jones and Al Hubbard. Numerous other institutions supplied invaluable help, including the National Baseball Hall of Fame Library, the Library of Congress, the Chicago Historical Society, the Boston Public Library, and the St. Louis Mercantile Library. Thanks also to Ranger Elaine Brasher of the US National Park Service, for showing me around St. Louis historical sites and sharing her insights on the city's history, and to Phil Swann, for urging me to never give up.

Many thanks to Lisa Kaufman, Brandon Proia, and their superb team at PublicAffairs for improving the book in a hundred ways.

Thanks go to my beloved children, Jean, Matt, and Josh, to whom the book is dedicated. Special thanks, of course, to my wife, Valerie, for her love and support—and her faith that the story of baseball's rebirth through German immigrants was one eminently worth telling.

APPENDIX:
AMERICAN ASSOCIATION, 1883

Final Standings

	W	L	PCT.	GB
Philadelphia Athletics	66	32	.673	—
St. Louis Browns	65	33	.663	1
Cincinnati Reds	61	37	.622	5
New York Metropolitans	54	42	.563	11
Louisville Eclipse	52	45	.536	13½
Columbus Buckeyes	32	65	.330	33½
Pittsburgh Alleghenys	31	67	.316	35
Baltimore Orioles	28	68	.292	37

Batting Leaders/*Batting Average*

1. Ed Swartwood (PIT)   .357
2. Pete Browning (LOU)   .338

3. Jim Clinton (BAL)   .313
   Dave Rowe (BAL)   .313
4. Long John Reilly (CIN)   .311

Home Runs

1. Harry Stovey (PHI)   14
2. Charley Jones (CIN)   10
3. Long John Reilly (CIN)   9
4. Chick Fulmer (CIN)   5
   Tom Brown (COL)   5

Runs Batted In

1. Charley Jones (CIN)   80
2. Long John Reilly (CIN)   79
3. John O'Brien (PHI)   70
4. Mike Moynahan (PHI)   67
   Harry Stovey (PHI)   67

Slugging Percentage

1. Harry Stovey (PHI)   .506
2. Long John Reilly (CIN)   .485
3. Ed Swartwood (PHI)   .476
4. Charley Jones (CIN)   .471
5. Pete Browning (LOU)   .464

On-Base Plus Slugging

1. Ed Swartwood (PIT)   .869
2. Harry Stovey (PHI)   .852
3. Pete Browning (LOU)   .842
4. Long John Reilly (CIN)   .810
5. Charley Jones (CIN)   .799

Runs Scored

1. Harry Stovey (PHI)   110
2. Long John Reilly (CIN)   103
3. Hick Carpenter (CIN)   99

4. Lon Knight (PHI)   98
5. Jud Birchall (PHI)   95
   Pete Browning (LOU)   95

Pitching Leaders/*Wins*

1. Will White (CIN)   43
2. Tim Keefe (NY)   41
3. Tony Mullane (SL)   35
4. Bobby Mathews (PHI)   30
5. Guy Hecker (LOU)   28
   George McGinnis (SL)   28

Earned Run Average

1. Will White (CIN)   2.09
2. Tony Mullane (SL)   2.19
3. Ren Deagle (CIN)   2.31
4. George McGinnis (SL)   2.33
5. Tim Keefe (NY)   2.41

Win-Loss Percentage

1. Tony Mullane (SL)   .700
2. Bobby Mathews (PHI)   .698
3. George Bradley (PHI)   .696
4. Will White (CIN)   .662
5. George McGinnis (SL)   .636

Innings Pitched

1. Tim Keefe (NY)   619
2. Will White (CIN)   577
3. Frank Mountain (COL)   503
4. Guy Hecker (LOU)   469
5. Tony Mullane (SL)   460.2

Complete Games

1. Tim Keefe (NY)   68
2. Will White (CIN)   64

    3. Frank Mountain (COL)   57
    4. Guy Hecker (LOU)   51
    5. Tony Mullane (SL)   49

Strikeouts

    1. Tim Keefe (NY)   359
    2. Bobby Mathews (PHI)   203
    3. Tony Mullane (SL)   191
    4. Guy Hecker (LOU)   164
    5. Frank Mountain (COL)   159

NOTES

3   *"out late at night"*: EDG, January 23, 1895.

4   *"handsome young woman"*: SN, January 1, 1898.

4   *"shrewd, cunning and pugnacious"*: AB, July 11, 1890. Reporter was W. I. Harris.

4   *"Base ball vicissitudes"*: BE, September 3, 1888.

5   *"peculiarities of German customs"*: Dacus, 383.

5   *"A great blessing"*: Bogen, 13.

5   *"conviviality, camaraderie and good fellowship"*: Olson, 134.

5   *"Beer and wine the German"*: Smalley, 5.

6   *"In the old countries"*: NYT, October 9, 1856.

6   *"Formerly Americans drank"*: CE, March 25, 1882.

6   *"its inhabitants are pious"*: Dacus, 383.

7   *"floating palaces"*: Kargau, 233–234.

7   *"These Western cities"*: Bishop, 497–498.

7   *"Little tables are put out"*: Ibid., 511.

7   *Von der Ahe . . . was born*: Familysearch.org, The Church of Jesus Christ of Latter-day Saints, Indexing Project Number J93019–2, Germany-ODM, Source Film Number 1051737.

8   *desperate for work*: Kargau, 208.

8   *"any grocery store worth its salt"*: Proetz, 58–59.

8   *On March 3, 1870*: Hetrick, 4.

9   *In time, he had*: SLGD, February 5, 1884.

9   *[Solari] rented it out*: SL, May 21, 1898.

9   *"interested in pretzels"*: SLR, June 6, 1913.

9   *Councilman J. B. Woestman*: Leonard, 618–619.

9   *bribery scandal that spring*: SLGD, April 1, 1876.

9   *"none but the best amateur"*: SLGD, March 2, 1876.

11   *newspaper exposé charged*: SLGD, August 3, 1877.

11   *"But the baseball-loving public"*: Spink, 46.

11   *"gazed at the beggarly array"*: SLGD, June 16, 1879.

12   *"It was 'Eddie'"*: SLGD, February 7, 1905.

12   *"contained a weather beaten grandstand"*: Spink, 46.

13   *"a cricket field"*: SLGD, March 20, 1881.

13   *devoted to wing shooting*: AB, July 11, 1890.

13   *"no use for us"*: Spink, 47.

14   *"When he pulled out"*: Palmer 2, 70.

14   *"It was agreed as we all sat":* Spink, 46–47.

15   *"Had they remained":* BE, January 6, 1889.

15   *"seemed cold and bleak":* Spink, 298.

15   *"There was of course no discipline":* Ibid., 48.

16   *"Base Ball is old in the world":* SLGD, June 6, 1881.

16   *"He took no interest in the game":* NYW, September 13, 1896.

16   *"not . . . an overpowering success":* SLGD, July 31, 1881.

16   *"ruffling the feathers of the club":* Ibid.

16   *Three months later:* SLGD, October 9, 1881.

16   *called on his political connections:* As Jeffrey Kittel suggests. See This
       Game of Games blog, June 4, 2009.

Chapter 2: The Beer and Whiskey Circuit

20   *"I'd rather be a lamppost":* Spalding 1, 208.

20   *set off for Chicago:* Wyant, 100.

20   *"clear-headed, farsighted, and successful":* Spalding 3, 5.

21   *"going to expel you":* Spalding 1, 312.

21   *"living from hand to mouth":* Ward, 25–26.

21   *"I heard him entreat":* Spalding 1, 229.

23   *until June 1885:* The rule was revised at a special meeting of the American
       Association owners at the Girard House in Philadelphia on June 7, 1885.

23   *"Lipman Pike has":* CCR, William Hulbert letter to Freeman Brown,
       September 8, 1881.

24   *"Address to Players":* Spalding 2, 85.

24   *"Beer and Sunday amusements":* CE, July 29, 1880.

24   *"We respectfully suggest":* CE, October 31, 1880.

26   *"Truthful Jim" Mutrie, was on hand:* CE, November 6, 1881.

27   *"mushroom beer stands":* Orem, 17.

28   *"The sole purpose of the League":* CCR, William A. Hulbert letter to H.
       D. McKnight, November 8, 1881.

29   *"I have been ailing:"* CCR, William A. Hulbert letter to H. D. McKnight,
       November 18, 1881.

29   *"He admired the game very much":* BC, April 15, 1882.

30   *"men should be so devoid":* Quoted in PI, January 22, 1882.

30   *"attitude toward the so-called American Association":* CE, December 25, 1881.

30   *"It grieves me to say":* CE, August 23, 1882.

31   *"brains seems to have run to his paunch"*: PI, December 11, 1881.

31   *"tried to smother us"*: PI, January 8, 1882.

31   *"present at Mr. Hulbert's bedside"*: Spalding 3, 7.

32   *"some 500 hoodlums"*: SLGD, May 9, 1882.

32   *"In the League cities"*: Ibid.

32   *"The Alleghenys in the early part"*: CE, October 15, 1882.

33   *Louisville hosted balloon rides*: Orem, 21.

33   *"Can you imagine the difference"*: NSJ, February 19, 1899.

34   *"low trickery" professionals employed*: SL, August 20, 1884.

34   *"raging, tearing, booming"*: BG, April 9, 1889.

34   *five of the Association's six teams*: CL, August 8, 1882.

34   *"You cannot afford to sneer"*: CE, September 23, 1882.

35   *"worked up to a fever-heat"*: CE, October 24, 1882.

35   *"was a splendid one"*: CE, October 26, 1882.

35   *"I think that in 1884 Chicago"*: Ibid.

35   *"will be war to the knife"*: CE, October 1, 1882.

36   *"at home singing lullabys"*: CE, October 7, 1882.

36   *"young America is with plum-pudding"*: Ibid.

36   *hillbilly from "across the river"*: Ibid.

37   *"will be expelled"*: Orem, 50.

Chapter 3: The Minstrel Star

39   *"inexhaustible coal and iron fields"*: Glazier, 398.

39   *61 public drinking fountains*: Statistics from Encyclopedia, 696.

39   *of 145,000 buildings*: Coolidge, 274.

39   *"unbounded supply of fresh water"*: Ibid., 229.

39   *"smallest and cheapest house"*: Ibid., 236.

40   *Born on August 27, 1838*: Details of Lew Simmons's career from Rice, 126.

41   *contributed to the cause*: Cazden, 368.

42   *"slight appreciation of his efforts"*: NYC, January 6, 1883.

42   *"pretty work!"*: Ibid.

43   *"Sharsig's capital consisted of"*: Spink, 71.

43   *"went around among the newspaper offices"*: SN, December 10, 1887.

43   *"destined to be as popular"*: PI, June 26, 1881.

43   *"kept no books"*: Spink, 280.

43   *revived baseball's "old-time popularity"*: NYC, April 7, 1883.

44   *"there is not a greater ladies' man"*: NPG, September 15, 1883.

44   *"Ladies and gentlemen will be protected"*: NYC, April 7, 1883.

45   *"we decided to get solid players"*: PI, April 1, 1883.

45   *"All of the Athletics' season tickets"*: PI, January 21, 1883.

45   *"large enough for all"*: NYC, March 31, 1883.

45   *"landscape gardeners"*: NYC, April 14, 1883.

45   *"Although not yet completed"*: Ibid.

46   *"[leading] off with a three-bagger"*: Ibid.

47   *"We seem to be drifting"*: AGM, Mills to Louis Kramer, Esq., December 22, 1882.

47   *"It requires no keen sight"*: NYC, December 2, 1882.

47   *"Kilkenny fight"*: NYC, December 30, 1882.

47   *"If they can play together"*: CE, December 10, 1882.

47   *"although his club has suffered as badly"*: PI, December 17, 1882.

47   *"slept on the matter"*: NYC, December 23, 1882.

48   *"narrow-minded views"*: NYC, February 17, 1883.

48   *"If Hulbert made"*: National, 41.

48   *"started the game on a new career"*: PI, March 18, 1883.

49   *"Philadelphia public's confidence"*: NYC, April 21, 1883.

49   *"money talked to the tune"*: Ibid.

49   *"all-important for the Athletics"*: Ibid.

49   *"On squeezing through"*: Ibid.

50   *"otherwise it will become"*: Ibid.

50   *"The defeat won't do"*: Ibid.

50   *"unworthy of an amateur club"*: PHI, April 17, 1883.

50   *"Simmons has become quite gray"*: NPG, May 12, 1883.

Chapter 4: The Moses of St. Louis

53   *"almost wintry at the ball park"*: MR, April 2, 1883.

54   *"in military precision"*: SLGD, April 2, 1883.

54   *"old and slovenly uniforms"*: Ibid.

54   *"When St. Louis plays Cincinnati"*: MR, April 2, 1883.

55   *"played to the grandstand"*: SN, November 17, 1900.

56   *"his first promotion"*: Sullivan, 234–235.

57   *"baseball tide had come in"*: Ibid., 237.

57   *"plain Ted Sullivan"*: Spink, 286.

57 *"mind of his own"*: Sullivan, 237.

57 *"He perfumed my atmosphere"*: Ibid., 238.

58 *"enter the gilded cavern"*: Ibid.

58 tried to lure Deasley back: CE, October 26, 1882.

58 *"Loftus on the field"*: DDT, September 21, 1879.

59 *"now an ice wagon"*: CE, September 22, 1882.

59 *"I had to cut and slash"*: T. P. ("Ted") Sullivan, "Breaking Into Fast Company," BM, April 1910, 55.

60 *"Very much of the remarkable"*: NYC, February 17, 1883.

60 *"a magnificent walnut"*: NYC, March 3, 1883.

60 *"Ever since his engagement"*: Quoted in CE, July 31, 1882.

60 switch hitter: MR, July 22, 1883.

61 *"changed his delivery"*: BA, July 19, 1882.

61 *"polish his buttons"*: SLPD, August 17, 1904.

61 *"a great hand"*: Ibid.

61 had a widowed mother: SL, November 19, 1884.

61 *"that chap's heft"*: MR, April 2, 1883.

61 *"Tony does not 'kill'"*: PI, January 21, 1883.

61 *"many a one a roasting"*: SLGD, March 18, 1883.

62 *"lively waiter"*: SLGD, April 13, 1883.

62 *"immense blackboard"*: SLGD, May 6, 1883.

62 *"provided with a compartment"*: SLGD, March 26, 1883.

62 4,000-pound roller: SLGD, March 18, 1883.

62 wrapping their hooves: SLGD, April 5, 1884.

62 On St. Patrick's Day: SLGD, March 18, 1883.

63 *"brawny fists"*: PI, July 2, 1882.

63 *"mark him"*: Ibid.

63 *"If he should some day break a limb"*: SL, July 29, 1885.

63 *"lithe and spry"*: SLGD, March 18, 1883.

63 *"throws like lightning"*: Ibid.

63 *"Dot poy Latham"*: CT, October 8, 1883.

63 *"Latham is the mouth"*: SN, May 26, 1888.

63 *"Why do they laff"*: Wallop, 52.

63 failed to provide any money: SL, February 3, 1886.

63 *"gratification of unnatural desires"*: SLGD, November 29, 1887.

63 *"little thought what havoc"*: SN, July 12, 1886.

64   *"had a good word"*: SLGD, March 21, 1883.

64   *"It is a generous offer"*: NPG, May 12, 1883.

65   *"remarked that he hoped"*: MR, March 21, 1883.

65   *"an immediate favorite"*: MR, April 2, 1883.

65   *"commenced to whoop up"*: SLGD, April 2, 1883.

65   *"seldom heard"*: SLGD, April 8, 1883.

65   *"letting the eager sightseers"*: SLGD, April 9, 1883.

66   *"their new red jackets"*: SLGD, April 8, 1883.

66   *"decidedly unprofessional"*: SLGD, April 15, 1883.

66   *"fair-minded spectators"*: Ibid.

66   *"It is bold, dashing"*: MR, April 29, 1883.

66   the *"Little Nicols"*: MR, September 16, 1883.

66   *"credit to one of Cole's Arabs"*: MR, April 29, 1883.

66   *"It is not the first or the last"*: SLGD, April 29, 1883.

67   *"St. Louis calls for something"*: MR, April 30, 1883.

67   *"commenced to ply me"*: Sullivan, 254.

67   *"Chris whispered in my ear"*: Sullivan, 115.

Chapter 5: The Shrimp

70   *"O. Hell"*: CCG, June 13, 1883.

71   *"St. Louis had it pretty bad"*: MR, June 6, 1883.

71   *"momentous storm clouds hung over"*: PD, May 31, 1883.

71   *"most tumultuous applause"*: Ibid.

72   *"so few breathing spells"*: PP, May 31, 1883.

72   *"none too many holidays"*: NYH, May 31, 1883.

72   *children stared at Jumbo*: PHIP, May 31, 1883.

72   *"little shrimp"*: NPG, May 19, 1883.

73   *had to rebuild his career*: Nemec 1, 119–120.

74   *"most remarkable memory"*: SABR Baseball Biography Project, Bobby Mathews, http://sabr.org/bioproj/person/e7ad641f.

74   *had won nearly 200 major-league games*: Official Major League Baseball statistics cited here come from www.Baseball-Reference.com.

74   *"Bobby is tough"*: SL, May 6, 1883.

75   *glanced off his bat*: PHI, May 30, 1883.

75   *pulled a handkerchief out*: PHIP, May 31, 1883.

76   *"a standing position"*: Spink, 186.

77   *"but few equals for pluck and coolness"*: NYC, August 12, 1882.

78   *"bullets shot out of a rifle"*: PI, January 14, 1883.

78   *"stops to question the cost"*: PI, June 24, 1883.

78   *"sharp, hard hitter"*: BG, May 22, 1883.

78   *"putty ball"*: MacDonald, 149.

79   *"such a tantalizing smirk"*: SN, April 23, 1892.

79   *"dead outlaw and desperado"*: Orem, 7.

79   *"he, of the ungodly grin"*: CE, October 4, 1882.

79   *"grin and kick and spout"*: CCG, April 16, 1882.

79   *"Bradley is not a pitcher"*: CE, October 4, 1882.

79   *"Never count on a ball player"*: PD, May 21, 1883.

80   *"Bradley's ascension"*: SLGD, June 3, 1883.

80   *"every other club in the association"*: CE, June 5, 1883.

80   *"by dint of pushing, threats"*: PHIP, May 31, 1883.

81   *"Athletics will be second"*: PI, June 3, 1883.

Chapter 6: Who's in Charge?

83   *"beautiful beyond compare:"* CCG, May 2, 1883. Caylor had left the *Enquirer* to join this paper.

83   *"sweet, silvery voice"*: Thompson described in CCG, July 28, 1883.

84   *"making good use of everything"*: CE, May 6, 1883.

84   *"buzz of excitement"*: CCG, May 2, 1883.

84   *"price of so many"*: CE, May 2, 1883.

84   *"best quality white bunting"*: MR, April 29, 1883.

85   *"drooping down the staff"*: CCG, May 2, 1883.

85   *"caught a passing breeze"*: Ibid.

85   *"would pitch if desired"*: Ibid.

85   *"comment on his personal habits"*: Axelson, 74.

85   *"quiet, earnest, silent team work"*: CCG, May 2, 1883.

85   *"transposed into a general picnic"*: CE, May 2, 1883.

85   *"openly violated the pitching"*: CCG, May 2, 1883.

85   *"refused to enforce"*: Ibid.

86   *"he was too d—n fresh"*: Sullivan, 267.

86   *"My dear Mr. White"*: Ibid., 267–268.

86   *"friends in the grand stand"*: CE, May 2, 1883.

86   *"great pitch of excitement"*: Ibid.

86   *"universal admiration"*: MR, May 2, 1883.

86   *"the excitement ran intense"*: CE, May 2, 1883.

87   *"never find a policeman"*: Nemec 1, 522.

87   *"wild with noble rage"*: CCG, May 2, 1883.

87   *"accepted as a big lift"*: MR, May 2, 1883.

87   *"attack of inflammatory rheumatism"*: CE, May 3, 1883.

87   *"tired of hearing the sharp whizz"*: Ibid.

88   *"brought about disaster"*: CCG, May 3, 1883.

88   *"same player who ran into Powers"*: CE, May 3, 1883.

88   *"This young man"*: CCG, May 4, 1883.

88   *died of a crippling rheumatoid condition*: Nemec 1, 91–92.

88   *"anything else but a sick man"*: CE, May 4, 1883.

89   *"buzzing of the championship bee"*: Ibid.

89   *"citizens with a brass band"*: CE, May 6, 1883.

89   *"a statement as vicious"*: SLGD, April 29, 1883.

90   *"not been enjoying his usual"*: Ibid.

90   *"full on the side of the head"*: MR, April 21, 1883.

90   *"He staggered and fell"*: Ibid.

90   *"unwarranted by the circumstances"*: MR, May 6, 1883.

90   *"It is hoped"*: Ibid.

90   *"made preparation to start"*: Ibid.

90   *"Sullivan was happy last night"*: OSJ, May 7, 1883.

91   *"watching matters more closely"*: MR, May 12, 1883.

91   *"permanently crippled"*: NYC, December 30, 1882.

91   *"could not do himself justice"*: SLGD, May 19, 1883.

91   *"Being a little angry"*: Sullivan, 238.

91   *"All right, Ted"*: Ibid.

92   *"never went to sleep"*: Axelson, 103.

92   *"aggressiveness and fearless spirit"*: Sullivan, 239.

92   *"mashing two fingers"*: LC, May 14, 1883.

92   *"It sounded like a drum"*: MR, May 25, 1883.

93   *"poor fellow uttered a groan"*: SLGD, May 25, 1883.

93   *"desire to cripple any man"*: LCJ, May 27, 1883.

93   *"get his neck broken"*: SLGD, July 24, 1883.

93 *"didn't dodge worth a cent"*: Ibid.

93 *"huge sheet of green velvet"*: MR, May 7, 1883.

93 *"well worth the price"*: SLGD, May 17, 1883.

94 *"a little humiliating"*: MR, May 25, 1883.

94 *"canopy with a base ball design"*: MR, May 27, 1883.

94 *"swayed perceptibly"*: MR, May 29, 1883.

94 *"dollars to doughnuts"*: SLGD, May 29, 1883.

94 *called in German-born Edmund Jungenfeld*: SLGD, June 12, 1883.

95 *box of expensive cigars*: Ibid.

96 *"came in from the field"*: PHIP, June 8, 1883.

97 *"toughest and roughest gang"*: SL, June 17, 1883.

97 *"sunburned and warrior-like"*: SLGD, June 17, 1883.

98 *"offered fabulous sums"*: MR, May 25, 1883.

98 *"went away empty-handed"*: MR, June 30, 1883.

98 *"big around as a bean pole"*: SN, July 27, 1887.

Chapter 7: The $300 Special

99 *"huddled like kittens"*: SLGD, June 18, 1883.

100 *"practice in the laundry"*: MR, June 18, 1883.

100 *"vigorously hissed"*: SLGD, June 18, 1883.

101 *"One of the objects of the uniform"*: MR, June 18, 1883.

101 *"Nicol started for it"*: SLGD, June 18, 1883.

101 *"so blanked stingy"*: Ibid.

102 *"just as Roseman came"*: SLGD, June 19, 1883.

102 *"Stone-wall Sandwiches"*: MR, June 20, 1883.

102 *"all anxious and willing"*: MR, June 21, 1883.

102 *"sown in clover"*: MR, June 20, 1883.

102 *"sight was like"*: SLGD, June 19, 1883.

102 *"so forgot their humanity"*: MR, June 20, 1883.

103 *this was no ordinary note*: DEN, June 26, 1882.

104 *"The only way to secure competent men"*: CE, October 27, 1882.

104 *blue flannel, double-breasted jacket*: SLGD, March 13, 1883.

104 *"He only needs a whisk"*: MR, May 16, 1883.

105 *"Ball players are up to constant tricks"*: SL, August 6, 1884.

105 *"nine beautiful young ladies"*: SN, June 7, 1886.

106 *"driver's lips were badly cut"*: SLGD, June 14, 1883.

106 *"seems to be a b-a-d man"*: CCG, July 2, 1883.

106 *"Mother, may I slug the umpire?"*: CT, August 15, 1886.

106 *"Goaded by uncalled for"*: SL, May 7, 1884.

107 *"drove the side of his face in"*: BG, July 10, 1883.

107 *"best umpire in the country"*: LC, July 6, 1883.

107 one of the best umpires ever: CCG, September 20, 1883.

107 *"really refreshing to see Kelly"*: OSJ, September 28, 1883.

107 *"most painful lack of breeding"*: PD, June 5, 1883.

107 *"scattered in small fragments"*: MR, May 17, 1883.

108 *"coolly stopped the game"*: BG, May 20, 1883.

108 *"I can candidly assert"*: MR, May 14, 1883.

108 *"uncertain skies were watched"*: MR, June 29, 1883.

109 *"everything at Von der Ahe's expense"*: Quoted in MR, September 14, 1883.

109 *"the same old 'Brad'"*: MR, June 29, 1883.

109 *"a very cordial reception"*: NYC, July 7, 1883.

109 Athletics' exhibition games: PHIP, June 29, 1883.

109 *"virtually a battle"*: MR, June 29, 1883.

110 *"perfect storm of hisses"*: NYC, July 7, 1883.

110 *"hung onto the bag"*: SLGD, June 29, 1883.

110 *"cursed the umpire"*: Ibid.

110 *"crepe all over the city"*: PI, July 1, 1883.

110 *"baseball caldron was boiling"*: SLGD, June 30, 1883.

110 *"break up the American Association"*: Ibid.

111 St. Louis intended to jump: DEN, June 26, 1883.

111 *"atmosphere of glee"*: SLGD, June 30, 1883.

111 *"All went merrily"*: Ibid.

112 *"Bring Daniels on"*: Sullivan, 204–206.

112 *"Kelly was all right"*: Ibid., 205.

112 *"solid amphitheater of humanity"*: MR, July 2, 1883.

113 *"stout, fleshy man"*: MR, July 3, 1883.

Chapter 8: Base Ball Mad

116 *"seems to be base ball mad!"*: BG, August 19, 1883.

116 *"tendency to run to extremes"*: LC, July 16, 1883.

117 *"Think how grieved"*: SL, December 31, 1884.

117 care of a doctor: CCG, June 19, 1883.

117   *"looked like a young lake"*: Ibid.

117   *"This nerved us"*: PI, June 24, 1883.

118   *"wipe out the disgrace"*: Ibid.

118   *Cub Stricker had a strange dream*: Ibid.

119   *"howled themselves hoarse"*: CCG, June 21, 1883.

119   *"fever is growing"*: CE, June 24, 1883.

119   *"walked up to their bat bag"*: CCG, June 21, 1883.

120   *"sent in the balls"*: CE, June 22, 1883.

120   *"came out to smell"*: CCG, June 22, 1883.

120   hire a *"cheap boy"*: CE, June 24, 1883.

120   *"We are alive"*: PI, June 24, 1883.

121   *"boss Hades on earth"*: PI, July 8, 1883.

121   *he had freakishly collided*: Nemec 1, 265.

121   *"threw off his silk hat"*: PI, July 8, 1883.

122   *"nineteen grease spots"*: Ibid.

122   *"I can assure you"*: Ibid.

123   *"It was pure carelessness"*: CCG, July 1, 1883.

123   *"His only excuse"*: CG, July 5, 1883.

124   *"mistake cost three runs"*: CG, July 1, 1883.

124   *"If any one thinks"*: CCG, July 5, 1883.

124   *"We do not intend"*: CCG, July 2, 1883.

125   *"holy terror of 'Tricky Tony'"*: Palmer 2, 65.

125   *death of President James Garfield*: quoted in BG, July 20, 1883.

126   *"Pete is not as stupid"*: Palmer 2, 65–66.

126   *noticed that Big Dan*: Ibid., 118–119.

127   *"the Prince of Bourbon"*: Orem, 11.

127   *"maudlin in the extreme"*: Ibid., 27.

127   *total of $140 in fines*: LC, July 10, 1883.

127   *"Browning and Leary"*: CCG, May 20, 1883.

127   *"So far as we Cincinnatians"*: CCG, July 10, 1883.

128   *"The present champions"*: LCJ, July 11, 1883.

128   *"We have hoped beyond"*: LC, July 14, 1883.

128   *"Old Energy sat"*: Ibid.

129   *"It isn't much use"*: LC, July 14, 1883.

129   *"local club is immense"*: LC, July 20, 1883.

129   "K-E-E-P C-O-O-L!": LCJ, July 23, 1883.

129   "out into the woods": Ibid.

129   "ten-dollar gold piece": LC, July 30, 1883.

129   "Physically, he is a ghost": LC, July 15, 1883.

130   "light of a great joy": LC, July 11, 1883.

130   "a great hairy, shaggy Siberian mammoth": LC, July 24, 1883.

130   "fair face of Margaret Fresh": LC, August 5, 1883.

130   "Margaret Fresh shrank convulsively": LC, August 25, 1883.

131   "as proud as a boy": CE, December 30, 1882.

131   "a light paralytic stroke": SLGD, July 26, 1883.

132   "just bet your life": SLGD, July 28, 1883.

132   "able to walk": SLGD, July 27, 1883.

132   "Cincinnatis' chances for the flag": CG, July 5, 1883.

132   "Four fine double plays": CG, August 1, 1883.

133   most celebrated scam of the season: CG, July 28, 1883.

134   in a cartoon published: CG, July 31, 1883.

Chapter 9: First-Class Drunkards

137   "forming a picturesque scene": MR, July 16, 1883.

137   "very curious implement": Orem, 7.

138   "It went off with a boom": MR, July 16, 1883.

138   "Gleason is suffering": MR, July 3, 1883.

138   "much like broiling a steak": Axelson, 48.

138   "horizon searchers": DEN, May 16, 1883.

138   "wretched fielder and a very moderate batter": BG, July 6, 1883.

138   "highest terms as a batsman and fielder": MR, July 3, 1883.

139   "Nothing wrong with that man": MR, July 4, 1883.

139   nowhere to be seen: Orem, 68.

139   "hit one bird with a double stone": Sullivan, 114.

140   "a queer character": SL, May 26, 1903.

140   "market for flesh and blood": NPG, August 4, 1883.

140   "engaging players by the bunch": CE, July 10, 1883.

140   "a man of fine physique": MR, July 10, 1883.

141   debut with St. Louis: SLGD, July 13, 1883.

141   "spirituous liquors": BG, July 22, 1883.

141   *"I have determined . . . to"*: MR, July 4, 1883.

142   *generally good for little else*: CT, October 2, 1881.

142   *"who will play base ball?"*: PD, May 29, 1883.

142   *"beds of flowery ease"*: Quoted in NPG, September 15, 1883.

143   *"He will soon find"*: NPG, July 14, 1883.

143   *"spunk of a louse"*: NPG, August 25, 1883.

143   *"slugging and brutal kicking"*: CE, June 25, 1883.

143   *"story was unjust"*: PD, July 10, 1883.

143   *"'lushers,' in other words drink too much"*: Ibid.

143   *"good drinkers on my team"*: SN, December 31, 1887.

144   *"forte is not managing"*: Quoted in CE, September 3, 1883.

144   *no brother was ill or dead*: CT, August 11, 1878.

145   *hotel late after a night*: BG, May 23, 1883.

145   *"There was a time"*: PD, May 29, 1883.

145   *"dumped 'the Only Nolan'"*: CE, June 24, 1883.

145   *Bodeman's Grove*: SLGD, July 25, 1883.

146   *"Latham, I've fined you"*: SLPD, July 27, 1883.

146   *wearing padded pants*: MR, August 5, 1883.

146   *"went through the boards"*: MR, August 6, 1883.

147   *"poor Mansell down in the hole"*: MR, August 10, 1883.

147   *"transported with considerable difficulty"*: MR, August 9, 1883.

147   *"Over the Rhine saloons"*: Quoted in NPG, August 25, 1883.

147   *"an infamous misrepresentation"*: MR, August 10, 1883.

147   *"grand and lofty act"*: CE, November 11, 1883.

148   *"made things lively for"*: OSJ, August 13, 1883.

148   *"Lewis was dropped"*: CCG, August 14, 1883.

148   *"a hard ticket"*: BG, August 17, 1883.

148   *"told them it was time"*: MR, August 30, 1883.

148   *"Throwing two or three beer glasses"*: CE, August 19, 1883.

149   *"contemptible and malicious"*: SLPD, August 18, 1883.

Chapter 10: Cap Anson's Nightmare

151   *"tainted with black blood"*: TB, August 11, 1883.

152   *he caught "magnificently"*: SLGD, April 26, 1883.

152   *"looming up as a great man"*: SL, July 22, 1883.

152   *"dog under the wagon"*: PD, April 18, 1883.

152 *"fancy they were not as fond"*: Anson, 10.

152 *"they had come to kill me"*: Ibid., 11.

153 *a "little coon"*: Ibid., 148.

153 *"no account nigger"*: Ibid., 150.

153 *out in public on a leash*: Palmer 1, 315–316.

154 *"center field the cedar trees"*: Sullivan, 154–155.

154 *"You and we are different races"*: Donald, 367.

154 *"Who believes that Whites and Blacks"*: Morris, 80.

154 *"against the admission of any club"*: BPC, December 19, 1867, quoted in Brunson, 197.

155 *"account of his being a colored man"*: PI, July 31, 1881.

156 *"prejudice of the Eclipse"*: LCJ, August 22, 1881.

157 *"shook the dust of Louisville"*: Ibid.

158 *"plucky catcher, a hard hitter"*: NYC, January 27, 1883.

158 *"one of the most efficient"*: MR, April 24, 1883.

159 *"the league failed to organize"*: DD, May 7, 1883.

159 *"not only be a novelty"*: MR, April 24, 1883.

159 *"worked like trained professionals"*: SLGD, April 25, 1883.

159 *"mince-meat of the colored clubs"*: SLGD, April 27, 1883.

159 *"champion moke club"*: NPG, May 13, 1883.

159 *"coons are doing good work"*: NPG, September 1, 1883.

160 *"Coons Carry Off the Cake"*: RR, June 20, 1883, quoted in Brunson, 214.

160 *"caught between the bases"*: MR, April 25, 1883.

160 *"rare opportunity to see"*: CCG, May 12, 1883.

160 *"colored club were a well behaved"*: CCG, May 13, 1883.

160 *"suspended in the barber shops"*: DEN, June 22, 1883.

161 *"blacked up"*: Ibid.

161 *"dancing around the home plate"*: Ibid.

161 *"curious or enthusiastic Caucasians"*: SLGD, August 13, 1883.

161 *"not quiet for a moment"*: Ibid.

161 *"hunted up a little darkey"*: CCG, June 30, 1883.

162 *"great favorite with his fellow"*: OSJ, April 23, 1883.

162 *"with no damned nigger"*: TB.

162 *"a gentleman and a scholar"*: OSJ, August 11, 1883.

163 *"weakened like a whipped cur"*: NPG, September 15, 1883.

163   *"management of the Chicago Ball Club"*: CCR, John Brown to C. H.
       Morton, April 11, 1884.

164   *"best catcher I ever worked with"*: NYA, January 11, 1919.

164   *"the undersigned, do hereby warn"*: SL, September 24, 1884.

165   *"conscientious player"*: TB, September 24, 1884.

165   *"Several representatives declared"*: NDJ, July 15, 1887.

166   *"a howl was heard from Chicago"*: White, 83.

166   *"law is a disgrace"*: SL, March 14, 1888.

166   *"Just why Adrian C. Anson"*: White, 83.

Chapter 11: Flinging the Watch

169   *"We feared Philadelphia"*: CCG, July 28, 1883.

170   *twisted his ankle so badly*: PHIR, August 1, 1883.

170   *clocked that summer*: PP, August 3, 1883.

170   *handsome badge*: PI, August 5, 1883.

171   *"losing their grip"*: BG, August 24, 1883.

171   *stopped in Providence*: PP, August 28, 1883.

172   *"does not look as well"*: BG, August 29, 1883.

172   *one half-game ahead*: This was not technically a lead, because the Asso-
       ciation awarded the pennant to the team with the highest winning per-
       centage at the end of the season.

174   *"lovers of baseball"*: NYJ, December 4, 1911.

174   *"Why don't you go to the Polo Grounds"*: Ibid.

175   *"employee was busy"*: NYH, April 8, 1883.

176   *"mind of his own"*: Sullivan, 237.

176   *"Nothing could be more unfounded"*: MR, August 28, 1883.

176   *"even the players laughed"*: BM, February 1910, 55.

176   *"It's no use now"*: NYT, August 31, 1883.

177   *"better let his manager run"*: NYC, September 8, 1883.

177   *"retorted warmly"*: MR, August 31, 1883.

178   *"Chris had been interfering"*: BM, February 1910, 55.

178   *"I have brought this club"*: NYT, August 31, 1883.

178   *"He says he was badly treated"*: PI, September 9, 1883.

179   *"Mr. Von der Ahe thinks"*: SLGD, August 31, 1883.

179   *"GOOD-BY, SULLIVAN"*: MR, August 31, 1883.

179   *"not exactly a dude"*: CCG, May 13, 1883.

180 *"has plenty of style":* Quoted in SLGD, April 8, 1882.

180 *put a gun to his own chest:* Details from CT and CIO, November 11, 1882.

180 *"completely infatuated with him":* Quoted in CE, November 19, 1882.

180 *"weary and excited":* CT, November 14, 1882.

180 *"played a brilliant game":* MR, August 31, 1883.

180 *"There were some warm words":* SLGD, September 9, 1883.

Chapter 12: Jumping Jack

183 *"a ton avoirdupois":* MR, July 3, 1883.

184 *"with doubtful chances":* PHIP, September 4, 1883.

184 *dislodging some of his teeth:* PHIR, September 1, 1883.

184 *"great strength of the St. Louis Club":* PHI, September 4, 1883.

185 *"The Banner in Sight":* MR, September 4, 1883.

185 *"If he is effective":* PHIR, September 4, 1883.

185 *public speaker and philanthropist:* Daggett, 211.

185 *"intensely interested":* Hyson, 445.

186 *Yale's glee club:* NYT, December 8, 1883.

187 *"He can only play":* DEN, July 9, 1883.

187 *"this big soap-bubble":* NPG, August 11, 1883.

187 *"his particular jumping act":* BCA, August 21, 1883.

189 *"There was perfect silence":* Quoted in NPG, October 6, 1883.

189 *"taught exclusively at Yale":* PHIP, September 5, 1883.

189 *"You don't know whether":* NPG, October 6, 1883.

190 *"The boys soon came up":* NYT, September 5, 1883.

190 *"his prance showed little":* PHIP, September 6, 1883.

191 *"tripped and fell":* PHIR, September 6, 1883.

191 *"things began to look shaky":* Ibid.

191 *"no less than 13,500 pasteboards":* PHIP, September 7, 1883.

192 *"Corey dared not move":* PHIR, September 7, 1883.

192 *"muffed" it "most ingloriously":* SLGD, September 7, 1883.

192 *"With one accord every heart":* PHIR, September 7, 1883.

193 *"turned and ran with the ball":* Ibid.

193 *"The shout raised was instantaneous":* Ibid.

193 *"ST. LOUIS SURRENDERS":* PHIP, September 7, 1883.

193 *"the sheerest hard luck":* MR, September 12, 1883.

194 *"crowd began to call out":* MR, September 8, 1883.

194 *"as if shot"*: PHIR, September 9, 1883.

194 *"game was of the burlesque order"*: NYC, September 15, 1883.

195 *"This is what beat you"*: PI, September 9, 1883.

Chapter 13: Hurricane in St. Louis

197 *cigar store and "Athletics headquarters"*: PI, August 26, 1883.

198 *"happy-go-lucky crowd"*: Spink, 72.

198 *"watched their movements as steadily"*: Quoted in NPG, December 23, 1883.

198 *lost his hearing*: SN, January 15, 1887.

199 *secret from his parents*: BG and BS, July 7, 1883.

199 *"greatly amused the spectators"*: PI, September 16, 1883.

200 *"strongest college battery ever"*: CCG, September 16, 1883.

201 *"as unruly as a colt"*: CCG, September 19, 1883.

201 *"so disliked here as he"*: CCG, September 20, 1883.

202 *"grin which had adorned"*: CE, September 20, 1883.

202 *"Oh! how he suffered"*: CCG, September 20, 1883.

202 *"long and tedious journey"*: MR, September 9, 1883.

203 *"old and trampish-looking"*: SLGD, September 10, 1883.

203 *"a gong sounded"*: MR, September 10, 1883.

203 *"grounds look brighter and prettier"*: SLGD, September 8, 1883.

204 *"straightened out"*: Ibid.

204 *"was especially applauded"*: SLGD, September 10, 1883.

204 *"made five corking hits"*: SLGD, September 11, 1883.

204 *"Browns can not play ball"*: SLGD, September 14, 1883.

204 *"That settles it!"*: PI, September 16, 1883.

204 *"Nothing short of a miracle"*: MR, September 14, 1883.

204 *"I brodest dot game"*: PI, September 23, 1883.

205 *"a very unpleasant duty"*: MR, September 15, 1883.

205 *"Lewis was a fine"*: SLGD, September 15, 1883.

205 *"terrific thrashing"*: MR, September 16, 1883.

205 *"could not afford to lose"*: SLGD, September 16, 1883.

206 *"How's that for a balk"*: SLGD, September 17, 1883.

206 *"Go on! Go on!"*: MR, September 17, 1883.

206 *"tried a left-handed"*: SLGD, September 17, 1883.

206 *"tip-toe of expectations"*: SLGD, September 19, 1883.

207 *"scooted away over the field"*: Ibid.

207 *"like a ray of hope"*: MR, September 20, 1883.

208 *"Thank God there is"*: SLGD, September 19, 1883.

208 *a "tug of war"*: MR, September 8, 1883.

208 *"as an added inducement"*: MR, September 21, 1883.

209 *"scoundrels to cowardly assassinate"*: Quoted in WP, April 8, 1882.

209 *"sky blue and clear"*: PHIP, September 22, 1883.

209 *"carriages, buggies, drays"*: MR, September 22, 1883.

209 *motion was "clearly illegal"*: PI, September 9, 1883.

210 *"to his own disgust"*: SLGD, September 22, 1883.

210 *"greatly admired by his Excellency"*: Ibid.

211 *"pretty bad looking object"*: MR, September 26, 1883.

212 *"Excitement was at"*: NYC, September 29, 1883.

212 *"creating a panicky feeling"*: SLGD, September 22, 1883.

212 *"A regular hurricane"*: NYC, September 29, 1883.

212 *"as if to get his coat"*: Ibid.

212 *"Go on! Play ball!"*: Ibid.

212 *"blew the ball far back"*: Ibid.

213 *"with the air of a person"*: SLGD, September 22, 1883.

213 *"Everybody expected to see"*: SLGD, September 23, 1883.

213 *"Athletics missed Mathews"*: NYC, September 29, 1883.

213 *"jubilant crowd filled the field"*: Ibid.

213 *"We were completely robbed"*: PI, September 23, 1883.

214 *"Great Caesar, the string"*: Ibid.

214 *"moving, surging dark mass"*: SLGD, September 24, 1883.

214 *"Fashionable circles were also"*: PHIP, September 24, 1883.

214 *"reminds me of Derby day"*: Ibid.

214 *"the great human stream"*: SLGD, September 24, 1883.

214 *"thousands were huddled and squeezed"*: Ibid.

215 *"groaned beneath the unwonted pressure"*: PHIP, September 24, 1883.

215 *"On the tops of the roofs"*: SLGD, September 24, 1883.

215 *"That it was a red-letter day"*: Ibid.

215 *"gathering was beyond a doubt"*: MR, September 24, 1883.

216 *"drop his bat and walk around"*: SLGD, September 24, 1883.

216 *"caused the small boys to cheer"*: Ibid.

217 *only through "pure pluck"*: MR, September 26, 1883.

217 *"Then, standing erect"*: PHIP, September 24, 1883.

218   *"relentlessly forwarded"*: SLGD, September 24, 1883.

218   *"HE WRECKED US"*: MR, September 24, 1883.

218   *"as they were driven out"*: PHIP, September 24, 1883.

218   *"Athletics leave here"*: Ibid.

218   *"base ball is mighty unsartin"*: SLGD, September 28, 1883.

Chapter 14: Limping Home

219   *Simmons had already negotiated:* WP, November 2, 1902.

220   *"chewed up four cigar stumps"*: LCJ, September 27, 1883.

221   *"debated between innings"*: PHIP, September 27, 1883.

221   *"burned the wires"*: WP, November 2, 1902.

221   *"on the ragged edge"*: CE, September 27, 1883.

222   *"very wild and hard to hold"*: LCJ, September 28, 1883.

222   *no meat but chicken:* Orem, 11.

222   *"crowd yelled repeatedly"*: LCJ, September 28, 1883.

223   *"Lew Simmons's manners"*: NPG, November 24, 1883.

223   *"whole heart in the Athletics"*: Quoted in NPG, July 14, 1883.

223   *"brought his cane down"*: LCJ, September 28, 1883.

223   *"full share of condemnation"*: Quoted in MR, September 29, 1883.

223   *"These orders were disobeyed"*: Ibid.

224   *"excitement all over the city"*: Ibid.

224   *"cup of sorrow overflowed"*: WP, November 2, 1902.

224   *"boys would not even let me around"*: Ibid.

224   *"Give us a show"*: Ibid.

224   *"wanted to beat the team"*: Ibid.

224   *"DANGER AHEAD"*: PHIP, September 28, 1883.

225   *"grace of the Supreme Being"*: LC, September 28, 1883.

225   *"if Louisville won that game"*: WP, November 2, 1902.

226   *"worked up to a fever heat"*: PHIP, September 29, 1883.

226   *"While lying flat"*: NYC, October 6, 1883.

226   *"It was impossible"*: PHIP, September 29, 1883.

227   *"rent the heavens"*: Ibid.

227   *"with joy in my heart"*: WP, November 2, 1902.

227   *"the boys got there"*: PHIP, September 29, 1883.

227   *"Men threw their hats"*: PHI, September 29, 1883.

227   *"men could be seen stopping each other"*: PHIP, September 29, 1883.

227   *"Now it is settled"*: PHIR, September 29, 1883.

Chapter 15: A Great Boom for Base Ball

229   *"quick, nervous, dashing, brilliant"*: PEB, September 29, 1883.

229   *"Athletic became a by-word"*: PI, October 14, 1883.

230   *"Have you the fever"*: PHIR, September 30, 1883.

230   *"certain degree of carelessness"*: LCJ, October 1, 1883.

231   *"made up in warmth"*: PHIP, October 2, 1883.

231   *"still somewhat discomposed"*: Ibid.

232   *"He was good natured enough"*: Ibid.

232   *"man whom everyone wanted to see"*: Ibid.

232   *"positions round the windows"*: Ibid.

232   *"rush was made for the windows"*: Ibid.

233   *"climbing on each other's shoulders"*: Ibid.

233   *"It was time to cheer"*: Ibid.

234   *"Half a dozen young ladies"*: Ibid.

234   *"set up a deafening chorus"*: Ibid.

234   *"advance fife and drum corps"*: Ibid.

234   *"If the crowds were great"*: Ibid.

235   *"great boom for base ball"*: PI, October 7, 1883.

235   *"swarmed on door steps"*: PHIP, October 2, 1883.

235   *"dense mass of human beings"*: PHIR, October 2, 1883.

235   *barouches passed the Hotel Lafayette*: PHIP, October 2, 1883.

235   *"glittering combination of lanterns"*: Ibid.

235   *"the lady friends of the club"*: Ibid.

235   *"created considerable amusement"*: PHI, October 2, 1883.

236   *Marchers carried*: PHIR, October 2, 1883.

236   *"Der ish von thing"*: PHIP, October 2, 1883.

236   *"'Twas Bradley's smile"*: PHIR, October 2, 1883.

237   *"Dignified-looking citizens"*: Ibid.

237   *"was one continuous smile"*: PI, October 7, 1883.

237   *"The uproar was tremendous"*: PHIR, October 2, 1883.

237   *"terrific blasts upon a score"*: Ibid.

237   *"many a man and boy"*: PHIP, October 2, 1883.

237 *"have made their names more widely known"*: Ibid.

238 *A man fell from a tree*: This and other mishaps from PHIP and PHI, October 2, 1883.

238 *"rose in their carriage"*: PHIP, October 2, 1883.

239 *"Oysters on the Shell"*: Ibid.

239 *"Nothing in the history"*: PI, October 7, 1883.

240 *"Not the least pleasant feature"*: PHIP, October 2, 1883.

240 *"delighted with everything"*: PI, October 7, 1883.

240 *whopping $78,320*: PHIP, September 29, 1883.

240 *purchased a fruit farm*: PI, July 8, 1883.

240 *"cozy family homestead"*: NYC, March 15, 1884.

240 *"led by colored grooms"*: MR, October 6, 1883.

241 *"a wire screen"*: SLGD, October 6, 1883.

241 *"nimbly jumped down"*: MR, October 6, 1883.

241 *profit of $50,000*: SLGD, January 27, 1884.

Epilogue: When They Slide Home

243 *"most glorious and satisfactory ever known"*: Wright & Ditson's Base Ball Guide 1884 (Boston).

243 *"The class of patron"*: Ibid.

244 *"The month of May"*: Reach's Official American Association Base Ball Guide 1884 (Philadelphia), 7.

246 *"received much praise"*: NYC, January 26, 1884.

246 *"A friendship began"*: NYT, October 21, 1936.

246 *"Frequently he expressed"*: WH, December 23, 1910.

247 *"I am just as happy"*: REG, January 24, 1920.

247 *"In response to loud calls"*: SH, April 6, 1904, 3807.

247 *"Old! That's a misnomer"*: Ibid.

247 *"the heyday of baseball"*: WP, November 2, 1902.

248 *killed by a beer truck*: NYT, September 3, 1911.

248 *"thing might break"*: CCG, October 11, 1883.

248 *"A whiter-faced set of men"*: Ibid.

248 *"elevator must have fallen"*: Ibid.

249 *"Mr. Caylor was never rugged"*: Quoted in SL, October 30, 1897.

249 *"characters of Dickens"*: CE, June 1, 1937.

250 *"His nose was broken"*: CE, October 16, 1883.

250 *showed up at a Phillies-Reds:* KDF, August 30, 1939.

250 *"one of those old time heroes":* Nolan folder, HOF.

251 *"got into the gambling game":* NYT, March 28, 1926.

252 *"He had such a powerful physique":* Ibid.

252 *"Negro race will be":* Walker, 29.

253 *"This team was the wonder":* Spink, 50.

253 *"That silver dollar":* BIP, March 27, 1941.

253 *"He put the watch":* Sullivan, 115.

254 *"But I would rather have won":* BM, February 1910, 55.

254 *"a great hustler":* BM, May 1910, 75.

254 *"reason may be found":* Axelson, 66.

254 *"It doesn't bring in":* Ibid., 68.

255 *"In all the years":* Spink, 177.

255 *inventing the use of tarpaulins:* NYC, March 15, 1884.

255 *"about the coolest":* SN, June 18, 1887.

255 *narcissistic Tony Mullane:* Nemec 2, 99–102.

256 *"I'm a daisy on the diamond!":* SL, November 14, 1888.

256 *"the worst third-base coach":* Ritter, 86.

257 *"King George had only":* Allen, 38.

257 *reportedly totaled $300,000:* BG, January 29, 1899.

258 *"a numerous army of flatterers":* Cash, 199.

258 *watch with the hotel clerk:* NYS, December 23, 1906.

258 *"He looked about":* SL, April 22, 1899.

259 *"makes me feel good":* Deutsch, 83.

259 *"First base is enlightenment":* NYS, June 15, 1913.

259 *His pallbearers included:* NYT, June 9, 1913.

SOURCES

Newspapers and Magazines

AB: *Auburn* (New York) *Bulletin*

AC: *Auburn* (New York) *Citizen*

BA: *Baltimore American*

BC: *Buffalo Courier*

BCA: *Buffalo Commercial Advertiser*

BE: *Brooklyn Eagle*

BG: *Boston Globe*

BIP: *Binghamton* (New York) *Press*

BM: *Baseball Magazine*

BP: *Boston Post*

BPC: *Ball Players' Chronicle*

BS: *Baltimore Sun*

CCG: *Cincinnati Commercial Gazette*

CE: *Cincinnati Enquirer*

CG: *Cleveland Gazette*

CIO: *Chicago Inter-Ocean*

CL: *Cleveland Leader*

CT: *Chicago Tribune*
DD: *Dayton* (Ohio) *Democrat*
DDT: *Dubuque Daily Times*
DEN: *Detroit Evening News*
EDG: *Elmira* (New York) *Daily Gazette and Free Press*
EM: *Everybody's Magazine*
FWG: *Fort Wayne Gazette*
FWN: *Fort Wayne News*
FWNS: *Fort Wayne News Sentinel*
HER: *Hudson* (New York) *Evening Register*
JG: *Janesville* (Wisconsin) *Gazette*
KDF: *Kingston* (New York) *Daily Freeman*
LC: *Louisville Commercial*
LCJ: *Louisville Courier-Journal*
MR: *Missouri Republican* (St. Louis)
NDJ: *Newark Daily Journal*
NPG: *National Police Gazette*
NSJ: *Nebraska State Journal* (Lincoln)
NYA: *New York Age*
NYC: *New York Clipper*
NYH: *New York Herald*
NYJ: *New York Journal*
NYS: *New York Sun*
NYT: *New York Times*
NYW: *New York World*
OSJ: *Ohio State Journal* (Columbus)
PD: *Pittsburgh Dispatch*
PEB: *Philadelphia Evening Bulletin*
PHI: *Philadelphia Inquirer*
PHIP: *Philadelphia Press*
PHIR: *Philadelphia Record*
PHIT: *Philadelphia Times*
PI: *Philadelphia Item*
PP: *Providence Press*
RCD: *Rochester* (New York) *Democrat and Chronicle*
REG: *Reno Evening Gazette*

RR: *Rockford* (Illinois) *Register*
SH: *Seen and Heard* magazine (Philadelphia)
SL: *Sporting Life*
SLGD: *St. Louis Globe-Democrat*
SLPD: *St. Louis Post-Dispatch*
SLR: *St. Louis Republican*
SN: *Sporting News*
TB: *Toledo* (Ohio) *Blade*
USG: *Utica* (New York) *Saturday Globe*
UST: *Utica* (New York) *Sunday Tribune*
WH: *Washington Herald*
WP: *Washington Post*

Important Magazine Articles

Bishop: Henry William Bishop, "St. Louis," *Harper's New Monthly Magazine* 68, no. 46, March 1884.

Hyson: John M. Hyson Jr., "Women Dentists: The Origins," *Journal of the California Dental Association*, June 2002.

Richardson: Sophia Foster Richardson, "Tendencies in Athletics for Women in Colleges & Universities," *Appleton's Popular Science Monthly*, February 1897.

Smalley: E. V. Smalley, "The German Element in the United States," *Lippincott's Monthly Magazine of Popular Literature and* Science, April 1883.

Wyant: Elizabeth Wyant, "A Merchant of Early Chicago: Four Letters of Eri Baker Hulbert," *Journal of the Illinois State Historical Society* 28, no. 2, July 1935.

Collections

AGM: Abraham G. Mills papers, New York Public Library
CCR: Chicago Club Records, Chicago Historical Society
HOF: National Baseball Hall of Fame Library

Books

Allen: Lee Allen, *The Cincinnati Reds* (Kent, OH, 2006).

Andreas: A. T. Andreas, *History of Chicago, From the Earliest Period to the Present*, vol. 3, *From the Fire of 1871 Until 1885* (Chicago, 1886).

Anson: Adrian C. Anson, *A Ball Player's Career* (Chicago, 1900).

Axelson: G. W. Axelson, *Commy: The Life Story of Charles A. Comiskey* (Chicago, 1919).

Benson: Michael Benson, *Ballparks of North America: A Comprehensive Historical Reference to Baseball Grounds, Yards and Stadiums, 1845 to Present* (Jefferson, NC, 1989).

Bogen: F. W. Bogen, *The German in America, or Advice and Instruction for German Emigrants in the United States of America* (Boston, 1851).

Brunson: James E. Brunson III, *The Image of Black Baseball: Race and Representation in the Popular Press, 1871–1890* (Jefferson, NC, 2008).

Burrows: Edwin G. Burrows and Mike Wallace, *Gotham: A History of New York City to 1898* (New York, 1999).

Cash: Jon David Cash, *Before They Were Cardinals: Major League Baseball in Nineteenth-Century St. Louis* (Columbia, MO, 2002).

Cazden: Norman Cazden, Herbert Haufrecht, and Norman Studer, *Folk Songs of the Catskills* (Albany, NY, 1982).

Coolidge: Susan Coolidge, *A Short History of the City of Philadelphia from Its Foundation to the Present Time* (Boston, 1887).

Dacus: J. A. Dacus and James W. Buel, *A Tour of St. Louis; or, The Inside Life of a Great City* (St. Louis, 1878).

Daggett: Leonard M. Daggett, *A History of the Class of Eighty-Four, Yale College, 1880–1914* (New Haven, CT, 1914).

Deutsch: Jordan A. Deutsch, Richard M. Cohen, Roland T. Johnson, and David S. Neft, *The Scrapbook History of Baseball* (Indianapolis, 1975).

Donald: David Herbert Donald, *Lincoln* (New York, 1995).

Encyclopedia: *Supplement to the Encyclopedia Britannica*, vol. 4 (New York, 1889).

Glazier: Captain Willard Glazier, *Peculiarities of American Cities* (Philadelphia, 1886).

Hetrick: J. Thomas Hetrick, *Chris Von der Ahe and the St. Louis Browns* (Lanham, MD, 1999).

Isenberg: Michael T. Isenberg, *John L. Sullivan and His America* (Urbana, IL, 1988).

James: Bill James, *The New Bill James Historical Baseball Abstract* (New York, 2003).

Kargau: Ernst D. Kargau, edited by Don Heinrich Tolzmann, translated by William G. Bek, *The German Element in St. Louis: A Translation from German of Ernst D. Kargau's* St. Louis in Former Years: A Commemorative History of the German Element (Baltimore, 2000).

Kelly: Mike "King" Kelly, *"Play Ball"*: *Stories of the Diamond Field and Other Historical Writings About the 19th Century Hall of Famer* (Jefferson, NC, 2006).

Lardner: James Lardner and Thomas Reppetto, *NYPD: A City and Its Police* (New York, 2000).

Leonard: John W. Leonard, ed., *The Book of St. Louisans* (St. Louis, 1906).

MacDonald: Neil W. MacDonald, *The League That Lasted: 1876 and the Founding of the National League of Professional Base Ball Clubs* (Jefferson, NC, 2004).

McFeely: William S. McFeely, *Frederick Douglass* (New York, 1991).

Miner: Margaret Miner and Hugh Rawson, *The Oxford Dictionary of American Quotations* (New York, 2006).

Minstrel: *Minstrel Songs, Old and New* (Philadelphia, 1883).

Morris: Roy Morris Jr., *The Better Angel: Walt Whitman in the Civil War* (Oxford, 2000).

National: Lee Allen, *The National League Story* (New York, 1961).

Nemec 1: David Nemec, comp. and ed., *Major League Baseball Profiles, 1871–1900*, vol. 1, *The Ballplayers Who Built the Game* (Lincoln, NE, 2011).

Nemec 2: David Nemec, comp. and ed., *Major League Baseball Profiles, 1871–1900*, vol. 2, *The Hall of Famers and Memorable Personalities Who Shaped the Game* (Lincoln, NE, 2011).

Nye: David E. Nye, *Electrifying America: Social Meanings of a New Technology* (Cambridge, MA, 1990).

Olson: Audrey L. Olson, *St. Louis Germans, 1850–1920: The Nature of an Immigrant Community and Its Relation to the Assimilation Process* (New York, 1980).

Orem: Preston D. Orem, *Baseball from the Newspaper Accounts, 1882–1891* (Altadena, CA, 1966).

Palmer 1: Harry Clay Palmer, J. A. Fynes, Frank Richter, and W. I. Harris, *Athletic Sports in America, England and Australia* (Philadelphia, 1889).

Palmer 2: Harry Clay Palmer, *Stories of the Base-ball Field* (Chicago, 1890).

Proetz: Arthur Proetz, *I Remember You, St. Louis* (St. Louis, 1963).

Rice: Edw. Leroy Rice, *Monarchs of Minstrelsy, from "Daddy" Rice to Date* (New York, 1911).

Ritter: Lawrence S. Ritter, *The Glory of Their Times: The Story of the Early Days of Baseball Told by the Men Who Played It* (New York, 1966).

Schlereth: Thomas J. Schlereth, *Victorian America: Transformations in Everyday Life* (New York, 1991).

Smith: Page Smith, *The Rise of Industrial America: A People's History of the Post-Reconstruction Era* (New York, 1990).

Spalding 1: Albert G. Spalding, *America's National Game* (New York, 1911).

Spalding 2: *Spalding's Official Base Ball Guide* (Chicago, 1880).

Spalding 3: *Spalding's Official Base Ball Guide* (Chicago, 1883).

Spink: Alfred H. Spink, *The National Game* (St. Louis, 1910).

Sullivan: "Ted" Sullivan, *Humorous Stories of the Ball Field: A Complete History of the Game and Its Exponents* (Chicago, 1903).

Twain: Mark Twain, *Life on the Mississippi* (New York, 1901).

Walker: M. F. Walker, *Our Home Colony: A Treatise on the Past, Present and Future of the Negro Race in America* (Steubenville, OH, 1908).

Wallop: Douglass Wallop, *Baseball: An Informal History* (New York, 1969).

Ward: Geoffrey C. Ward and Ken Burns, *Baseball: An Illustrated History* (New York, 1994).

White: Sol White, *Sol White's Official Base Ball Guide* (Philadelphia, 1907).

INDEX

EDWARD ACHORN, a Pulitzer Prize finalist for Distinguished Commentary, is an editorial page editor with the *Providence Journal*. He is also author of *Fifty-Nine in '84: Old Hoss Radbourn, Barehanded Baseball, and the Greatest Season a Pitcher Ever Had*. His reviews of books on American history appear frequently in the *Weekly Standard*. He lives in an 1840 farmhouse outside of Providence, Rhode Island.

PublicAffairs is a publishing house founded in 1997. It is a tribute to the standards, values, and flair of three persons who have served as mentors to countless reporters, writers, editors, and book people of all kinds, including me.

I. F. STONE, proprietor of *I. F. Stone's Weekly*, combined a commitment to the First Amendment with entrepreneurial zeal and reporting skill and became one of the great independent journalists in American history. At the age of eighty, Izzy published *The Trial of Socrates*, which was a national bestseller. He wrote the book after he taught himself ancient Greek.

BENJAMIN C. BRADLEE was for nearly thirty years the charismatic editorial leader of *The Washington Post*. It was Ben who gave the *Post* the range and courage to pursue such historic issues as Watergate. He supported his reporters with a tenacity that made them fearless and it is no accident that so many became authors of influential, best-selling books.

ROBERT L. BERNSTEIN, the chief executive of Random House for more than a quarter century, guided one of the nation's premier publishing houses. Bob was personally responsible for many books of political dissent and argument that challenged tyranny around the globe. He is also the founder and longtime chair of Human Rights Watch, one of the most respected human rights organizations in the world.

·   ·   ·

For fifty years, the banner of Public Affairs Press was carried by its owner Morris B. Schnapper, who published Gandhi, Nasser, Toynbee, Truman, and about 1,500 other authors. In 1983, Schnapper was described by *The Washington Post* as "a redoubtable gadfly." His legacy will endure in the books to come.

Peter Osnos, *Founder and Editor-at-Large*